Rocky Road
By the Time I Get To Phoenix

by

Clive Smith & Bip Wetherell

Copyright @ 2023 Clive Smith and Bip Wetherell

All rights reserved

ISBN # 979-8861428682

The rights of Clive Smith and Bip Wetherell to be identified as co-authors of this work have been asserted by them.

We have tried to describe factual events and actual locales and convey situations and conversations from our memories and the memories of those mentioned within this book as they were faithfully and honestly conveyed to us.

Chapters

1. Wish You Were Here
2. One of These Nights
3. Long Hot Summer
4. Play That Funky Music
5. Take It To The Limit
6. Melody Makers
7. No More Heroes
8. Jim Fotheringham
9. Don't Leave Me This Way
10. Blowin' In The Wind
11. Stayin' Alive
12. The Road To Argentina
13. Knickers and Knobs
14. Scene Stealer's First Offence
15. Chrome Molly
16. Tony Haselip

17. I Will Survive

18. Energised

19. On The March

20. Keep The Candle Burning

21. New Horizons

22. Energy 1980

23. Ashes To Ashes

24. Startin' Over

25. Bitter Memories for Pat and Yvonne

26. The Battle of the South Atlantic

27. George Reilly and the Rocket Man

28. Live Aid

29. Biographical Sources

30. Author Briefs

"Rocky Road - By the Time I Get to Phoenix" is the third part of the trilogy documenting the social side of life in Corby from the 1950s to 1980s

"Its Steel Rock and Roll To Me" - Clive Smith and David Black published 2004

"Alive In the Dead of Night" - Clive Smith and David Black published 2010

Acknowledgements

Stuart Allen, Ian Bateman, David Black, John Black, Mike Bosnic, Pete Buckby, Leon Cave, Bob Clark, Tony Cousins, Derek Cowie, John Crawley, Andy Dickson, Mick Dickson, Rick Dodd, Craig Douglas, Ian Eccles, Mick Ferguson, Bob Grimley, John Grimley, Nigel Hart, Alex Henderson, Liz Hill, Dave Irving, Stewart Irving, Fred Jelly, Roger Johnson, John Kenrick, Reggy Knowles, Franny Lagan, Dave Martin, Willie McCowatt, Angus McKay, Pat McMahon, Richard Oliff, Chris Page, Tim Penn, Colin Pheasant, Polly Short, Dennis Taylor, "Taffy" Thomas, Bip Wetherell, Iain Wetherell, Doug Wilson, Kelvin Woods, Trevor Wright, Jim Wykes

In Memory…

Dedicated to the memory of those who contributed and sadly are not around to see the publication. Projects like writing and compiling the stories of our history, it's inevitable that this is so. First of all on a very personal level I lost my wife of 40 years, Sue after a two-year long battle with cancer in 2014. The third book in the trilogy that saw the story of Corby's social history covering the 1950s to the 70s, "Its Steel Rock and Roll To Me" and "Alive in the Dead of night" was originally going to be titled "No Occupation Road". This was on schedule until the diagnosis of Sue was revealed, and as you can imagine, and those who have gone through it, will know all too well, life came to a crashing halt. My co-author for the books, David Black also took the decision to step back and retire from his very successful printing business.

Over the years since 2014 "No Occupation Road" was resurrected a couple of times but the enthusiasm wasn't there. In 2017 my friend, Bip Wetherell, got me interested in working on a subsequent project, helping to write the autobiography of world-famous session drummer and one time Johnny Kidd and the Pirates and Tornados sticks man Clem Cattini. Together we travelled the country meeting Clem's contemporaries from the halcyon pop days of the 50s and 60s. The enthusiasm and will was back and on the encouragement of Pat McMahon and David Irving whilst on vacation in Spain, I was stimulated enough to once again, attempt to conclude the trilogy, which I decided after being on the shelf for so long, deserved another chapter, covering the decade of the 1980s.

Bip came along for the ride and after a couple of false starts with titles "steel Got the Blues" and "No Occupation Road" it was felt a fresh beginning was required and we came up with "Rocky Road," and acronym for Rockingham Road, one of the oldest streets in Corby. "By the Time I Get To Phoenix" was later added, the Glen Campbell 1960s hit suddenly seeming a perfect subtitle with the revamped Steelworks site becoming known as Phoenix Parkway encompassing a shopping precinct. Asda sits right on the land where the Blast Furnaces once lit up the Corby sky.

"Rocky Road" is in memory of those who were an integral part of the story covering 1975 to 1990. They include Mick Ferguson, Mick Harper, Mick Haselip, Billy Mathieson, Bob Grimley, Ian Eccles, Franny Lagan, Ricky Geoghegan, Dougie King, Bob Crawford, Ned McGuigan, Steve Short, Mike Bosnic… others I have missed please accept my apologies.

All will never be forgotten.

Preface

The 1970s often felt like a hangover from the 60s. "Baby boomers" were settling down, getting married, having families. The decade is remembered, apart from the dreadful fashions and the ever-changing music scene, as a decade that was forever in a state of flux and confusion, bedevilled by constant industrial action knackering the country.

Described as the decade fashion forgot, how can you forget, apart from the mini-skirts and hot pants, which were delightful on the eye, the bell bottom flares, maxi dresses, platform shoes, kipper ties, boob tubes, tank tops?

Musically there was as many diverse trends as that of the 1960s. In the wake of the demise of the Beatles, the singer/songwriter phase came along with Joni Mitchell, Crosby, Stills and Nash, Neil Young, Jackson Browne, James Taylor, Carole King, The Eagles, Elton John, Melanie.

"Glam" Rock brought dynamism into the mainstream with T Rex, Slade, David Bowie, Roxy Music, Sweet and Mud.

A counter to this frivolity, Prog Rock trundled along with Yes, King Crimson, Van Der Graf Generator, Emerson, Lake and Palmer, Atomic Rooster.

All swept away with the tsunami of Punk.

Piercing through this amalgam of cultural diversity was Fleetwood Mac of The Buckingham / Nicks "Rumours" era. Cast aside as driftwood the earlier incarnations of the Mac, the 60s Blues in the Peter Green, Danny Kirwan and Jeremy

Spencer years, the Christine McVie / Bob Welch / Bob Weston soft rock of the early 70s, the Mac were revitalised with the arrival of Lindsay Buckingham and Stevie Nicks.

Corby's reputation as a hotbed of talent was reinforced with the Bumper/Scene Stealer, Chrome Molly, Auction, Canned Rock, Energy bands striving to make a breakthrough.

"Rocky Road" covers the period from 1975 to 1990. Interwoven are the stories and headlines that circumvented the globe and linked events with those closer to home, including the Falklands War, Live Aid. Also some local sportsmen who made their mark.

The 1975-80 period also covers the slow demise of Corby's steelworks, the finality of it all. The aftermath which is documented in an extra chapter to take the story to the 90s.

There are stories included which attempt to give a different angle and some insight into what it was like to work in the cacophony and grimy environment of the Steelworks, and for the Royal Mail which when I started in 1978, I found to be entrenched in out of date and often bemusing Victorian practices. Bip Wetherell has contributed greatly with his memoirs of running successful pubs and entertainment businesses throughout the area during this time span. Providing venues for a generation which probably wasn't appreciated as much as he deserved. But that's my opinion.

I believe the stories will resonate with a number of readers.

Hope so anyway.

Clive Smith

Part One

Wish You Were Here

1975

Occupation Road and Rockingham Road are two of the oldest streets in Corby, the latter more commonly known as Rocky Road. Which could also have been a metaphor for the late 70s situation Corby found itself in during this period. Back in the 1950s the Rocky Road shopping precinct housed the fire station, the Odeon cinema, shops of all kinds, and the famous "Tips". Tipaldi's Cafe where all the youngsters hung out during the Teddy Boy days listening to the Jukebox playing Bill Haley and Elvis Presley records.

Rock Road Shops 1950s

Occupation Road was actually named after a farm that was once situated near Tanfields Road, midway between the junctions of Studfall Avenue and Rockingham Road. In the 1950s it was a hub of activity with an abundance of shops and amenities. Perks the Greengrocers with its pungent smell of cheese, fruit, vegetables, confectionary and ham slicing machine on the counter. The Co-Op with its butchers and Recreation Hall. David Cory's newsagents with its little window hatch where people queued outside in all weathers to buy a newspaper on the way to work. Security conscious Cory didn't let the punters into his shop in the early mornings. Allan's the bakers, a cobblers, coal merchant, Mobil Garage, Hairdressing Salon, Charles" Off Licence all provided whatever one desired.

Our Lady's Catholic School, Samuel Lloyds Senior School, Rockingham Road Juniors and a Grammar School Annex at it's rear, covered the education requirements. Corby Town Football Club was opposite the Sea Cadets Hall. Stewarts and Lloyds' Recreation Club, "The Welfare," was wedged between the St. Columba Church Hall and the football ground. Nellie's Bin and Martin's cafe was a sanctuary for teenagers who wished to dance or listen to music with a bag of chips and a coke.

Polly Short grew up in Corby and moved to London in the 1960s. She later lived in Australia and the United States before returning to the U.K. in the 1980s. With connections in the music business Polly worked behind the scenes at the Live Aid Concert at Wembley in 1985. Which we will return to a little later.

She recalled her memories of Corby and the 1950s when we met in Whitstable, Kent, where she lived at the time, in 2014. "I remember going to get groceries from Perks. It had those green and white mosaic tiles on the walls. Old fashioned scales and I always loved the Spam they sold! I seem to remember one of the girls I went to infant and junior school with got a job there. All the staff wore immaculate white overalls and hats. I also remember going to the Co-op and Cory's newsagents at the very end of the shop parade which had a sub post office inside. I lived in Lodge Green Road so it was only a few minutes" walk to the shops in Occupation Road."

If Polly had visited Corby in the 1970s she would have found little had changed. Apart from a monstrous ugly concrete chimney stack that resembled a lighthouse and dwarfed the steelworks Sinter Plant where it was situated, and overlooked the "Rocky Road" end of Occupation Road. The cobblers and coal merchant had long gone but everything else was pretty much the same. It was still a main bus route through the town with the United Counties 291 taking workers back and for to the steelworks on the alternative shift work patterns. Flower beds were still a feature.

Mention "Little Scotland" around the country and recognition is often instant. Such is the reputation of Corby. Walking down a lane in Southport, Lancs one day, I stopped to ask a couple of guys for directions to the football ground. First thing they asked, "Whereabouts in Scotland you from? I told them Corby. "Where there was a steelworks?"

"Yes," I replied. "I worked there in the 60s, contracting. I remember the place was full of Jocks, couldn't believe all the Scottish accents."

Though somewhat diluted nowadays in the 2000s, Hogmany in Corby was still embraced with all the enthusiasm and fervour as it was in Glasgow, Aberdeen or Edinburgh. Pipers wandered the streets lamenting "the Northern Lights of Aberdeen," "the Bonnie Banks of Loch Lomond," bringing many a tear to a glass eye. Soirees throughout the night were ubiquitous with Kenneth McKellar (Roamin' In the Gloamin') and Andy Stewart (Donald where's yer troosers) providing a soundtrack from BBC's White Heather Club on the box (Tele) as "first footers" were welcomed in with their bottles of Scotch and the traditional lump of coal.

Corby police were well-versed and conversant with over excitement and indulgence during the New Year festivities but New Years Eve 1975 was to go down as one of their busiest Hogmanys on record. Called out to a number of incidents, including a fracas on their very own doorstep in the now derelict Elizabeth Street Station culminated with two windows in the Co-op town centre store opposite being smashed and several revellers arrested and invited to spend the night in the cells.

The Co-op Store, "smashing place" reckoned Davy

P.C. "Taff" Skinner was witness. "One was a yuletide regular, Davy Collins, well-known as he slept on the bus station benches. Davy threw a brick through the Co-op window every Christmas and waited to be lifted to be taken to Bedford nick. He liked his turkey as much as the next man. One year when he didn't show up, Bedford Prison actually phoned Corby Police to check if he was ok!"

Collins may well have been viewed as a reprobate but he was a local legend who once thanked Corby magistrates for handing him a three-month prison sentence after he'd kicked in a large plate glass window at Corby police station with his boot. He'd walked into the station, laid down on the floor and refused to move. Turfed out by the sergeant, he returned, stretched out on the floor again, and was ejected a second time. On his way out he put his boot through the window.

"You'll have to spend the next three months in prison Collins," Magistrate W.T. Montgomery informed him.

"Thank you very much sir," said Davy!

Davy Collins was also remembered by landlord Jim Tibbs of the Nags Head in the High Street, Corby. "Closing time lunch and evening was a nightmare, the punters just didn't want to leave. Davy Collins, who I got fed up barring him for tapping drinks was always the last one out -- and I think I gave up in the end. There for the grace of God and all that. The Nags was one of the oldest establishments in Corby, prominently placed just a stone's throw away from the steelworks. To say the Nags had some characters would be putting it mildly. Disney had nothing on them. Being close to the Works we were first port of call for all those who were on Backshift or Nightshift."

"On Friday lunchtimes when the workers used to go down to pick up their wages, I had to put on five bar staff to keep up. Cards were quite the thing - no matter how many times you told them they couldn't play brag/poker or any other card game that meant money was on the table, they took no notice at all. Wives were known to come in the bar on Friday lunchtimes to get the shopping money or there might not be any when they got home. Taxi drivers were also regulars. Every morning after they had done the works run, Flanagans, Donovans, Knights all did well with the trade from the Nags, the drivers who shall remain nameless because most of them were on the dole, used to like playing pool and we had two of the first pool tables in Corby. I couldn't believe how much money they could take in a week at 10p a game."

"We also had a video juke box, well it wasn't really a video, more like a super eight and the film used to get stuck and burn a hole in the box. The engineer would come out and splice the film together so when the record played, and there was a topless girl dancing around in the kitchen, it would suddenly jump to the living room then jump again to the garden then again to the bedroom and then back to the kitchen, it was hilarious. The police raided us one night and took it away saying it was obscene, I never saw it again."

Corby's reputation wasn't overly appreciated by Judge Nancy Wilkins at Northampton Crown Court. She was less than impressed, condemning Corby "as a town not conducive to respectable living," adding, "I am told it has the biggest beer consumption in the country." Her outburst followed the prosecution of a Corby man for assault after his explanation, "I don't feel I've had a good time unless I've spent half of my weeks wages in a night's drinking". If the miscreant in question had been a celebrity, film star or a footballer, he'd have been hailed as a hell raiser. As it was, he was hailed a pain in the arse and Nancy fined him £110 for his trouble.

Council Leader Kelvin Glendenning was incredulous on hearing this. Ignoring the bad form of the hell-raiser he refuted Nancy's claims, "I can't believe Miss Wilkins has any first-hand knowledge of Corby. I will be delighted to welcome her as a guest for a day and let her judge for herself what the town has to offer. Corby has the best living environment in the county in terms of quality housing, cultural and recreational facilities. No other town in the country can match our modern town centre, festival halls complex and sport amenities." Whether Nancy accepted the invite and came over to meet Kelvin for a coffee in one of the town's finest bistros, the Bus Station Cafe, Fine Fare Cafe or Finlays Cafe on Corporation Street wasn't reported.

Davy Collins wouldn't have taken any notice but back in November 1974 British Steel chief Monty Finniston had declared, "The future of Corby and it's steelworks is safe and exciting," words that would prove to be as hollow as the tubes produced at the Corby plant as just a few months later, Finneston released a statement that sent a chill through the town. "Britain's six major steel centres are to be concentrated in Scotland, Port Talbot, Llanwern, Scunthorpe, Teeside and Sheffield." No mention of Corby. A town relying totally on its steelworks.

A town where every family bar none would be affected if the complex was allowed to go into decline. The script was being prepared.

Reaction to Finniston's statement, which also included "The BSC is losing £3 million a week and the workforce should ideally be trimmed to 50,000," plus Chief Executive Bob Scholey's prediction that "losses could reach £375 million a year unless stringent economies were made" was swift.

John Cowling, Corby Councillor and National Executive of the ISTC (Iron and Steel Trades Confederation) warned, "This could lead to the first national steel strike since 1926. If the BSC want to pursue the issue we will have no alternative but to use every means of persuasion possible."

Corby Steelworks

Scholey was unrepentant. "Solutions to reduce the following years" wages bill of £145 million have to be found to prevent the BSC borrowing to pay its workers. Decisions are bound to mean redundancies, virtually no overtime and the probability of stopping the guaranteed working week."

He did give a glimmer of hope when he added, "Although the national position is bleak, the position at Corby's giant iron and steel tube making plant is distinctly brighter despite a fall in orders from the building industry."

Which gave Frank Smyth, chairman of the Joint Branches committee of the ISC (Iron and Steel Corporation), a vestige of reassurance, "Though the statement fails to differentiate between steel production and other sections of the industry, it is hopeful Corby's steelworks will still be a viable project at the turn of the century. Steel production into the 1980s may not be secure but the future of the Corby Tubes division is bright. It is the biggest in Britain and could be the biggest in Europe."

Full employment in the steelworks meant Corby's pubs and clubs were flourishing. Darts and Dominoes teams criss-crossed the town during the week along with their vociferous supporters to the town's watering holes which all had their share of characters. The Open Hearth on Studfall Avenue, which sadly closed in 2014 and was eventually converted into flats, was typical.

Clive Smith was full-time barman at the Hearth, serving pints and "a hof and a hof" to crabbit "auld" domino players and being constantly told "you wouldn't last five minutes in Aberdeen" by daytime drinker octogenarian Willie McHattie. "On arrival by taxi Willie would be escorted to his table by Jimmy Cramp, a retired former Guide in the steelworks, attired in torn jeans, open necked shirt, neckerchief, long hair, a moustache that made him resemble Jason King off the TV. Cramp used to wind everyone up, good naturedly, calling the barman 'twat' when being served with his pint and Sovereign cigarettes. Everybody loved him though!

For selection to the domino team it appeared that you had to be aged at least 50, as Bip Wetherell explained when asked why, during his time as full-time barman at the Hearth, he wasn't part of the successful cup winning squad of 1972. "I wasn't old enough," Bip said dolefully.

Thick skin to survive behind the bar was necessary. In the Open Hearth, John Ogilvie scowled with a look that would drop you down dead if the head on his pint was too big. "You got a tie to go with that collar!" he'd rasp. A pint with little head would receive commensurate abuse from his pal Willie Porter. "Put a head on it big yin, it looks likes maiden's water!"

And the stories you heard were better than those you heard on the TV. "Wee" Joe Gallagher liked to tell the tale of when he was a soldier during the second world war, entrenched in hills overlooking a bay in the Mediterranean where a Hospital ship was anchored. "The medics came round looking for blood donations to help the wounded and I gave a pint. A short while later the Luftwaffe came over and dropped a bomb right down the ship's funnel. I couldn't believe it. I looked at my mate and said, "There goes my pint of blood!"

Lack of humour threatened the renewal of a licensee's application from one of the town's longest serving landlords, Albert Hardy at the Pluto in Gainsborough Road. Another pub closed down in 2010 when Corby police condemned it as a haven for crime and a magnet for drugs. Councillor John Cowling argued that Albert's banter with his customers was rude and insulting when magistrates reviewed his case, claiming Hardy had insulted him when he called in for a drink one Wednesday evening. Pluto regular Rab Taylor refuted Cowling's appraisal, telling the court that Hardy provided the main entertainment at the pub. "His banter is the best entertainment going. I drink there five or six nights a week. He takes the piss out of everybody!"

The license was granted. The Open Hearth, an otherwise nondescript alehouse, had been transformed since rugby player Alan Smith took over as Landlord in September 1967. Alan established the pub as a leading venue for discos, folk nights, cabaret and country and western nights. By 1975 the times were a-changing though. The Hearth's loyal "backroom" punters had outgrown the discos, grown bored with the cabaret nights and moved on. The Shire Horse, Nags Head, Maple Leaf, Candle, Raven had all jumped on the bandwagon, offering, if nothing else, a change of scenery. Darts and dominoes leagues were also beginning to show signs of decline. Left behind by the Pool teams when tables were introduced into the town's bars in 1974 to rapidly became the most popular pub sport, albeit chiefly aimed at the younger clientele.

As the numbers, and takings, dwindled, Alan's attempts to revitalise the Hearth with the soul-destroying "Free and Easy" nights proved to be the final straw, the death knell. 'singalong with Bob" or whoever it was owned the organ, didn't catch on and the last rites of Alan's tenure were being read. Alan called it a day in May 1975, admitting, 'the time was right to get out, I was flogging a dead horse in the end."

After his days at the Hearth, Alan built up a successful stock taking business in the brewery trade, before handing over the reins to his son Adrian on his retirement. Adrian later became famous in the 1990s as "Britain's Strongest Man," performing on television and shows all-round the country as "The Mighty Smith"!

Taking over from Alan at the Hearth was his former barman and resident DJ, Bip Wetherell, who by now had a blossoming disco business besides continuing to play keyboards with his soul band Granite.

Following his days behind the decks at the Hearth, Bip had acquired a regular disco gig at the Shire Horse in Willowbrook Road, and the Nags Head in the High Street, (demolished in the early 2000s to make way for a Care Home), where Jim Tibbs had offered him as much time as he wanted to promote live music as well as his discos. Bip's younger brother Stuart was recruited to work alongside him, and soon built up his own reputation as a DJ, and he also fronted his own short-lived band The Headboys.

Bip's success in the disco business was noted by Trevor Upton, director of Arden Taverns who owned four pubs in Corby. He asked Bip if he'd be interested in resuscitating the Open Hearth, an opportunity he accepted, after some contemplation. "As long I could be allowed to continue with the discos at the Shire and the Nags, and sing with my band."

An agreement was reached and Bip duly took over the Hearth with his wife Elaine, just two weeks after Alan Smith had left.

"We had Tamla who was just two years old when Trevor rang," Bip recalled. "I had given up Uni in my second year as I was doing up to ten gigs a week with the disco business and I had to make a choice. Money or a degree. I dropped out and concentrated on the business. We were doing alright as we had just bought our first house in Cecil Drive for the sum of £3000. So this day the phone rang, and it was Trevor Upton who I'd met whilst working at the Hearth.

"How would you like to be landlord of the Open Hearth?" he asked.

"Landlord? Me?" I replied, gobsmacked. Landlords were big men with gold sovereign rings on their fingers and they were all, in Corby, a lot older than 24 years old. I discussed it with Elaine and we decided to go for it. So, after an interview at Head Office, and a visit from the Licensing Sergeant in the Police to prove we were fit and proper people to become licencees, we moved into the Hearth in May 1975. And the first thing we did was buy a dog. There was no alarm systems in those days so the brewery insisted we had an Alsatian and they would pay us £5 pounds a week to cover its food and medical bills. So we had our first dog and as we now lived in a pub, we called it Sherry."

"How were we going to get the Open Hearth busy? Well the first thing we did was clean it. Saddle soap for the nicotine-stained ceiling, polish for the linoleum bar floors. Carpet cleaner for the lounge carpet which we actually found to have quite a nice pattern on it. Elaine's Mum and Dad, Annie and George Knight, and her two sisters Wendy and Pam were a great help and it was a good idea to employ family as the stocks and takings were always spot on."

"The first time I was sacked was at the Open Hearth when the Discos had been that successful, the Lounge had needed to be extended and refurbished to accommodate the level of business we were achieving. We were closed down for three months while we waited for the brewery to complete the job. By this time I had finished as Full-time Barman at the Hearth and was at Kettering Technical College studying for the "A" levels I needed to get into Uni. The long-term plan was I wanted to be an English teacher teaching primary school children. So the Disco work was my only income. I'd just bought a new Mini Van and distinctly remember asking Alan Smith if I would definitely be back doing the disco's when we re-opened, so I could keep up my H.P. payments on the van. He confirmed that I would. Well the fateful phone call came on the Thursday before we were due to start the disco again on the Saturday. Apparently, the brewery had done such a lovely job on the new lounge that Beryl, Alan's wife, didn't want the disco crowd to ruin it, so they were going to do "Cabaret Nights" instead."

"So you don't need me anymore?" I asked.

"No," was the reply.

"We're doing Cabaret."

I couldn't believe it. The two disco nights had paid for the new look and extension ten times over. Were they mad! Elaine was with me when I took the call. She could see I was upset. This was when she made the best decision of our married life. "No problem" she said, "We'll just take the crowd to another pub." I didn't know what she meant.

"But the Open Hearth is the 'in' place," I said.

"Don't be silly, the "in" place will be wherever you take it. Let's go round the pubs, see who's got a back room they don't use, and make a deal."

I would never have done anything like this if it wasn't for Elaine. She always wanted to go into business and here was her golden opportunity. Funnily enough the first pub we went to, the Shire Horse, the landlord said, "Bip, I've been waiting for someone like you to fill my pub, when do we start? Mind you, I get to keep all of the bar take."

"No problem," said Elaine, "we'll pay for the security, the advertising, and the DJ's wages, so we'll need all the door money."

So that was the deal. We went from £6 pound a week to £100 which was a lot of money in the early 70s. We used to put candles on the tables and point the disco lighting at the mirrored ceiling to create a nice atmosphere. I started the very first night with "A Horse With No Name" by America just to get things going nice and easy. The pub was packed by the third week. Elaine had been right. I was playing the records and she took the money on the door. 20 pence on a Tuesday. 40 pence on a Saturday.

We tried to limit the numbers but every week some lads would break the toilet windows to get in, so in the end we crammed 200 into a room that was built for 50. It was bedlam. A brilliant atmosphere. And a very happy landlord. I'll always remember he drove a Ford Zodiac when we first met but when the brewery moved him onto a bigger pub in Leicester, he was driving a Jaguar. You always knew when a Landlord was doing well. He would drive a big posh car and have several gold sovereign rings on most of his fingers.

The disco business was booming. I can distinctly remember having six bookings all on a Saturday. Three weddings and three gigs at night. I spent all morning setting the kit up at the various venues, going round to make sure the DJs were doing their job and then going back to the Shire Horse to do the final spot. Elaine would help me. Honestly she was the only woman I knew that could set up a set of disco equipment. Speakers, amps, microphones at the correct setting, no problem.

In the Open Hearth, I started the Jam session on Sunday lunchtimes with the core of musicians from the Corinthian pub where "jams" had been such a success. Guitarists John and Bob Grimley, saxophonists Bob Crawford and Bob Clark, bassists Jack Murphy and Jim Smith, drummers Billy Mathieson and Johnny Heron all played when available.

We also introduced an "Album" night on a Monday and with the Discos at the weekend we were soon busy enough to meet the brewery targets and then some. And we enjoyed working at the Hearth as it had a really nice living accommodation and we earned extra money by renting our house in Cecil Drive out."

Clive Smith: "When my brother, Alan, handed in his notice to the brewery I decided it was time for me to move on too. I'd been working behind the Hearth bar for over six years in varying capacities and I was ready for a change of scenery. After Bip had left, Alan started the cabaret nights on Saturdays which were very successful, bands like Auction and Scenery providing the entertainment, and the good old fashioned "Chicken or Scampi in the basket" were introduced. When this began to wane Alan tried the "Free and Easy" nights which did my head in. I was asked by a feller from the brewery, a Mr. Kent, if I'd be interested in taking over from Alan but I was just getting back with my future wife Sue, we'd split some five years earlier, and I'd had enough of working in the pub. Life was changing, I wanted a fresh start in all departments."

"So there was I, trekking down the old familiar route, Occupation Road in January 1975, with the words of my old foreman in the C. W. Mills, Andy Sneddon, echoing in my ears, "You'll be back!" That was in April 1970 when I thought I had escaped the environs of the steelworks, along with my pal Ted Foster, forever. I had started work as an office boy in the engineering shop in December '65 failed an apprenticeship interview in '66 and spent the years in between on shift work in the C.W. (Continuous Weld Mills).

CW Mills

The intervening years was spent working behind the bar at the Hearth, building sites, stints with Shanks and McEwans and the Lancashire Steel plant in the "Works" where I had a constant day job with the title of Bog Ore Man. Which wasn't something to mention or brag about when chatting up the women in the Open Hearth! It wouldn't impress I figured. The prospect of returning to the "Works," and the noise, the filth, the 'double decker egg and bacon toasties' in the less than salubrious canteens, not to mention the shift work, filled me with dejection. Trudging down Occupation Road that miserable January morning, the thoughts were gnawing away at me. "Is this it? For the next 25 years?"

But I was back, in the EWSR as a tube inspector. Feeling like I'd been re-captured after five years on the run. Feeling as if the gravitational pull of the steelworks had dragged me back in. Like the Apollo spaceships returning to earth's orbit from the Moon. Bit dramatic but that's how I felt!

Meantime, Ted Foster had gone his own way, and we'd lost touch, until.... hunched over a mug of tea and newspaper early one dayshift, a voice disturbed my concentration. "Excuse me pal, can you point me in the direction of the foreman's office?" There was something unerringly familiar about that voice. Looking up from page three of *The Sun,* I was astonished to see Ted looking down on me.

"Aw no!" he blurted out in disbelief. I couldn't believe it either! We both cracked up laughing, shared a few expletives. It turned out that Ted too was less than enamoured at being back in the "Works". We were both Pink Floyd fans and as it happened, Floyd released their classic album this year, "Wish You Were Here". The title, an irony not lost on either of us.

My first week as a Tube Inspector in the EWSR was spent measuring tailpieces of steel strip cut off from coils at the back end of a Mill with a micrometer and recording them for posterity on sheets of paper. The most mundane job imaginable. "Does anyone look at these reams of figures I've scribbled down?" frequently crossed my mind. Left adrift with the micrometer and pen for doodling gave plenty of time for deep thought. Bored to death. I imagined a lapse of concentration could end up with my hand being chopped off in the contraption that severed the tail ends of the coils. Somehow I couldn't imagine me being in this place for the rest of my life. And I was determined I wouldn't be.

Tales of horrific accidents and fatalities in the steelworks were legion, often grossly exaggerated. One was of a steelworker who fell into a ladle of molten metal. His dad, working alongside, did the merciful act by pushing his son's head under with a brush. Believe that if you will. Many moons before, in Motherwell Steelworks, a similar incident had been recorded when a worker fell into a ladle of molten metal, and was dragged out with only severe burns to his body. Which is hard to believe given the extreme temperatures but nonetheless it was reported in the *Motherwell Times* as an accident. Not a fatality. So the Corby "accident" seems far-fetched by any extreme. It was a tale vehemently disputed by former Blast Furnace worker John Crawley over a pint in the Rockingham Arms. "That story was a right load of bollocks" John said. "I worked with a Kettering bloke called Tony in the Blast Furnaces and we were talking about all the accidents in the "Works" and I told him about the poor lad who fell into a ladle. He laughed out loud. Then repeated what I said, "What a load of bollocks!"

"Watch this," he said. He picked up a cat that was wandering by. There were millions of them in the Works, wild, mangy looking things, many with an eye or an ear missing, half a leg or something. Tony threw the cat towards a ladle. Before it got anywhere near it, the cat exploded!"

Which sounds like another tall tale, but John swore it was true. Myth or not, many men were maimed, or died in the "Works". Run down by trains, falling off chimney stacks, electrocuted, crushed, burned to death. And I'm inclined to add, many probably died of boredom."

Despite rumours that the Steelworks was doomed, life continued as normal. George Bradshaw worked in one of its most unwelcome environments, the Soaking Pits. Deep below ground gas heated chambers where ingots of steel were placed to ensure their temperature would be uniform before they were processed in the Rolling Mills. "You had to be 21 before you did that job" George claimed. "It was man's work. The pits were cleaned twice a week. They were left to cool for two days but would still be white hot when you went into them with a jackhammer to drill away the scale from the floor and walls. It was hard work in horrible conditions. The heat was intense, ten minutes and the wooden planks you stood on started smouldering, and you had to get out. Health and Safety? Don't make me laugh. There was no such thing. No hard hat, no goggles. Clogs and overalls was the only protection. It was a crap job but the money was good."

The prospects of an oil boom lifted spirits when oil fields were discovered under the North Sea off the northern coast of Scotland. The discovery promised to have a dramatic impact on the North East of Scotland and likewise, the British economy. Scotland and the Shetland Islands rapidly became gripped with oil fever and Aberdeen fast became a "boom" town. The oil brought jobs, opportunities and workers from around the world. The lure of earning big money proved an irresistible temptation for Scottish expatriates, many of whom had left in search of work south of the border in years gone by. Unsurprisingly, the number of inquiries for jobs in the oil business from Corby was well above the national average, as an employment officer from Aberdeen revealed, "At one time, when there were no jobs here, we used to export people to Corby. Now the work's here, they're wanting to come back."

The good news about the oil was counteracted by demands from hospital workers for a pay increase of 74%, the miners with a 35% demand and the rail workers with 33%. Leading Chancellor Denis Healey to puncture the oil euphoria by proclaiming, "higher wage claims will see higher unemployment." The pay demands came simultaneously as the cost of electricity was rising by a record 33%, and TV license fees going up, a colour licence from £6 to £18 and black and white an extra £1 to £7. Which despite many complaining, was value for money if only for watching Meg Richardson getting married to John Bentley on "Crossroads" this year. The nightly soap with its dodgy scenery and duff actors was well worth seven notes by any stretch.

When it was announced that the cost of posting a letter was set to rise, it was deemed by many as pushing the envelope too far. First class from fourpence halfpenny to 7p and second class from threepence halfpenny to 5p was decreed outlandish but the increases were explained unapologetically by Post Office Chairman, Sir William Ryland who whined, "They still fall short of what is necessary to get us out of the red."

A crime wave, undoubtedly sparked off by the rising price of potatoes, occurred in Wellingborough during August with spud thieves doing the rounds. Allotment holders were beside themselves. Horace Newbury, secretary of

Wellingborough Allotments Society was livid. Horace, who also had half of his onions pilfered, raged, "It could be because of the rising prices of vegetables but it's more likely people are just too lazy to grow their own!"

Two women were eventually summoned to appear at Wellingborough Court for pinching three rows of King Edwards. They were caught red-handed by Horace who was spying with his binoculars and attempted to apprehend them. The ladies sped off in their car, forcing him to leap out of the way. Horace clocked the registration number and reported the incident to the police. Both women were fined £10 with £6.70p costs which was a considerable amount to pay when spuds were advertised as 2p a pound at Cransley "if you pick your own and the weather is permitting. Please bring your own buckets."

In the light of all this, it came as no surprise when Jim Callaghan's Labour government announced its intentions to abandon plans to build the Channel tunnel, which had been talked about as far back as the 1880s when construction had actually started in France near Calais, and at Folkestone on the UK side. Back then it was claimed that British Generals didn't trust the French and feared an invasion, which prompted the construction company to consider having a soldier permanently on guard to "pull the plug and blow the tunnel up" if our Gallic cousins did indeed invade. The French, indignant at such a suggestion, then pulled their own plug on the operation. Nearly a century later, the umbilical chord between Britain and the rest of Europe was still a quarter of a century away from completion.

Following two 'disastrous' election campaigns the Conservative Party was in a state of transition. A vote of no confidence was called against leader Ted Heath and in a leadership contest Margaret Thatcher defeated the part-time sailor to become the first woman to take the helm of a British political party. Edward du Cann, Chairman of the 1922 Backbench Committee was thrilled, "We have a new and rather exciting leader, Mrs Thatcher will make the Tory Party distinctive."

And it would be under Thatcher's generalship that work on the tunnel re-started in 1987, eventually opening in May 1994 during her successor John Major's reign as Prime Minister.

One of These Nights

A staple of many a band's repertoire in 1976 was The Eagles' "Take It Easy" and "One Of These Nights". Country Rock was in vogue with The Eagles carrying the mantle whilst Crosby, Stills, Nash and Young spent their time arguing amongst themselves.

Mick Harper of Auction wasn't following the trend, releasing his first solo record "I'm Crying" in July on Retreat Records, described by one music journalist as, "A Disco/Soul effort with falsetto-ish vocals, strings, wakka-wakka guitar and spoken sections a la Barry White."

The song was composed by Chris East and produced by Ray Cameron who is better known for being the father of comedian Michael McIntyre. Chris East also wrote "My Kinda Life" for Cliff Richard which was released in 1977 and reached No. 15 on the UK singles chart. "I'm Crying" should have been a hit too. Listen to "I'm Crying" on Youtube and You'll wonder how it wasn't. It was a great record which surely deserved success.

Mick had been on the scene for over a decade as vocalist with The Ray Brett Combo, The Cervezas, Formula Five and The New Formula. He was currently playing a summer season at Pontins Holiday Camp in Southsea along with guitarists Derek Cowie and Reggy Knowles, drummer Billy Mathieson and bassist Jim Smith as Auction. A bright future was predicted for the band but unfortunately, the summer was to end in acrimony.

Auction

Derek Cowie said, "The Pontins gig was scheduled to run for around five months but came to a premature end when Mick's record was released. We had agreed beforehand that if opportunities came along for television or radio work, we would all be in it together, but then Mick changed his mind and intimated that we were surplus to requirements if such an occasion did arrive. It did cause an upset and talk of unrest within the band soon resounded around the camp. Pre-empting Mick's departure, and no one could deny him the opportunity to make a go of something he had craved for longer than the rest of us, we recruited a Bluecoat called Perry, a Liverpudlian who was a great singer and also a great impressionist. Our hand had been forced, but we felt we had to do something. Mick was stunned. Perry came back to Corby with us and we rolled on with a name change, calling ourselves Steps."

"I'm Crying" failed to make the charts but not long after, Mick joined the Nottingham based group Paper Lace who had achieved chart success with "Billy Don't Be A Hero" and "The Night Chicago Died" in 1974. As happens in the music business, success can often be fleeting and for Paper Lace the hits would soon dry up when the punk revolution evolved. Pop bands, cabaret bands, rock bands were all destined for the exit door. Reminiscent of when the Beatles came along and signalled the end for the Acker Bilk's, Frank Ifield's, Adam Faith's, Tornados, as Shadows guitarist Bruce Welch told us when me and Bip interviewed him for the biography of Tornados drummer Clem Cattini in 2019, "We knew we were finished when the Beatles came along. I said to Clem, "We've had it now." "I know," he said.

So it was that punk signalled the end for Paper Lace. Mick had long dreamt of making the "big time" but the fates were against him. Paper Lace disbanded in 1979 and Mick returned to Corby where he continued to perform with a number of bands for many years and is still acclaimed by many to be the best soul singer to ever come out of Corby. A proclamation Alex "Scoop" Gordon, well known scribe in the 1960's, concurred with. Scoop was chief music writer for the *Evening Telegraph* and *Corby Leader* and he believed that the one thing that prevented Mick from making it big was his disablement, his false arm.

Talking in 2012, he opined, "The music business is all about image and I believe Mick suffered because of that. He was one of the most talented vocalists in the country, able to sing anything from blues, pop, gospel, rock. He deserved to have succeeded, but that's the business for you."

Mick sadly passed away in 2012.

Derek Cowie was still playing into the millennium, mainly in Germany with a long-time German friend, Hans Adam who I first met in Greece when I was on holiday during the beer festivals. There was a jam session in a bar and I borrowed a guitar and sang the Everly Brothers's "Walk Right Back". The guy providing the backbeat was Hans. We hit it off right away. He was a drummer with a band called The Runaways and he invited me over to Germany after the holiday. I later fixed up a gig for them at The Raven in Corby. It was their ambition he told me. Not to play the Raven, but to play in Britain!

Derek was born in Peterhead, came to Corby in the early 1960s with his family when the employment situation in North East Scotland became too severe. Long before the "oil boom".

His first job was with British Relay, a television company installing "piped" TV across the town. 'this is where I met Reggy Knowles who was to become one of my closest friends."

Derek had been keen to follow in his father's footsteps and become a piper. He said, "But that changed after I went to the Playhouse Cinema in Peterhead and saw the 'the Girl Can't Help It" starring Little Richard, Eddie Cochran, Chuck Berry and all the other American stars. Thoughts of becoming a bagpiper took a back seat and I worked hard to save enough money to get myself a guitar. A paper round, butcher's round, delivering bread rolls."

He added, "I'd do anything to enable me to get a guitar. Eventually I saved enough and purchased a Hofner Blonde Bass guitar for £25 from Sinclair's Music Shop, Aberdeen.

Then along came the Beatles and I was instantly a fan. In the 60s Corby had a number of established bands. The Size Seven, Midnighters, Crusaders, Invaders, Drumbeats, Phantoms, Rising Sons to name but a few. Most of us aspiring guitarists used to watch Jack Stewart, Dennis Priddy and Archie Brown to pick up tips and see how they played the riffs. Archie was ahead of them all, his playing of Chuck Berry's 'Johnny B. Goode' was amazing. Everybody was still tapping into Bert Weedon and Hank Marvin and the Shadows as The Stones and Beatles stuff was beyond most of us those days."

When word was out that a professional bass player from Scotland was in town, "A ruse by Reggy Knowles!" Derek laughed, Reggy and Charlie Parr from the Drumbeats came knocking on his door to tell him they needed a bass player to replace the departing Ted Ward.

"I still remember Charlie's reaction when I spoke. I had a strong Peterhead accent. "Christ," Charlie said, "a foreigner from Scotland!" He couldn't understand a word I was saying. I joined the Drumbeats and was with them for a year or so and then Reggy became disillusioned with the music scene and went on a near six-year sabbatical. That was the end of the Drumbeats and along with Billy Mathieson I joined Ricky Geoghegan's group The Comancheros which lasted a couple of years until Ricky eventually decided to go solo. That was when me and Billy teamed up with Mick Harper and Jim Smith to form Auction. And funny enough, Reggy then joined us. That was the best time of my life, particularly playing American air bases supporting the likes of Waylon Jennings and Willie Nelson.

Less memorable was a six-weekend residency we had at the Heathrow Hotel where we had to doss in a dressing room. After the third week we were really getting tired of it and one night a security guard with the name tag Crosby pinned to his lapel knocked on our door at 3am, and asked us gruffly what we were doing there. Mick jumped up and startled the guy. 'look Bing, either give us a song or eff off!" Next morning he was back and Billy gave him some verbal. That was it. We were given the sack!

Another memorable gig was in Merthyr Tydfil, a right rough looking joint. We played a club there and before we started, the MC told us, 'look boys, if they don't like you, we'll close the curtains!" Talk about giving us confidence! As it happened they did like us and we had a great night. Funny thing happened after the gig though when we loaded our van up and realised we were short of fuel. Jim spotted a crane parked up, grabbed a three-foot piece of tube and decided to try and siphon the diesel out of its tank into a five-gallon drum we had. Only trouble was, the crane's owner was looking out of his window and came chasing after us! We made a dash for it and found a lay-by to hide in, turning off our lights. After all that excitement, all we managed to get was about half a bloody pint!

Yet another riotous night was at Corby Civic, a dance called "A This Is Your Life Tribute to Nellie," for fund raiser Nellie Connaughty. All the bands, who had long been friends and rivals from the 50s and 60s ended up fighting each other! The Size Seven, Auction, Ricky and the Avengers, Harry Garter's Elastic Band, others who I can't remember were all on. It started over nothing, a silly accusation from one of the band members to another. Les Carter, a 'regular" in the Rockingham Arms and a guy not averse to a bit of action, was acting as a roadie when I went to enquire what was going on between one of the singers and a drummer.

"Nothing to do with you, Cowie," he said. So I nutted him! Somebody then took a swing at the Seven's Brian Dowell. Big Brian chinned him and sent him flying. Then it really kicked off. A real battle of the bands! The police were called in to sort it out. All those years when the bands played Nellie's Bin and there was never any trouble. It was amazing. Here we were, respectfully married and grown up, whatever - and everybody was trying to knock the crap out of each other!"

Elastic Band guitarist Frank Mullen remembers: "It was a good night until somebody stole our singer Pat Lavin's wife's handbag. Somehow the bag ended up next to Billy Mathieson's drums, somebody must have chucked it up on stage. Pat accused Billy who was totally mystified. Next thing, the two of them were battling away. Derek Cowie then joins in and before long, everybody is on stage fighting each other. It then spilled on to the dance floor. It was crazy. I stood back with drummer Alistair Brodie and watched them get on with it. I asked Pat what was missing, he told me £2. "All that for £2!" I said to him. It reminded me of Glasgow, I couldn't believe all this carry on. Pat's shirt was ripped right open, it was hanging off him, others were nursing cuts and bruises. What Nellie made of it I've no idea!"

A more peaceful night at the Civic was when jazz legend Stephane Grappelli appeared. A concert which was recorded and mentioned in Grappelli's biography, "A Life in Jazz". The subsequent CD was later released in 2003 on the Storyville Label with the sleeve notes explaining the somewhat surprise recording.

Stephane recorded frequently during the last three decades of his life and previously unissued recordings like this 1975 concert at Corby Festival Hall have continued to turn up. On this occasion lead guitarist Diz Dizley, rhythm guitarist Ike Isaacs and bassist David Moses accompany the violinist. The set is fairly typical, concentrating on standards from the 1920s through the 1940s, starting with a chugging but brisk take of "I Can't Believe That You're In Love With Me". The marvellous duet by Grappelli and Dizley of "Smoke Gets In Your Eyes," Grappelli's inventive treatment of "(Back Home Again In) Indiana" and the crowd pleasing 'sweet Georgia Brown" are among the highlights. It is simply amazing that Stephane Grappelli never seemed to go on autopilot as he played a song for the hundredth (or possibly thousandth) time, this CD is a valuable addition to his already vast discography.

The Annual Corby Arts Festival, an important fixture on the Corby calendar and awaited on with great anticipation went ahead again in spite of concerns about its expenditure with Supremo Trevor Wright more than optimistic.

"This festival will be as good, if not better, than those in past years. Beer gardens and late bars are an added attraction and the very idea of a week-long orgy of music and entertainment and fun seems to bring out the best in Corby people. The high spot must be jazz singer George Melly but a dose of Slavonic tonic in the form of Ivan Stepenov's Balalaikas, providing a couple of hours of colour, gaiety and folk song are bound to cause some interest."

A troupe of Morris Dancers kicked the week off by embarking on a tour of local villages, East Carlton, Middleton, Rockingham and Gretton before they headed back to the Town Centre where they vied for attention with the German Velbert Fire Brigade band. Late night events included The Kursaal Flyers, a Southend rock band who were the subject of a BBC documentary this year, playing in the Willow Room on the Monday. Fatso, with former Bonzo Dog guitarist Neil Innes in the line-up and who featured in the TV series 'Rutland Weekend Television" were support. Tuesday was the 'late Night Jazz" spot with John Chiltern's Feetwarmers featuring George Melly who was described in *Melody Maker* as "Britain's number one jazz singer, a major British discovery of the 1970s". Even though he had been around since the 1950s! "Fame, that dangerous bird, has brushed my cheek once more!" George proclaimed.

Corby Festival programme featuring George Melly

"George Melly was a right case," Trevor said. "I was wondering if I would recognise him when he turned up. Then all of a sudden this short squat chap arrived, with a yellow top hat, green jacket and red trousers on. "Ah! that has to be

George!" I thought. He was brilliant as well, amusing too with his tales. In the bar after the show I introduced him to a local Evening Telegraph reporter who was keen to interview him.

"Do you mind?" the reporter asked George.

"Not at all," George replied.

"Do you want a drink?" George asked the reporter, and before he had a chance to reply, he said to the barman, "get him a double whisky".

George started knocking them back. The reporter was trying to ask him questions and each time, he was given another large whisky! He didn't get much of a story, but at the end of the night, he was steaming!

Trevor's enthusiasm for Slavonic music failed to ignite the interest he had hoped for but all the same the Telegraph reporter, don't know if it was the same one, wrote, 'the small audience went overboard as the nationally costumed band put on a fine show in true Russian style.

Better received was the return of Bluesman, 66 year-old cousin Joe, sustained by white wine and menthol cigarettes, and billed by Trevor as a "gospel wailing, jazz playing, rock and rolling, soul shouting, tap dancing bluesman from New Orleans." An all-rounder then.

Disappointments came with the late withdrawals of jazzman Ronnie Scott, due to ill health, and the Chapman Whitney Streetwalkers who were down for the Saturday Night Rock show. Tony Coe, (Pink Panther theme with Henry Mancini and one time member with the Humphrey Lyttleton and Johnny Dankworth bands) covered the Scott spot whilst ex Small Faces bass player Ronnie Lane filled in with his new band Slim Chance. The week was finished off with a performance from the Halle Orchestra, conducted by Owain Arwell Hughes.

Despite accruing debts of around £700, the Arts Festival was given the thumbs up to continue for the following year in 1976, albeit in a more refined and limited form after some considerable debate in which a number of councillors were in favour for calling time on the event.

The running of the Civic Centre was reported to be costing around £73,500 a year. Of thirteen shows in a six-month period up until the 31st of March, only three had made a profit. The overall loss stood at £2,119. Most profitable evening was the performance of "Ballet for All" by the Royal Ballet Touring Company, which made £214 and a gig by rock 'n roll band Mud, the "Tiger Feet" group, which made a profit of £52. That's right, that's right... 52 notes.

Not so well received and disappointing for the promoters Ned McGuigan and Kenny Payne was American star Tim Rose (Hey Joe, Morning Dew), who played at the Civic in January. It was Ned and Kenny's second promotion, following on from folk singer Bridget St. John which Ned revealed had recorded a loss of £200.

"We need 275 people to break even for Tim Rose," Kenny confessed beforehand. Regrettably, the hall was again only half full. For those who couldn't be bothered to turn up, they missed a show described as "a faultless performance from the Virginian folk singer" in the *Evening Telegraph*.

Tim Rose was relatively unknown in Britain it has to said but back home in the States he was a big star, a close friend of Barry Maguire (Eve of Destruction), Mama Cass and the Mamas and Papas (Monday Monday etc). Adding this to the advertising might have helped the promotion but hindsight is a wonderful thing.

More successful was Scottish folk singer/comedian Billy Connolly who also made an appearance in January. His bawdy humour couldn't have gone down better anywhere else than in Corby, which included a gag about him travelling through a village called Husbands Bosworth on his way to Corby, "How much is yer... husband's Bosworth?" Billy roared with laughter. As did the audience!

The former ship building welder had split with his friend Gerry Rafferty in The Humblebums in 1971 to pursue a solo career as a folk singer. His anecdotes, presentation and repartee came to the fore in-between songs and he was encouraged to develop this side of the business. It was the beginning of a career that would launch him to worldwide fame.

Away from the Civic, a "Rock 'n Roll" event was organised by Corby Rugby Club members Aivors Zakss, Roger Clark and Rob Purdie in September, to be held in a marquee on the Rugby Club ground at the Rockingham Triangle at the north end of the town.

The Rugby Club had become a popular venue with Alan Wetherell's Touchdown Disco and Live Music on Sunday Nights. The disco clientele was aged in their late-teens and early-twenties, made up basically with rival clans from the Phoenix and Kingfisher pubs. Great friends most probably but virtually every week when tanked with cans of Tennants lager or Brew XI, there would be a scrap to sort out. Rock nights were less frenzied with punters more interested in enjoying the music of Corby's Bumper, Northampton bands Scenery, August Bank Holiday and others, including a band called Iron Maiden. It seems unbelievable but it turns out they weren't the famous Heavy Metal band that went on to worldwide acclaim. This Iron Maiden were a local band, Kettering I believe. It was enough though for bassist Steve Harris of the famous Maiden to contact the Kettering outfit to tell them they would have to change their name, as it was already registered. A claim to fame there for somebody!

To help in the organisation of the Marquee event, Rob Purdie enlisted Franny Lagan who became one of the town's leading entrepreneurs over the coming decades. Franny, born in 1952, was from Coleraine, Northern Ireland. His family moved to Corby in the 1950s, like thousands of others, in search of a new start and employment in the town's steelworks.

Corby's entrepreneurs Franny Lagan and Trevor Wright

Leaving school (Pope John) in 1969 with four O Levels, Franny confessed, "I didn't have a clue what I wanted to do. I was supposed to be doing my A levels but I jgot more and more bored with it which didn't go unnoticed by my teacher. That's when I decided to jack it in and look for a job. I wasn't interested in being a welder or fitter, more a white-collar worker. I tried for three, one of which was a trainee manager at the Fine Fare supermarket in Corporation Street.

Somehow though that didn't feel right. I thought I'd probably spend half my time as a glorified shelf stacker. I ended up taking an office job at the Cold Draw Plant (CDS) in the Tubeworks. That was a good little number and became even better when my gaffer, a Welshman called Ron Lyden, called me and said "I've got just the job for you boyo." He realised I was good with figures and thus gave me a job sorting out percentage sheets and such things. It also gave me plenty of free time and inadvertently led me to a career path I hadn't visualised. Coming up to that Christmas, Ron asked me if I would be interested in organising a festive bash for everybody in the CDS. I thought I'd give it a go and the first person I contacted was my friend Tom Howarth who apart from being a DJ with his own disco was also involved with the Hamblin's set up at Corby Bowl, which obviously incorporated the Exclusive Club, the forerunner to Shafts.

"Do you think You'll get enough people to fill the club?" Tom asked. I was confident, "watch me," I told him. Back at work, I began to phone up everybody I knew who worked in offices all around the works. Tickets were a modest 10p and leading up to the big night, the phone was red hot as more and more people heard about it and wanted to go. It was a great success and sparked off my interest in an entrepreneurial career.

Rob Purdie asked me if I could sort the tickets out for the marquee event, which were priced at the princely sum of 30p, and I printed them off on a cheap printing machine, which with hindsight, anybody could have copied with ease. Rob couldn't believe it when I showed them to him. "Is that it?" They were good enough though. The marquee itself was organised by the rugby club's entertainments chief, a guy called Roger Clark who was affectionately known as Roger the Dodger!"

Searching for a good title for the Bank Holiday event, Franny admitted he stole the name, 'midsummer" from the Wembley Stadium gig featuring the Beach Boys and Elton John on June 21st.

"Though the local bands, Stutz, Auction, Harry Garter and so on could hardly replicate Elton John and the Beach Boys, interest in the gig intensified once we got our teeth into the promotion. I spent days handing out flyers to everybody that happened to be passing through the Town Centre. "Give one to your friends, take them to work," that was along with me telephoning everybody at work and sticking flyers all-round the Works and the town. It worked. I sold around 330 on my own. They reckon that nearly a thousand turned up!"

Rugby player Bob Smith helped out on the day. "What I remember is that we worked our socks off behind the bar, it was bedlam. We sold Tennant's lager by the sleeve, 24 cans in a pack. It was crazy! Next day during the clean-up, the hedgerow along Rockingham Road was awash with empty yellow and blue cans, millions of them!"

Pat Lavin, extrovert singer with Harry Garter's Elastic Band, had a vivid memory of the event.

"It was a hot day and I suggested to the rest of the band that we should wear shorts, just to be different. We started our set with Ian Hunter's "Once Bitten Twice Shy" with me walking up to the mic and saying "Ello!" which was Hunter's trademark. The crowd, who'd been drinking all afternoon, pelted us with beer cans! We had to take cover. It was all a bit of fun, nobody got hurt. In fact, everybody thought it was a great laugh!"

Pat and his band were often courting controversy and they were in the headlines again following a gig at a Lodge Park School Leaving Party. Headmaster Mr. Rumbelow thought they were disgusting, lurid and promoting sex. Years later Pat met a girl up the town centre who reminded him about the dance, "I remember that night," she said, "it was brilliant!"

"We also played regularly at The Flying Fox in Lutterworth" Pat recalled, "a bikers pub. This was arranged by our keyboard player Pete Dyne, a self-confessed 'rocker". Despite that we always had the mod gear on. They thought we were a right bunch of queers! They always gave us a good shout though."

Pete said, "I was right into that scene, had the bike, the gear. The Fox was a great hang out which our gang used to frequent regular. I booked the band in and Pat nearly wet himself when he saw the punters. There was a hall up these narrow stairs and once you were up there, there was no other way out. Never thought of the fire hazard when I think about it! A ritual these Lutterworth rockers had was at the end of the night they formed a circle, like a huddle, and started jumping up and down on the dance floor, which would vibrate and looked as if it was ready to cave in at any moment. Course it never did but the first time you experienced it, it was pretty scary. The people in the bar underneath must have been sceptical though!"

Harry Garter and His Elastic Band apart, a report published by the Clothing Manufacturers Federation of Great Britain was scathing on the attitudes of the male half of the population.

"Our sloppy dress styles make the British the worst dressed men in Europe. The British male once prided himself as the Peacock of Europe but is now falling way behind his rivals in the world sartorial league."

The Federation report concluded that on average, a British male spent 74p a week on suits, jackets, slacks etc. Whilst the average German spent six times as much and as a result, "is usually immaculately turned out." Which probably explains the decline and disappearance of so many men's outfitters from the High Street down the years. Corby Town Centre once boasted George Allan, Hepworth's, Burton's, Abington's, Roadnights, Millets, John Collier. Only George Allan's remained into the millennium.

With the year coming to an end, 'disco" was becoming increasingly more popular as the "progressive music" genre began to wane. Rick Wakeman's 'myths and Legends of King Arthur" performed on Wembley Ice Rink was stretching it way too far for many.

Rick, keyboard player with The Strawbs and Yes, even confessed once that during a gig with Yes in Manchester, he was that bored playing 'tales Of A Topographic Oceans," now there's a pretentious title if ever there was one, he asked a roadie to get him a pizza, and he proceeded to eat it during the performance.

"There were a couple of pieces in the show where I didn't have much to do, and it was a bit dull. Half the audience were in a narcotic rapture, and the other half were bored and asleep."

Interviewed in the *New Musical Express,* David Bowie must have been at the gig.

"Rock is dead, it's a toothless old woman," said Ziggy Stardust and the Spiders From Mars star.

Part Two

Long Hot Summer

1976

The Rolling Stones were on tour for the first time in three years, promoting their latest album "Black and Blue," their first to feature new guitarist Ronnie Wood. On May 14th, they were appearing at Leicester's Granby Halls, a show which might have been hailed as explosive had a bomb scare not been proved to be a hoax.

As reported in the *Leicester News and Chronicle*, 'the Stones opened up with "Honky Tonk Women" which immediately had the capacity crowd on their feet and stomping. Oblivious to anything else going on, they were clearly unaware of a brigade of St John's ambulance men mingling and shuffling amongst their midst. A bomb scare, which proved to be a hoax, had the St. John's people scouring for "anything vaguely suspicious" in every row of the hall whilst the band played on."

Does seem rather odd that it was the St John's Ambulance people searching the aisles and arena and not the Army Bomb Disposal Unit but obviously they didn't take the threat seriously.

The *New Musical Express* hailed the return of the Stones with wit, mindful of the historical location, the apparent final resting place of one of our most famous Kings, Richard III. (Legend had it that Richard was a regular visitor to Leicester and had shuttled off his mortal coil in the city back in 1485. An archeological dig in 2012 proved the point when his remains were discovered under a car park). Richard had lain there in peace for over 500 years.

This was the NME's take on the show, "100 minutes of hot sweaty rock. Most impressive feature was the marvellous interplay between Keith Richards who looked like some rock and roll Richard III who had been through a greasy mangle, and new recruit Ronnie Wood who smiled like a mischievous chain-smoking Disney cartoon crow." Adding for good measure, 'Ronnie Wood looked like a 40 fags a day brillo pad!"

With the Stones Mark III back in business it was somewhat ironic that their idol Chuck Berry, "No Particular Place To Go," was playing in Leicester the same month, in cabaret at Baileys Night Club.

The music press must have been delighted to have the original bad boys of British Rock back, such was the blandness of the music scene, the Stones apart, and Swedish phenomenon Abba who had emerged on the scene after their victorious 1974 Eurovision Song Contest. A Beatles revival with the release of all their original singles in original covers was another highlight. Record companies jumped on the bandwagon and the 1976 charts would also see re-entries by Dion's 'the Wanderer," Elvis Presley's "Girl of My Best Friend," and The Who's 'substitute" amongst a plethora of reissues.

Conversely, whilst all this had the "baby boomers" besides themselves with excitement, the Wurzel's "Combined Harvester" had rock fans scratching their heads at the depths of banality the charts had plummeted.

The scene was set for a change and by the end of the year, Punk would arrive and sweep away the dross and nostalgia, sending shock waves through the Establishment, just as the Teddy Boys, Mods and Rockers and Skinheads did before them.

The Stones however would continue to roll, long after the Punk fad, and others to follow, to prove if nothing else, that not only were they the self-styled "greatest rock and roll band" - but the longest surviving too.

***

Whipping up a storm at home and causing havoc across the country at the beginning of the year were hurricane force winds of 105mph. Twenty-two people lost their lives in weather described as the worst since 1953. Railways were severely affected, as ever, with the perennial leaves on the lines and overhead power supplies collapsing, whilst in Southend, a light aircraft was blown onto the tracks near the airport, which was, well, something different..

High winds also brought down a crane in Manchester. A pinnacle on the main tower of Worcester Cathedral crashed through the roof and in Corby, two dozen families were evacuated from Counts Farm Road flats on the Exeter estate when gales ripped the roof off, sending tons of debris crashing to the ground.

Carnage on the Exeter Estate

A result of all this carnage was that Summer was being written off, such is British pessimism and obsession with the weather. Long before the term "Climate Change" entered our vocabulary. How wrong could the doom mongers be? The 1976 Summer saw excessive heat suffocating the country, resulting in the longest and most severe drought Britain had experienced in over 200 years.

When the hurricanes subsided, the heatwave in Britain started in earnest. Fifteen consecutive days in southern England saw the temperature rise above 32 degrees, resulting in reservoirs and rivers drying up. With water running short, Prime Minister Jim Callaghan introduced a powers bill to enable water authorities to redirect supplies. He also appointed Denis Howell as Minister for Water to control the drought. Denis started with a campaign to get the public to limit their use of water. Millions of stickers and leaflets were produced to publicise ways of saving water.

Stickers to place above taps to remind you to turn it off and not leave it running unnecessarily.

Suggestions like putting a brick in lavatory cisterns to reduce the amount of water used in a flush were encouraged. Short films were made for television and a cinema release. The public were asked to bath with a friend. Which might have gone down well in some quarters but not all. "U Turn Me Off" slogans emblazoned on T Shirts moulding the female breast sold several thousand. Which did go down well. Ideas to ease the situation included towing an iceberg from the North Atlantic, which was a barmy idea if ever there was one, and laying an emergency pipeline down the middle of motorways, reversing the flow of rivers, importing water in giant tankers from Norway.

Emergency measures to prevent a national disaster were eventually introduced in August as forest and heath fires raged throughout the month. The Fire Service, stretched to breaking point, introduced Green Goddesses to pump waste water and sewage to fight the blazes. The South West Water Authority had 10,000 standpipes ready in anticipation of water rationing. Homes in South Wales had water turned off at 7pm. Public toilets in Corby Town Centre were put on a three-day week in an attempt to save water. A flush restriction policy meant shoppers would be inconvenienced except on market days. Farmers saw their harvest ruined, agriculture suffered half a billion failed crops. The cost of a cauliflower soared to 45p. Housewives were warned that Brussel sprouts would cost 5p each by Christmas, precipitating a surge in frozen food panic buying.

If this wasn't bad enough, housewives - why was it always assumed it was only housewives who did the shopping? -

were dealt another massive blow after a Common Market farm deal made in Brussels hit dairy products. Butter went up 8p a pound to 45p. Cheese up 4p a pound and milk a 1p a pint. Housewives, and I guess a few of their better-halves, were livid.

Agricultural Minister Fred Peart was oblivious to the concerns. "I'm confident 1976 will turn out to be a good year for farmers" he proclaimed confidently. William Molloy, Labour MP for North Ealing was less than convinced. 'the Brussels dagger is pointing straight at the heart of British inflationary recovery."

The introduction of Denis Howell as the Minister of Drought was later praised by Sheffield MP, Roy Hattersley. "Denis was a brilliant appointment. He used to go to drought ridden areas carrying an umbrella to demonstrate his confidence that it would soon begin to rain. A cheerful but blunt figure, his catchphrase was, "Every bucket of household water saved will be less to carry from the standpipe later."

A folk song was even dedicated to the minister. "Save a bucket a day for Denis, keep industry on the move, It's work and safety first and last is your thirst, So You'll have to use the birdbath to flush the loo. Throw away your hose for Denis, put your garden tools in to pawn, sit and watch your flowers die 'neath the blue and cloudless sky, you'll be beautifully rested and as brown as a lawn."

Not exactly Bob Dylan or Jake Thackray, but it made a lot of people smile. Roy as well I suspect!

The drought was also a cause of dismay for contestants at the World Conker Championships held in Ashton, near Oundle.

"It's a poor year for horse chestnuts," cried competitor Pat McMahon, "you couldn't make it up!"

Pat normally selected his conkers from the Chestnut trees at Kirby Hall, (one of the great Elizabethan houses of England) and nurtured them before the eagerly awaited contest. Baking them in other words.

With the yield down this year, hundreds of conkers were flown in from Jersey and Pat had to settle for a random conker out of a basket. The winner was a Mexican, Jorge Ramirez, making his debut. Delighted with his success he then stunned the organisers by refusing to return in 1977 to defend his title and so the trophy was Mexico bound, never to be seen again.

"He was a right bandit!" Pat exclaimed.

Much to everyone's relief, rain did eventually arrive at the end of August, though restrictions in some places remained until October. And with some irony, the autumn became one of the wettest on record! Meteorologists later explained the phenomenon, "In the 60s and early 70s, there were very few warm summers. People were not used to the Mediterranean type heat wave. A blocking anti cyclone, the Water Boards" dread, parked itself above the British Isles."

***

The winds of change bellowing around the country in those early months, and Counts Farm Road, were also being felt in the steel industry, which instigated a mass meeting at Corby Festival Hall in January by Corby steelworkers to discuss their concerns over the town's future as a major steel producer.

Fears had first surfaced in 1972 when the Government announced, following a fourteen-month review by the Minister of State for Industry, Lord Beswick, a ten-year development strategy to convert British Steel from a large number of small-scale works using largely obsolete equipment, to a more compact organisation with highly competitive plants, with a cutback of 44,000 jobs. The news was undoubtedly a shock for Corby steelworkers but then councillor Kelvin Glendenning astonished everyone with his insensitivity by telling a planning committee that houses backing onto the Blast Furnaces in Stephenson's Way should be demolished. 'the whole area should be levelled off and made into an amenity. Not many people want to live near Blast furnaces." Kelvin suggested.

As it happened, ten years down the line, nobody would live near the Blast Furnaces!

It was close by the steelworks that clothing magnate Frank Brierley started building his empire, selling socks from an old furniture van parked in the White Horse carpark with posters adorning messages like 'Welcome to the madhouse!' and 'Don't stand there looking - buy something!'

Following a few years away and his supermarket business reportedly collapsing like a "precarious stack of baked bean tins," Frank was back, making a welcome return to Corby, and defiant. "I shall sell my last pair of tights only when St. Peter calls me" he roared.

Frank had a string of self-service supermarkets at Northampton, Leicester, Wellingborough, Peterborough and Birmingham. Following years of success as the pirate of town centres, he left the helm by giving up his managing directorship to become life president. It was then the new Brierley helmsman tried to change the indoor market image. The tills stopped ringing, and the Brierley fortune was lost.

Returning with new vigour after a humiliating and degrading trial in a London court, which saw him acquitted of all charges of conspiracy and handling stolen goods, he was ebullient, saying, "I'm not posh, never have been. I'll never make any money. I sell everything as cheaply as I can. I want to help poorer people so that they know if they want a jumper and can't afford one, they'll get one at Frank Brierley's."

Frank's image, and that of Corby, wasn't helped by a comment from Chamber of Commerce member Bert Cripps that the town was "tatty and untidy." A comment that prompted an angry response from the Chairman of Corby Environmental Services, Jimmy Kane.

"Mr. Cripps should visit other towns and compare them to Corby. I have travelled the length and breadth of the country and every time I am in another town I deliberately visit the town centre to see how the cleanliness, facilities and amenities compare with ours. We are among the best."

1976 was proving to be an 'annus horribilis' for the town. In April, British Sealed Beams, one of the town's biggest employers outside of the steelworks, announced the impending closure of their factory on the Earlstrees Industrial estate, with the loss of 530 jobs. Which was hot on the heels of York Trailers and Golden Wonder announcing redundancies.

British Sealed Beams

British Sealed Beams boasted one of the most popular social clubs in town, catering for its hundreds of workers along with those opposite at Golden Wonder on Earlstrees Road. The 'Beams' was thriving most weeknights and every weekend with 'live' music, discos, darts and dominoes teams, and bingo. Along with the Rangers Club and Corby Rugby Club, 'Rocky Road" (Rockingham Road) was reminiscent of Mathew Street in Liverpool for entertainment. This might be exaggerating a bit but the town's taxi owners did a roaring business conveying revellers to these dens on the outskirts of Corby. So the disappointment felt with the news of the factory closure was tangible. The Rangers and Corby Rugby clubs may have been rubbing their hands with glee at the possibility of absorbing the trade but much to the relief of the Beams members and their associates, a committee was formed to take over affairs and the venue was relaunched under a new banner as The Earlstrees Club.

The Earlstrees Club formerly known as The Beams

***

When Sir Henry Chisholm retired as Chairman of Corby Development Corporation, a political merry-go-round was set in motion. Prime Minister Harold Wilson followed Henry's lead and he too called it a day, handing in his resignation to the Queen after thirteen years as leader of the Labour Party. Harold was succeeded by Jim Callaghan, described as "big, relaxed and handsome," staving off a challenge from what some might have said, the less handsome Michael Foot.

Liberal leader Jeremy Thorpe was next through the departure door, resigning in June after what he claimed was a witch-hunt over homosexual allegations. David Steel stepped into his shoes.

The comings and goings wasn't confined to the British Isles. Heads of government were rolling around the globe. Peanut farmer Jimmy Carter was elected America's 39th President during celebrations to commemorate the nation's 200th birthday. Jimmy running "as an honest outsider and reformer," defeated the residing incumbent of the White House, Gerard Ford. Carter appealed to many voters after the Watergate scandal as Ford was seen to being too close to his predecessor Richard Nixon's administration.

During the campaign, Carter promised a "blanket pardon for Vietnam draft dodgers" which went down well but his credibility took a battering when he admitted in an interview with *Playboy* to "lusting in his heart" for women other than his wife. The bounder.

On the other side of the globe, China was plunged into turmoil when Chairman Mao passed away at the age of 82. Chaos ensued. Ideological cleansing began with attacks by Red Guards on so-called "intellectuals" to remove bourgeois influences. Millions were forced into manual labour and tens of thousands were executed. Mao's successor Hua Guofeng ordered the arrest of four leading radicals, including Mrs. Mao who was charmingly described as "filthy and contemptible - like dog's dung!" A case of "say what you mean..."

Angola was also in turmoil following its independence from Portugal. Cuban forces, backed by Russia, fighting UNITA (The National Union for Total Independence of Angola) prompted a tirade from Margaret Thatcher during a speech in her capacity as opposition leader. Her diatribe slamming Russia for their involvement was received with amusement in Moscow. The Kremlin dubbing her "the Iron Lady". Which appeared to delight her.

Civil War had erupted in Angola when rival groups, MPLA (Popular Movement for the Liberation of Angola) and UNITA fought for the right to rule. British mercenaries joined the fight against the Marxist regime, tempted by the pay packet of £150 a week. Among them were Corby men Jimmy Rhinds and Peter McAleese, Carl Fortuin from Kettering and Tom Chambers from Wellingborough, who was one of the first to return home after he'd witnessed the cold-blooded murder of eight prisoners shot on his first day in action. Tom revealed to the *Evening Telegraph* that he had been in fear of his life. "We were worried because if we demanded to come back we'd also be executed."

Tom also spoke about the recruiting campaign, "Many were not even trained soldiers and others, especially the SAS guys were kill hungry. We were told to look for a man wearing a brown suede coat under the clock at Paddington Station and to ask him if his name was Frank. About twenty others were also there, with police looking on, obviously aware of what was going on."

Frank whisked the group off to the Park Court Hotel where they were given a short back and sides haircut and an open briefing on what they could expect in Angola. They were also informed that "no money was necessary as everything was free, including the women". Their pay packets would be forwarded on to their wives or partners. (Which never happened.) From Heathrow the band of mercenaries was flown to Brussels before moving on to Zaire where they were billeted in a palace in Kinshasa, supplied by President Mobuto. A few hours later they were flown by light aircraft to a camp near the Angolan border and a group, which included Tom, was selected for a rescue mission, a three-hour journey by troop carrier fifty miles over the border. Ten of their comrades were holed up by the MPLA. This is where the eight prisoners were captured and executed, prompting Tom Chambers to reconsider his future.

Another drama unfolding was in neighbouring Uganda, where a hijacked Air France plane, flying from Israel to Paris, landed with 250 passengers on board. The hijackers, two from the Popular Front for the Liberation of Palestine and two from Germany's Baader-Meinhof gang, diverted the plane to Entebbe where they were joined by three more colleagues before demanding the release of 53 militants held in jails in Israel and four other countries. Uganda's President, Idi Amin, arrived at the airport to give a speech in support of the PFLP and supplied the hijackers with extra troops and weapons.

A deadline was set for their demands to be met or they would blow up the airliner and its passengers. 150 hostages were released but the hijackers continued to hold the remaining 100. Their plan was foiled with a dramatic raid by Israel's elite Sayeret Matkal to free the hostages on the night of July

3rd. Amin was humiliated by the surprise, believing that Kenya had colluded with Israel in planning the raid and hundreds of Kenyans living in Uganda were massacred soon afterwards.

The raid, and Adi Amin was immortalised in song by St Cecilia guitarist John Proctor who gave it to Corby band Honey to play in the finals of a talent contest, and caused a storm when they were subsequently banned from appearing at the town's Labour Club because it was felt the song was racist and unpatriotic. Club officials objected to the chorus,

"Idi Amin, Idi Amin, he wants to become our Queen. So everybody, stand up and shout, 'We love Big Daddy because he knocks us about'." Sounds fairly innocuous and Proctor was unrepentant, calling the Labour Club officials 'silly'.

If only they listened to the words of the song they would know it is meant to be satirical. I am putting the Queen on a pedestal and making Amin look the fool he is. The song runs to three verses and talks about the Entebbe raid and how Amin hopes to save the world from the "ultimate grave". My Adi Amin song is very topical and I am hoping both the song and Honey do well.

Honey was one of the sweetest bands on the circuit, originally with Pat Lavin, Pete Dyne, Paul Cross, John McCormack, Alex Henderson, Rita McCosker and Theresa Morgan and later on, Corrie Gillies.

They were used to the whims of workingmen's club officials as drummer Alex Henderson recalled, "We played all the usual haunts in Corby, the Silver Band, St Brendans, Labour Club, Ex Servicemans, British Legion, Sealed Beams,

Catholic Club etc. but mostly out of town. Committeemen were the same everywhere. Complaining we were too loud, could we keep it clean… you just had to put up with them. You know what it's like, give somebody a badge and it goes to their head."

Honey, one of the sweetest bands around

Pat McMahon recalls many a barney when he was working at the St Brendans Club where his dad Joe was Steward for a number of years. 'the band would start and you could guarantee a committeeman would straight away tell them, "you're too loud, turn it down." The punters didn't seem too bothered but dad used to shout back to the band, "turn it up!" So my dad and the committeeman would be arguing and shouting at each other and I remember on one occasion, the singer, might have been Pat Lavin, was shouting back, "Will you make your mind up!"

Alex Henderson; "We won a competition at the Civic Festival Hall when I think we were one of six acts/bands. We did three numbers "You Win Again" by Hot Chocolate, "I Only Wanna Be With You" by Dusty Springfield and the song written by John Proctor about Adi Amin. The prize for winning the talent contest was a gig to support Smokie at the Theatre Royal in Norwich. They had just made it into the charts with "If You Think You Know How To Love Me."

It was a gig keyboard player Pete Dyne has vivid memories of, confessing, "It was the first time I'd played in front of such a big audience. And I have to admit, I froze for a moment. But I soon got over it and enjoyed the experience."

Alex added, "We also played many RAF bases, once when we were support to Liverpool Express who were very big at the time after having a huge hit with 'You Are My Love'. Another memorable gig was at The Croft Club in Downham Market, which co-existed as a Nudist Club."

A gig witnessed by a reporter from the *Downham Market Weekly,* who clearly wasn't too impressed. "I wouldn't know if Honey are inhibited by a New Seekers image or not, but for me, Saturday didn't take off until the last spot when the boys took the show by the scruff of the neck and shook some life into it. Until then it had been pleasant enough but nothing to write home about. A five-piece line up of two guitars, drums, with a guy and gal lead vocalists. When you have a young lady in a group she's invariably the centre of attraction so it follows that she should have enough charisma to charm the birds off the trees but this agreeably voiced lass had a most doleful look about her and was distinctly lacking in personality.

Speaking to her afterwards, I suggested everything would look so much better if only she smiled a little. The answer I received was that she's not allowed to. Apparently where they normally operate, Corby way, folks go to see the boys in the band. Odd? Maybe, but then different parts of the country have their own ideas of what they want. Smart looking with music for listening to. But I reiterate that for one at least, it was the last set that made it, four, five-part harmony, bags of showmanship and driving numbers such as 'the Wild Side Of Life" and 'Tell Her'."

Play That Funky Music

After three years of travelling around Europe working in hotels, night clubs and discotheques, former Corby Grammar Schoolboy Dougie Martell was now settled down in Denmark. He was resident DJ at Daddy's Music Hall, formerly known as the Hard Rock Cafe, in Copenhagen.

Dougie's travels began in 1970 when he worked the summer season as a Redcoat at Butlins Holiday Camp, Skegness. Eighteen months later he was resident DJ at The Hive, Bournemouth, enjoying "the unique experience" of working with many famous acts and rock groups of the day. A Who's Who of the 'Underground' scene, East of Eden, Savoy Brown, Juicy Lucy, Supertramp, Renaissance, as well as chart toppers Chicory Tip, Love Affair and the 'Shotgun Wedding' man Roy C.

Doug Martell with Ed Stewart

Doug moved to Weymouth in 1973 and started his own Roadshow, touring the country with several important agents. It was in Weymouth that Doug won the prestigious national disc jockey competition sponsored by *DJ and Radio Monthly* magazine. The success brought in several national offers on top of a trip to the USA to see the TV and Radio world at work in the States.

In 1976 he was offered the residency in Copenhagen. An opportunity he grabbed and would find him working with famous names as diverse as Blues legend Muddy Waters and punk protagonists the Sex Pistols. Doug met his wife Jonna in Copenhagen, over the next ten years, in between having two children, they set up and operated the country's leading disc jockey agency. "Being the first foreigner to hold an entertainments licence was an enormous privilege" Doug proudly admits. He was also employed by a Scandinavian music paper as a photo journalist and met and interviewed many artists during their North European tours.

Doug eventually moved back to the U.K. with Jonna and children Kevin and Kiki in 1986, setting up a business in manufacturing flight cases and lighting effects. He continued to run his own very successful roadshow by night and was contracted work with Scandinavian Seaways to supply disc jockeys and equipment on their North Sea routes.

Of all the highlights of his career Doug sights his time with Blues legend Muddy Waters amongst the best. "He was a lovely guy. I was given the job as chaperone to Muddy. I helped him up and down the stairs in the Club, sorted out anything he wanted. He sat perched on a stool on the edge of the stage and was brilliant. People go on about all the great blues guitarists, Eric Clapton, Robert Cray and the like. Muddy Waters was up there with the best of them. A great guitar player. His fingers were so nimble and the licks he produced were remarkable. He had the audience captivated.

There was an aura about him, gave you a feeling of being in a great presence. I always felt he appreciated people who were courteous and kind. He invited me and Jonna over to his home in America but unfortunately we never got round to it, and sadly he died before we could take up his offer."

There's a story that in his later years, when Muddy started making the money he was long overdue, he'd call up his friend John Lee Hooker and the pair would jokingly brag about the cars they owned. If Muddy said he had a new Mercedes then Hooker would call back a few weeks later and tell Waters he had just bought a Mercedes with a phone in the back. It was a small perk in a long career of endless nights gigging, playing or recording for little return.

For playing blues didn't make much money unless you were somebody, as Waters told Charles Shaar Murray of the *New Musical Express* in 1977, 'the kind of blues I play, there's no money in it. You makes a good livin' when you gets established like I am, but you don't reach that kind of overnight million dollar thing, man…no way. If you play nuthin' but blues, it's hard to get big off of it. It takes years and years and still the kids come in and go, "Whose he?"

Doug said, "Phil Lynott of Thin Lizzy was another nice guy, although completely out of control. We used to have drinks together whenever we teamed up at gigs. Phil just didn't care about anything. His father-in-law, Leslie Crowther, TV Presenter of 'New Faces' fame, was always trying to get him to ease off the drink and other pleasantries but he didn't give a toss. He had no responsibilities whatsoever." This probably explains how he turned up one time for a Thin Lizzy gig at the Bowling Alley in Corby without a drummer. Three weeks before "Whisky In The Jar" hit the top of the charts.

Dougie King was the promoter and looking out from the stage, Dougie press ganged his friend Richard Oliff into stepping in. "He'll do it!" he shouted.

Richard, radio broadcaster and journalist, was an aspiring drummer with a group of friends calling themselves Wildlife at the time. He began his radio career with KCBC, which later became Connect FM in the 1990s. He joined the BBC in 2001 to present a daily consumer and current affairs programme, during which time he worked with TV personalities Alan Titchmarsh and Charlie Dimmock at the Chelsea Flower Show, broadcast live in front of an audience on the banks of the River Thames.

He later worked on HFM (Market Harborough) presenting the Drive Show before moving to Bournemouth in 2019 where he continues to work on the airwaves with Forest FM.

Richard Oliff

He remembers the Thin Lizzy night at Corby Bowl well. "Dougie King regaled audiences for years with that tale, they were great nights at the Corby Bowl. Chicken Shack, Medicine Head, The Pink Fairies, Van Der Graf Generator were amongst other top names who played there. I'd never heard of Thin Lizzy before that night though. Can't remember why they didn't have a drummer. Brian Downey was the incumbent of the seat but maybe he'd got lost somewhere en route!"

Whatever happened to Downey, Richard is name checked on the Thin Lizzy website for the gig at Corby Bowl April 18th 1972. In brackets - (Richard Oliff on drums).

Dougie Martell said, "The Sex Pistols played in Copenhagen (July 13th 1977) on their 'Anarchy Tour', and were terrible. For a start off they couldn't play their instruments any better than what I could. And I can only manage two chords! They were egged on and manipulated by their manager Malcolm McLaren. They started spitting at the crowd which went down really well. The crowd responded in fury, throwing bottles and glasses at them on stage. Rotten and Co threw them back, effing and blinding, all the stuff you see on their videos."

"They were pathetic really. Their dressing room was supplied with trays of sandwiches and stuff. They obviously thought it'd be good fun to decorate the room with them, splattering the walls and trashing the place. When the bouncers discovered the mess, they wanted to kill them. In the end, twenty minutes before the end of their set, the whole crowd just walked out and left them to it. They played to a massive empty hall, snarling and making arses of themselves all on their own."

"Amusingly, the *Melody Maker* sent their reporter Chris Brazier over to cover the gig and he did his best to shift the blame on to the Danes for a lacklustre and disappointing performance. He even had the nerve to call me a moron! Just because I was giving the support group Fumble, a 50s rock revival outfit a big push. The reporter slammed them as being passé, redundant, totally irrelevant! Mind you, I suppose when I told the punters – "This was the last piece of good music You'll hear tonight" - just prior to the Pistols stepping out - it wasn't appreciated!"

Chris Brazier later became co-editor of *New Internationalist* magazine. Covering myriad subjects from masculinity to maternal mortality, Panafricanism to the paranormal, and has edited country issues on South Africa, Burkina Faso, Western Sahara, Bangladesh, Iran, China and Vietnam. He has written regularly for UNICEF's annual The State of the World's Children report since 1997. (*Wikipedia*)

The Sex Pistols released 'Anarchy In The UK' in November and were due to promote the disc co-headlining a 19 date UK Tour with The Damned and The Clash, until it all went pear shape following a notorious TV appearance on the Bill Grundy *Today* show in December.

All but six gigs were cancelled by local councils and venue managers as their notoriety spread.

The Pistols were at their most obnoxious sitting on Grundy's television sofa, upsetting everyone with their obscene language which had headlines screaming outrage. For manager Malcolm McLaren, it was manna from heaven. For Bill Grundy, it cost him his job. The Pistols maintained they were goaded, insisting Grundy was drunk and ignorant.

Grundy was unrepentant, "The object of the exercise was to prove that these louts were a foul-mouthed set of yobs. That is what it proved. I had never heard of them before in my life. I didn't mind their dress. It is how they behaved. They hadn't endeared themselves to me before the programme started, but I only saw them for a few minutes, literally." I ended the programme by saying, "I don't ever want to see you again," and I meant it.

Watching the tea time show was Kelvin Woods who proudly claims to have been one of Corby's first punks. Kelvin worked at Corby Post Office in the early 2000s. He said, "That show was what got me hooked! I thought it was unbelievable. Until then I had been an avid Hot Chocolate (You Sexy Thing) and Sailor (Glass of Champagne) fan, long hair down my back. After that show I went out and had my hair shorn, spiked up. I tore a big hole in my tea shirt and wrote on the back of it, 'destroy Corby". Then I went out, and was set upon by a bunch of lads who kicked the crap out of me!

"It didn't put me off though. My brother Clive and a few mates started going to London to hang out around the Kings Road and McLaren's shop Sex. We used to have a laugh pretending to spew up in the street when busloads of tourists would go by. They always wanted to take photographs of this new craze, all these freaks hanging out with spiky hair, ripped shirts, chains and safety pins pierced in their faces. The trick was to get a tub of yoghurt, then take a mouth full and spew it out just as another bus went by! It was hilarious."

"One of the first gigs I went to was on Franny Lagan's bus to see the Buzzcocks at Coventry Locarno. I was wearing a pair of new PVC trousers and by the time we got to Coventry my bollocks were sweating and I jumped straight into a fountain in the City Centre to cool off! It was agony, my nuts were chapped! Later on I was beaten up in Greenhill Rise when I was wearing bondage trousers and a short tartan kilt! The jocks coming out of the Hazel Tree thought I was taking the piss!"

Dougie Martell was amongst the group of local DJs that emerged in the late 1960s, along with Kru Zakss, Bip Wetherell, Ian Eccles, Dougie King and Dennis Taylor. Joining this select band in 1976 and starting out on what would be a 40 year plus career was conker fan and future Corby Radio presenter Pat McMahon, along with Des Barber, Ian Bateman, Dave Irving, "Gillie" Gilfillan, Dave Mulheron and Simon Green.

Des Barber, far right bottom row, and Corby DJs floating around with the Carnival

"There were a number of us who stayed the 40-odd year course," Pat recalls, "we were never short of work, there was stacks going on. Discos in the pubs, nightclubs. Private parties, weddings."

Most of the DJs mentioned went on to radio work. Bip, Des, Pat, Dennis at Corby Radio, Dougie King with Corby and Hereward Radio and later Radio Forth in Scotland. Dave Irving has presented a breakfast time show on Harborough FM for over a decade and as of 2023 is still going strong.

Dave Irving, Harborough FM

His career kicked off with a gig at the Church of Epiphany in Elizabeth Street in 1974, which he recalled over a beer in the Ex-Serviceman's Club in 2022, "I asked Rev. John Ashcroft if I could use his mic from the pulpit and he said "No". I thought quickly and told him the proceeds were going towards the scout group. "Alright." he said. My brother Rob was behind the curtains waving a red lightbulb in a Saxa salt carton around, switching it off and on. That was my first light show! Not exactly Pink Floyd and technicolor dreams but good enough for the tranquillity of the Epiphany Church Hall!"

Dennis Taylor provided Dave with some work, once to stand in for him at the Raven for a children's party. Truth told, Dennis probably didn't want to do it! But it was good experience for me at the time. He was a bit of a hero to me. He had a T-shirt with Dennis Taylor - DJ and Star of Television" emblazoned on it. I thought, "Wow! Amazing."

Turned out his mother had spotted him in the crowd of Liverpool supporters at a Luton v Liverpool game on Match of the Day!"

Dave Irving also spent time during the 80s and 90s working and managing his parents' Off Licence in Pytchley Court, Corby which is where he obviously inherited his dad's sense of humour. He recalls his dad giving him a poser to think about, regarding selecting prospective shop assistants.

"Imagine this," my dad said, "I place a five pound note on the floor in front of the counter and three women come in. The first one looks around, stoops down and picks the fiver up and discreetly puts it in her purse. The second one picks it up and says 'someone must have dropped this" and puts it on the counter next to the till. The third one comes in, and says, "Keep this in case someone comes in and says they've lost a fiver". So which one of them would you choose to work here?" he asked.

Straight away I said, "The third one."

"No," my dad said, "the one with the biggest boobs!"

Besides the booze and cigarettes, we also sold sweets and we had a box of McCowan toffee bars on the counter which weren't selling. The kids weren't buying them. One woman who worked with us was well endowed in the upstairs department and she suggested a way of moving these toffee bars on. She undid the top three buttons on her blouse to reveal a generous portion of her assets, and placed the box of toffees on a table just below the counter. A couple of young lads, school kids, came in and she leaned forward, making out she was adjusting the box, to give them an eyeful. Well before you knew it, all their mates were coming in to buy the toffee bars as word spread. The box of toffees which we hadn't been able to shift for weeks suddenly disappeared within days!"

Ian Bateman was 14 when he started 'messing about with electronics' and used to build power supplies to convert AC to DC. "As a paperboy at Murray's shop on Welland Vale Road, I saved my money to buy electronic parts from shops on Edgware Road in London. I used to go down to the tip in West Glebe Park and look for old TVs to take the Printed Circuit boards for resistors and capacitors. Reading Practical Electronic magazines I found a company called TUAC who had ready-made modules, Mixers, Amplifiers and 4 channel flashing light assemblies. A carpenter friend made my DJ console boxes and Speaker Boxes. Two second hand BSR Turntables finished the job! These all got me going as a DJ, from home at the start. I wasn't a threat to pirate radio though, my transmitter only worked up to about 200 meters!"

"I spent hours in my bedroom playing singles back-to- back. Just a bit of fun. I left school when I was 15 and had more money to spend on records and more kit. In 1974 I asked

Alex Goodall at the Sealed Beams Club if I could have a go with their in-house kit on Friday Nights. After a couple of months, I became resident DJ and worked there for over 2 years. That's when I called in at Corby Rugby Club where Alan Wetherell was resident with his Touchdown Disco. The place was really taking off and I asked Alan if I could do a regular spot. He agreed, so I shared the work with Alan and Terry Woolmer. These were great nights. Disco Thursday and Rock Nights on Sunday."

"Through the disco nights, I gained work for weddings and parties which was great fun. One memory though was when I was asked to DJ in the Rugby club for the Corby Girls Netball end of season party. That was scary with all those ladies. One informed me that if I didn't play a montage of Motown they would drag me off the console and into the Rugby Club Showers! It was banter but believe me, nerve racking. Thankfully I managed to keep them happy on the dance floor!"

Bip and Elaine Wetherell begin life in the Nags Head in 1976. "Jim Tibbs had moved on and we were asked to take it on as it was double the size of the Open Hearth," Bip recalled. "The brewery thought that because we had made such a success of the Hearth we could do the same, and more, at the Nags. We were reluctant as the living quarters at the Nags were awful. Ancient, dirty. The Hearth had great living quarters. To try and put the brewery off I wrote out a list of alterations I wanted before we moved in, and also a good top up on our salary. Thinking there was no way they would accept it. The guy came back on the Monday, looked at the list, and said, "Right, move in on Wednesday!"

Although our attempts at trying to stay at the Open Hearth had failed, we soon got used to living in a much bigger pub. Our daughter Tamla was now old enough to go to Nursery school, freeing up more time for Elaine to work. The back room of the Nags had a stage, and a dressing room for the artists behind it. There was a dance floor, some basic lighting and a long bar to accommodate 300 customers we were licenced for. I kept the same format from the Open Hearth and added two additional nights, one an album night where Jim Marshall would play tracks from Yes, Pink Floyd, etc.

Because the room was too big for the level of mid-week trade, I made up room dividers that were pulled across to cut out the dance floor area that wasn't needed. So we had "Jam Nights" on a Monday, "Half Price drinks on a Tuesday, "Album Nights" on a Wednesday, "Country and Western" on a Thursday, Disco on a Friday, 'live band' on a Saturday, and a Double D. J. show on a Sunday with last but not least, "Indie Bands" at Sunday Lunchtime.

To give you an idea of how busy we were I used to open the door on a Sunday Lunchtime for the two-hour session (this was years before the dreaded all day opening). I would spend at least ten minutes saying good morning to everybody who had been queuing to get in before I could get behind the bar with the other nine bar staff. We used to have bands come from all over to play their own music, Gaffa, London Town, Bethnal Green to name but a few. The pub was rammed in the bar and the back room.

By the time we got everyone out of the midday session, the customers would go home, have their Sunday lunch, a quick afternoon kip, and be back down to the pub for the 'double DJ'. show which featured my brother Stuart and myself, either side of the stage, with our own disco decks and records, constantly trying to outdo each other with jokes and mad patter. The audience loved it. We even had one of my other DJ.'s, Pete Jinks, mark on a chalkboard who got the best response, it was hilarious. This went on for eight brilliant years. Every two or three years we would have a new audience as people got engaged and married and moved away. Only to bring a fresh batch of teenagers to the door. I often got criticised by my accountant for spending too much on live music but I still maintain today you cannot beat a brilliant band matched with a top DJ.

By this time, 1977, my son Glen was born. He was the perfect baby until the pub was shut and when everything went quiet we couldn't get him off to sleep. As my children have always come first I told my area manager we would have to leave. He then made a precedented decision to allow us to live out with Elaine's sister Pam moving in. At the time we were buying a house in the village of Middleton where we would eventually stay for 40 years.

So began 8 years of constant hard work, 14 shifts a week with no let up. We created an incredible busy pub with the added bonus that all the tills were full at the end of the night. Elaine and I won the brewery's Pub of The Year 6 out of the 8 years we were there and the prize was a fifty pound bonus. Wow!"

Take It To the Limit

One of the most popular bands to play at Corby's Sealed Beams/Earlstrees Club was Canned Rock who featured drummer and percussionist Pete Buckby, a homespun legend, having been a member of one of Corby's finest harmony groups in the 1960s, The Rising Sons, the highlight of their career was supporting Otis Redding at Boston Gliderdrome in September 1966.

Canned Rock

When the Sons went their different ways in 1967, Pete was setting his sights on joining the Merchant Navy, until he received a phone call that was to alter the course of his life.

"I was all set to join the merch," says Pete, "next day in fact, when I got a call from Joan Blakely, who was the manager of a Hitchin based band called The Endeavours. They had a residency in a Sheffield nightclub. Joan told me that Mick Harper had told her about me being at a loose end when she was searching for a new drummer. She asked me if I was interested, and if so, she'd pick me up at 8.30 next morning and take me up to Sheffield for an audition. I was in two minds but deep down I knew what I wanted most. So we went up to Sheffield and I met up with Don (Maxwell) and Doug (Kenna), watched them play, with another guy, Roger, and I thought they were crap! Awful.

They were more of a comedy outfit with Roger doing a skit on Sandie Shaw! It's not what I expected or was too enamoured with. However I joined, to be honest, they were on £19 a week each which was great money at the time.

Eventually, though, I had enough of hamming up "Puppet On A String" and told them I was quitting. I applied, believe it or not, for a job with the Hitchin Fire Service. I had an interview, found the panel of interviewers obnoxious and arrogant, told them what I thought, and next day, I received a letter saying "Sorry…"

My immediate reaction was "bollocks to them" and I phoned Don Maxwell up to tell him what had happened. To my surprise, and delight, he asked me if I would consider coming back to The Endeavours.

"We've tried about 40 drummers to replace you but all of them are crap, do you fancy coming back?" I jumped at the chance!

But with conditions. I told him I couldn't carry on with the comedy routines. If they take the music more seriously, I'd definitely come back. Don felt the same as it turned out. So we started again, under a new name, Candy Rock. I bought a set of Timpani and Tubular Bells and we went from Sandie Shaw to playing Queen and Holst Overtures.

We were signed up by Tony Aherne, the manager of the Barron Knights who'd achieved chart success with "Call Up the Groups" and "Merry Gentle Pops" in the early sixties. More comedy stuff! I needn't have worried though, through Aherne's connections we gained an audition to appear on televisions' ITV "New Faces" show, which you would have thought, we would have been overjoyed with."

The news, in fact, was received with trepidation.

Pete: "New Faces had a terrible reputation for its judges slagging off and demoralising acts, particularly Nina Myskow who revelled in the squirming and embarrassment of the artists. Aherne insisted we should do it all the same. It has to be said New Faces was essential viewing, as being a peculiar trait of the British, watching people suffer to the amusement of others was very entertaining."

New Faces was recorded at the ATV Centre in Birmingham and hosted by Leslie Crowther with a panel of judges assessing performances from ten acts looking for a break. Welsh singer Jennifer Jones won the inaugural show that also featured a bloke who blew up a hot water bottle until it burst. Which is hard to believe. How the guy thought he could get a show biz career out of doing this but there you go!

The panel, depending on who was available, would consist of showbiz personalities Tony Hatch, Mickie Most, Arthur Askey, Ed Stewart, Lonnie Donegan, Terry Wogan and Noel Edmonds. Plus the lady who would become infamous, Nina Myskow, a feature writer for teenage magazine *Jackie* and columnist for the *News of the World*.

On the strength of her contributions to New Faces, Nina was later snapped up by the BBC to become a regular performer on their "Grumpy Old Women" show.

The public tuned in by their thousands to watch Nina, Hatch and Most tear acts to pieces and it was said viewers were often stunned by insulting comments fired towards the more inept acts but I doubt that. As Pete Buckby reiterated, "There's something entertaining watching someone else's misery!"

Fortunately, Pete and Candy Rock, now renamed Canned Rock, "after Mickie Most told us he thought the name Candy Rock was rubbish," didn't have to endure any insults.

Nina and her co-panelists were impressed and Canned Rock went through to the final where they were up against an "up and coming" comedian, and ultimate winner, Jim Davidson.

Davidson went on to have a stellar career and to his credit, acknowledged Canned Rock in his autobiography "Close To the Edge", stating he genuinely feared he had no chance of winning the New Faces show. "Canned Rock were an excellent band, really professional, and I didn't want to go on."

As it was, with the points level at the end of the judging, it was down to the diminutive Arthur Askey to decide the winner and not surprising, you might think, the music hall veteran, famous for his signature song, "I'm a busy little bee," or whatever it was, went for his fellow comedian.

Despite the disappointment, the show did give Canned Rock a massive boost. "We had loads of work afterwards," Pete recalled, "right up until the Falklands War in 1982. We were playing regularly all three nights of the weekend at the Army, Navy and RAF bases, earning around £60 each when the average wage was around £30 to £40 a week.

When the Task Force set sail for the Falklands, the gigs dried up and I feared the worst. I thought we'd be bankrupt in a month. When victory was won, we were inundated again. All the bases wanted us back and we ended up playing six, seven gigs a week."

Eventually, it all came to an end when they grew tired of the toil and after twenty years of showbiz, Pete wanted back in the real world. "I think we were all feeling the same basically. I was wanting to settle down and have more time with my kids as I was away most of the time and I felt that I wanted to do something else."

Pete became "a keen boater," achieving his ambition of to be "Captain of your Ship" (Reperata and the Delrons 1967 hit), on the River Nene! A hobby that probably had it's seeds in his original desire of going to sea.

Pete said, "We decided to finish in 1984 with a six-week tour of Germany, playing the American air bases to get enough money to pay off our debts before quitting. But it ended in disaster. We were playing at Manheim where the electrics were dire. Our base player Doug was electrocuted on stage, blew a big hole in his arm. It was unreal. Our sound engineer immediately scrambled across the tables pulling all the cables out of every socket he could see. Beer and glasses went everywhere. Crazy thing was, the yanks thought it was all part of the act! They were cheering like hell. We came home and Doug wanted to get back to work after about a month so we decided to work solid for the next six months, playing all the venues we had ever played in Britain. Our final gig was at Brize Norton air base. After which I was glad it was all over."

Since his retirement from the full-time world of show biz Pete has enjoyed work in an assortment of capacities. The Fire Service in Corby, an undertaker in Kettering and shift manager in the Weetabix factory in Burton Latimer. Over the years he continued to play sporadically with a number of bands on an ad hoc arrangement. He is also an accomplished ventriloquist which was part of his armour during his undertaker days. Black humour is, some would say, essential for such an undertaking, if you pardon the pun. It did lead Pete into trouble once when accompanying a hearse to the Kettering Crem. Sitting aside of the coffin Pete tapped the box and wheezed "Let me outa here!"

His partner on the other side asked "What was that?" and Pete repeated the trick. Unable to stifle his giggles, he revealed his party piece and all four undertakers in the hearse started laughing their heads off. Unfortunately a member of the public saw them as they passed by, was disgusted, and reported them to the Head Office. Reprimanded as a matter of course, he performed his act to the boss who luckily saw the funny side of it and he too fell about laughing.

Canned Rock recorded three albums during their career. Their self-titled album, recorded at Derek Tompkins studio in Wellingborough, in 1976 included covers of "Bohemian Rhapsody," "Hocus Pocus," "Sabre Dance" and "Bridge Over Troubled Water". Two more albums would follow, "Kinetic Energy" in 1978 and "Machines" in 1982 which featured their tour-de-force 1812 Overture.

***

One of the biggest hits of 1976 was "Lost In France" by Welsh girl Bonnie Tyler. Watching Top Of The Pops on television at home in Corby when Bonnie made her debut on the show was her old friend Liz Hill, who remembers, "nearly falling off my chair when I realised it was the girl I knew as Gaynor Hopkins."

Liz had met Bonnie/Gaynor when along with another friend, Toni Carroll, they had attended an audition for a show band in Swansea. "Gaynor was a quiet girl who we dropped off at her home in Neath on our way back to Toni's parents," in Ystrad. She obviously went on to have a terrific career."

Liz's career began in the 1960s with the folk based band Paula's Chessmen, who later morphed into The Jacksons. Her brother, John Hill a guitarist with another folk group, The Carnations, used to take her along to gigs which is where she met Dave Dick and Ian Dixon who were in the process of forming the Chessmen.

Liz explained, "They were looking for a female singer, I guess in the vogue of Judith Durham and the Seekers, and it was arranged for me to go to Dave's house for an audition. I was that shy I sang "Summertime" while looking out of the windows, with my back to Dave and Ian. They must have been impressed enough as they invited me along the following week for a rehearsal and gave me a recording of a country and western song called "Once a Day" to learn, a good one for my range.

With another guitarist, Charlie Foote, we became Paula's Chessmen and spent two years doing the rounds of Working

Men's Clubs which eventually led to us to turning professional in 1968. Dave then left the group after contracting Meningitis and Charlie, Ian and I carried on as The Jacksons. We continued to work around the country playing places as far apart as Sunderland and Middlesbrough to the Penguin Club in Birmingham, where we were support to The Tremeloes and other top acts of the day.

Our agent then got us fixed up on cruise ships where we virtually worked non-stop for the next two years. The first stint was a three-month trip going back and forth from New York to Bermuda on the *Franconia*, and I lost a stone in weight from being sea sick!

The Jacksons featuring Liz Hill

After a break of a few weeks, we flew to Boston to meet up with the *Carmania* for a four and a half months gig cruising from Fort Lauderdale to the Bahamas and the West Indies, playing three shows a night and an 'Old Tyme Music Hall' with Ian and Charlie doing a dance routine, 'Me and My Shadow' and me dancing behind them. I also did a sketch where I wore a white dress. On top of which I had a pillow by my tummy with a white table cloth draped over it. Clutching a bunch of flowers, I came out singing, "There was I, waiting at the church..." One night, while I was singing, the safety pin holding up my table cloth gave way and I was left standing there in my little white mini dress and the pillow and table cloth by my feet. It brought the house down and I had a red face, but it was great fun.

When the work on the cruise ships came to an end, I started reading *The Stage* magazine, which was essential for finding work. There'd be a list of numbers for agents, band leaders and clubs looking for artists, but not all were as good as they sounded. One time, I phoned a number in a small town near Leeds and asked for a gentleman called Mick, as was specified. Mick came to the phone, in what appeared to be a pub, and asked me to come up for an audition. I travelled all the way from London by train, on my own, changed trains for the connection and arrived exhausted in this place at the back of beyond."

"Leaving the station, I noticed a car with its engine running and went straight over and asked if it was Mick sitting behind the wheel. He said it was, and he told me to jump in. I had a funny feeling about this, he was a big fat bloke, didn't give me the impression he was an entertainer or anything, even if there was an accordion on the back seat. Before we moved off, he told me, "we" were going to go to America, make a record, play in the big clubs. I began to feel uneasy and suddenly felt vulnerable. When he then said we were going to pick up a friend of his, a guitarist, I immediately got out of the car and ran back to the station. Maybe my imagination was running wild but then I saw this little old lady sitting on the platform reading a newspaper. "Terrible," she said, "all these young girls getting murdered around here!"

Liz eventually joined The Terry Reaney Show Band and found herself back on the cruise ships, this time on the QE2. The Reaney band also had a residency in a club in Stevenage and Liz had to learn three or four songs from the charts every week.

"After Terry Reaney, I went back to London and met up with Colin Rose who I had been going out with before the QE2 trip. We married in 1973, had a daughter Natalie in 1974 and I gave up singing until 1983 when I returned as a function band singer with The Nightbirds, performing at prestigious venues such as the Cafe Royal in Regent Street, top London hotels including the Heathrow and Gatwick Airport hotels, golf clubs in and around London. We also did some BBC radio work at Maida Vale studios where we were paid the princely sum of £142. 80p. I eventually retired in 1996, making a brief return to record a CD entitled "Everything But The Band" in 2005 at Ian Wetherell's Premier Studio in Corby."

***

Brothers John and Bob Grimley, regarded as two of Corby's finest guitarists, were making their own way in the music business, and having considerable success.

John teamed up with Chris Kefford, the original bass player of The Move, having turned down the offer to join 60s star Helen Shapiro, her of "Walkin" Back To Happiness" fame.

Kefford, otherwise known by his nickname of Ace had quit The Move in disillusionment in 1969, but was back and putting together a band to be called Rock Star.

He explained the reasons for his return after a long layoff from music during an interview for music mag *Spectrum*. "When I quit The Move, I never wanted to play again. I felt disillusioned. We'd worked our guts out for two years then when the Move made it, there was so much back-biting about us from other people in the music business that it pulled me to pieces."

Ace recruited the help of Wilf Pine, who he knew from The Move days and who had also been involved in various capacities with Black Sabbath, Black Widow, Stray and The Groundhogs. He was also a friend of the Kray twins, Ronnie and Reg, the infamous London gangsters.

It was with the Kray's elder brother Charlie that John and the Rockstar boys met up for a business lunch to discuss future plans, which left an indelible imprint on John's memory, if not for the musical direction than his palate. "I remember we had l'escargots for starters. Snails! And I didn't know whether to eat them or race them!"

John said, "Ace lived in this tiny old cottage in Worcestershire. We spent months rehearsing in that idyllic little sardine can. The ceilings were so low I constantly had lumps on the top of my head until I learnt to walk with a stoop. Even though we were skint, Chris's wife, Jenny, who was a lovely girl, allowed us to stay at their cottage, cooking meals etc. I was getting around £5 a week from social security and she wouldn't take a thing off us. I used to say to Chris, 'Let's go to the pub and spend it there then!'"

> **The Rockstar band rocks on**
>
> **Kefford heartbreaker 'fantastic'–new single?**
>
> THE CONTINUING saga of Rockstar: ... After five weeks' hard labour in the studio Ace Kefford's new band Rockstar underwent the acid test recently. Peter Knight Junior, managing director of NEMS records, came to hear them. His verdict: "Fantastic".
>
> Will Fine, Rockstar's manager, looked the picture of a worried man immediately before the great man's arrival. "I've listened to the boys so much that it's got to the point where I can't even trust my own ears," he says, "I was worried sick last night."
>
> His fears were soon assuaged by Peter Knight. While Fine sat with head bowed and fingers crossed Knight listened with obvious enjoyment to four completed album tracks.
>
> There were straight rock numbers, the other a heartbreaker penned by Kefford, which sent shivers down the spine even after the fourth hearing.
>
> "It's just like the old Move stuff, only it's got more balls," says Knight. "The only problem is deciding which one to release for your first single. Shall we sit down and talk?"
>
> "Yes," agreed a greatly relieved Fine. "We'll talk all right."
>
> *Rockstar in the studio* *Photo: Ian Dickson*

Rockstar featuring John Grimley

Spectrum stated Rock Star have been quietly "getting it together" in a country cottage in true rock biz tradition. Inkberrow in Worcestershire is something of a quiet place. Rather twee in fact. Still the band seemed unconcerned as to the effect their bedenimed and long-haired appearance might have as they sat down for a chat. Singer and guitarist Chris, along with bass player Terry Biddulph have been forming Rock Star for the past nine months or so. The band is signed to Rebel Records. Behind Rebel is none other than Michael Palin of Monty Python fame, so there is little danger of it being a fly by night outfit. The deal is for two singles and an album which the band hope to make a start on soon. "It is a tremendous break and we don't intend to blow it," said Chris. Rock Star will be going into IBC Recording Studios, London and working on a selection of songs written by both

Chris and guitarist Terry Ware. As yet, there are no plans for live work.

"This band is past the paying of dues stage," said Chris, "we have all done the pub circuit on a constant string of one-nighters."

The band have been rehearsing solidly for several weeks and have an impressive selection of tough but melodic rock tunes with a tightness that belies their time as a working unit.

Steve Rowland, who has produced hits for Dave Dee, Dozy, Beaky, Mick & Tich, P. J. Proby, The Pretty Things amongst others was asked by Wilf Pine to work with Rock Star and was very impressed. "I thought it was the hottest stuff I'd heard in London since 1967 when the Herd and the Move used to play the Marquee."

Everybody is working hard, doing straight eight-hour stints in the studio, and they plan to continue until they have recorded enough for an album. Then Pine will set about finding a recording contract for them.

"When we've recorded two hit singles," says Wilf, who is gambling his life savings on the project, "we'll be ready to go on tour, but not until we're 100% perfect." Wilf Pine kept his word and a month later champagne corks were popping when Rockstar signed a three year worldwide recording contract with MCA Records and their debut single "Mummy" was set for release on December 3rd.

Wilf Pine talked about the deal as Rock Star's Patrick McLachlan taxied down to the pressing plant just off Regent Street where acetates were being prepared. MCA were knocked out by the demo tapes and Pine liked their offer, so the deal was struck. At the same time he secured a publishing contract with Heathside Music and appointed David Apps of Evolution as Rock Stars agent. Apps plans to organise a tour to coincide with the debut album, tentatively scheduled for release in March."

Melody Maker gave Rock Star a great write-up in the November 20th issue with the headline. "Kefford heartbreaker fantastic". "After five weeks hard labour in the studio, Ace Kefford's new band Rock Star underwent the acid test recently. Peter Knight, managing director of NEMS records, came to hear them. Verdict, "Fantastic."

Wilf Pine had looked a picture of a worried man immediately before the great man's arrival. "I've listened to the boys so much that it's got to the point where I can't even trust my own ears. I was worried sick last night."

While Pine sat with head bowed and fingers crossed Knight listened with obvious enjoyment to four completed album tracks. Three were straight rock numbers, the other a heartbreaker penned by Kefford, which sent shivers down the spine even after the fourth hearing. "It's just like the old Move stuff only it's got more balls," said Knight. "The only problem is, which one we are going to release for a single."

All was far from rosy, however. John Grimley was growing tired, feeling he was carrying Tony Weir. "I spent hours in the studio re- doing his parts because he wasn't up to it. He was a passenger, he did my head in eventually. Then one night in the Marquee I'd had enough. Weir had been watching this guitarist play and when he came into the bar I asked him who it was. "A Canadian guitarist," he said, "he's crap. Pat Travers is his name." I couldn't believe it! I'd seen Pat Travers at Barberellas in Birmingham just a month previously and he absolutely blew me away. That showed me just what Weir knew. 'listen" I said to him, "I couldn't lick the boots of the guy who licks his boots! He's fantastic!"

Just then, Wilf appeared. "Alright boys?" he asked as he passed us.

Well, I was stoned. It was maybe why I went after Wilf and shouted at him, "No, we're not alright. I want you to get rid of Weir, he's a waste of space!" Or words to that effect.

He looked at me and said calmly, "Leave it until tomorrow."

I thought he was being dismissive and made the mistake of shoving him in the shoulder against a wall and repeating my demand. Next thing I know, he's belted me right in the face and knocked me clean out! I woke up in the hotel room next morning with a sore and bloody nose. Chris Kefford phoned to see if I was alright, and then asked me to go down for breakfast.

"Wilf's here, he wants to see you," he said.

Oh, no, I thought! I then realised I didn't have any shoes, or money and asked Chris what happened.

"We chucked you in the back of the van and took you back to the hotel. We took your shoes in case you pissed off." I went down, a bit sheepish and before anybody could say anything I said, "Look Wilf, do me a favour, just give me enough money for my train fare and I'll get going," feeling sure I was for the bullet.

"I've already handed out some train money this morning" he said. He'd sacked Weir. "I told you to leave it until tomorrow, didn't I!"

Rock Star promised so much but disappointing for John, Chris Kefford's project was ultimately aborted. In 2004 the Birmingham based music magazine *Brumbeat* featured Ace in a career retrospective, and wrote about the Rock Star single that never was.

"If further proof was required regarding Kefford's songwriting ability, this is it. The deeply personal "Mummy" and "Over The Hill" (turn the volume up to 11 for this one!) bring to mind classic-era Mott The Hoople or David Bowie."

Wilf Pine died in 2018, he was 74.

***

John's older brother Bob was now playing guitar with Bumper, a hugely popular band having replaced the departing Barry Monk. The line up also included Stewart and Jimmy Irving, Mick Haselip and Nigel "Nidge" Hart, another recent recruit who had replaced the original drummer Ned McGuigan.

Nigel's career started with Oundle-based combo The 49th Parallel. Interviewed in 2011, Nidge recalled his early beginnings and later career, post Bumper.

"Playing drums was all I was interested in. I was lazy at school and not really interested in any subjects. When I left, it was with no qualifications and no idea where I was heading. If somebody had told me then that one day I would play and count among my friends, Procol Harum guitarist Mick Grabham, Dick Parry, Pink Floyd's sax player on the 'Dark Side Of The Moon,' 'Wish You Were Here' albums, and Foreigner keyboard player Rick Wills, I would have laughed at them!"

49th Parallell featuring Nidge Hart on drums

49th Parallel failed to accrue any measure of success, as illustrated by the accompanying aside to the photograph of their debut in Nidge's scrapbook, "This is the one and only gig 49th Parallel did, and we didn't get paid for it!"

A change of name and musical direction was needed, and the choice maybe gave a clue as to the inspiration behind the name, The State Of Mind, and playing harder edged Cream and Jimi Hendrix material. Nidge was playing a twin bass drum kit, a rare commodity on the local scene, and rapidly building a reputation as a rock drummer. The band's preferred heavy rock style saw them change their name yet again, to a more suitable Brain Damage.

Striving to reach a wider audience, they moved en bloc to Liverpool where they lived in 'digs' in the district of Aigburth, south of the city. Signed to Playlord Enterprises Agency in Manchester they played venues such as Liverpool's famous Cavern Club, capturing an enthusiastic audience and fan base.

It was an exciting time for Nidge and his pals in the rarified atmosphere of the world-famous basement where the Beatles and other 60s rock stars learned their trade. In truth the Cavern in 1974 wasn't actually the genuine article. The original club was closed down in 1973 when British Rail enforced its closure to allow building work on a new underground railway system to commence. The ancient warehouses above the Cavern Club were demolished while the cellar itself was filled with rubble and left like a sealed tomb for the remainder of the decade.

The "new" Cavern was still a small and sweaty cellar, and still in Mathew Street, the entrance just 15 yards further up the road.

"Soon after the Cavern club closed in 1973, a new Cavern club opened at 7 Mathew Street, later renamed the Revolution Club. This club would later shut down and be reopened as Erics, which itself became a notable local music venue in the late 1970s." (*Wikipedia*)

Nidge said, "We lived in Liverpool for about a year, great city and great people. My abiding memory of the Cavern is the club being jam packed and the frenzied reaction of all the girls. It was brilliant, they used to try and tear all our clothes off! Let's say, we all pulled."

Brain Damage returned south twelve months later in 1975 exhausted, and went their separate ways. Following a short period of recuperation Nidge was back behind his kit with an outfit fronted by guitarist Tony Haselip, playing the pub and club circuits as Flash Harry, "which soon evolved into Gemini."

Nidge added, "I was approached by Tony Haselip's brother Mick who asked me if I'd be interested in having an audition at the Raven Hall to replace Ned McGuigan. I decided beforehand though to catch Bumper at the Central Hall in Kettering, and that sealed it for me, I thought they were fantastic. Bumper had a tremendous following and was clearly heading in the right direction."

Bumper entered a National Folk/Rock contest sponsored by the *Melody Maker* and EMI Records, and won through to the finals at the Roundhouse in Camden, London, a prestigious venue which was originally built as a turntable locomotive shed for the London & Birmingham Railway and opened in 1847.

"The Roundhouse was converted into a permanent cultural centre with a theatre, cinema, art gallery and workshops, committee rooms for local organisations, library, youth club and restaurant dance-hall in 1964. In 1966 it became an arts venue, the opening concert on 15th October being the All-Night Rave, in which Soft Machine and Pink Floyd appeared at the launch of the underground newspaper *International Times*.

During the next decade, it became a significant venue for UK Underground music events Middle Earth and Implosion. Bands to play at the Roundhouse included The Rolling

Stones, Jeff Beck, The Yardbirds, David Bowie, Jimi Hendrix, Led Zeppelin, The Incredible String Band, Fleetwood Mac, The Doors, Jefferson Airplane, Ramones, The Clash, The Jam, Elvis Costello, Paul McCartney, Otis Redding and Motörhead." (*Wikipedia*)

The prize for the winners of the Melody Maker/EMI contest was £2000 worth of equipment and recording time.during 2022 Stewart Irving recalled how it came to be that Bumper played the Roundhouse. "It was actually Franny Lagan who arranged the Folk/Rock contest. "I've entered for you" he told us. Twenty-eight area heats were held throughout the country. The first heat for us was at Warwick University which was successful and the second heat was at Barbarellas in Birmingham. The opposition was top rate and I thought we had no chance. Packing our gear up at the end of the night, we hadn't been told how we'd got on and I couldn't rest so I asked one of the promoters. He told us we were brilliant and yes we were through to the final at the Roundhouse! And, of course, to tread the boards where so many legends had played was mind blowing."

Bob Grimley said, "What a day that was. We were a bit concerned at first, all the other bands were greeted with loud cheers and shouting from their followers when they took the stage. When it was our turn it was more a mooted silence. We couldn't understand it. Then all of a sudden a crescendo of noise resonated around the arena when the hordes of Corby fans made their entrance. Turns out the coaches had been late getting away from Corby Rugby Club. They were well oiled by the time they arrived at the Roundhouse - and didn't the rest of the crowd know it!"

John Grimley was there to give his brother and the band support. "The Roundhouse, that does bring back memories. We all left the Nags, I think it was a Sunday afternoon, in a coach to travel down. Franny Lagan was on the bus as well. Stinking hot day so the cans of beer were not quite as cold as they should have been. I remember we all had a bloody good time in the Roundhouse, even though Bumper failed to win the day."

The panel of judges at the Roundhouse included the Head of A & R at EMI, Nick Mobbs, DJ "Whispering" Bob Harris, and former Jimi Hendrix bass player Noel Redding.

The *Evening Telegraph* was on hand to report. "Their brand of aggressive rock has built up a good following in Corby and coach loads of supporters travelled to see Stewart Irving 24, Jimmy Irving 23, Mick Haselip 25, Bob Grimley 25 and Nigel Hart 21 do battle. Attired in matching 'Godfather' gear. The Prohibition era dress seems to pull in the fans." Said singer Stewart, "We always try to play to our audience, this is why we have such a good following in the town. We go out there and grab them by the neck. That's the way they want it so that's the way we play to them." Bumper played two self-penned numbers, as well as their arrangement of Paul McCartney and Wings" "Norwegian Wood/Rock Show."

Bumper came a respectable third, collecting a prize of £150 plus a voucher for musical equipment. In second place was The Please Y'self Skiffle Band from Matlock and the winners were Stallion, who to pardon a pun, galloped through!

Afterwards, Bob Grimley was magnanimous, "It was a great day and the group was very happy with what we got. We would like to thank everyone who followed us throughout the competition."

Gavin Dare of Rebel Records was also impressed. Nidge Hart said, "Gavin signed us up for a record deal after watching us rehearse. We were taken out to a flash restaurant in Covent Garden for lunch to celebrate. Felt like the big time had arrived! With hindsight we maybe should have hung on a little longer. After the gig, Bob Harris, presenter of TV's biggest rock programme, 'the Old Grey Whistle Test," came back stage and whispered in that inimitable style of his, that he'd like to record us and it's fair to say we could have been down for an appearance on his show which would have been a real thrill and opportunity. Nick Mobbs from EMI also wanted to sign us but we had to tell him, and Bob, that we were tied up with Rebel Records."

Bumper

Gavin Dare booked the studio to record Bumper's debut album "First Offence" with Andre Jackeman as engineer. He was the composer of Monty Python's optimistic "Always Look On The Bright Side Of Life".

"First Offence" including the single, "Ballerina" were all compositions by Stewart and Jimmy Irving. Gavin Dare was supremely confident,

"Bumper's agreement with Rebel Records will last three years if both parties are happy after an initial six-month period. They play the kind of music that will sell records all over the world. Over the last six months we have seen around 300 bands and none of them are up to the same standard as Bumper. We are just sure they are going to make it. They are all talented individuals who can get together and make the most incredible sound. With our contacts overseas we can almost guarantee releases all over the world."

He also announced that he was planning to take the band to the international MIDEN festival in Cannes, France in 1977. "I can see Bumper emerging in the same image as 10cc and Queen."

***

Franny Lagan had also busy, setting up a business called Sidewinder Promotions with Aivors Zaks, Rob Purdie and Chris Johnstone "in an effort to get Corby onto the touring circuit of established bands." Sidewinders" inaugural promotion came during the 1975 Christmas period at the Raven Hall with Hard Road, shortly before they became Bumper, and Scenery from Northampton. The night was a great success with over 700 punters turning out. A series of

Spring gigs followed. Cisco, an eight-piece band playing a "vigorous selection of brassy Afro Rock" at Corby Youth Centre on February 28th with 300 punters in attendance.

Fumble, the band who impressed Dougie Martell and upstaged the Sex Pistols in Copenhagen appeared at the Raven on March 6, also to great acclaim despite a drop in numbers. "Fumble Fervour Rocks Raven Hall" was the headline in the *Evening Telegraph*. 'the key to their success must be their knack of dressing up old rock and roll numbers in a fresh and exciting way without losing the spirit of the original. The zeal of their act and excellent sound and equipment made the rock show a winner. Sheer rock and roll is the sort of music you either like or don't but it was still a pity more people didn't turn up to see the band."

Sidewinders' ambitions were established when they booked The Stranglers for the Raven Hall. Franny said, "We booked the Stranglers a year before they hit the big-time. They cost us around £70. Punk hadn't really taken off at this point and Corby certainly wasn't ready for it. When singer Hugh Cornwell started his mimicking masturbation act, spitting over the crowd, the punters were shocked, and many left the building, calling them sick bastards. Twelve months later this became common place with most of the punk bands."

Competing with Sidewinder, the Corby Festival Hall provided one of the highlights of the year when Australian rock band AC/DC played on June 24th. The gig was in the middle of their European "High Voltage" tour.

The Civic Centre venue was also striving to provide top class theatre for the town, promotions included "Coronation Street's" Pat Phoenix (Elsie Tanner) and husband Alan

Browning in February's offering, 'marriage Go Round". Pat also appeared, without her husband, in Liptons supermarket on Corporation Street, looking completely flustered when shoppers in the queue at the till realised who she was. 'she doesn't look so hot in the flesh" remarked snide postman Craig Douglas.

"Pyjama Tops," described as "a sex comedy," commenced a five-day run-on March 22nd, starring Bob Grant (On The Buses), Joyce Blair, Simon Merrick and Derek Roy. The play centred around the amorous capers of a group of people at the Villa Clare de Lune, "a spectacular newly renovated island retreat in the Caribbean," and the involvement of three pupils from a convent next door. The show, including nude swimming scenes in a glass fronted tank holding 17 tons of water, was greeted enthusiastically by a disappointing half full house.

The attendances were becoming a cause of concern for theatre manager Ross Jones who was rapidly becoming despondent. 'my Fat Friend," another comedy followed, featuring more TV stars, James Ellis (Z Cars) and Ann Stallybrass (Onedin Line).

"These are part of the current series of professional plays being brought to Corby over the next few months," Ross explained, but warned, 'this could be the last chance for townspeople to show they appreciate such entertainment. There's a strange feeling around the civic complex that if the top names lined up can't attract an audience - then no one can. The next play scheduled is 'murder With Love" starring Peter Byrne (Andy Crawford in Dixon Of Dock Green). These are all West End plays with West End actors. If they don't sell, the whole future of live theatre on the Corby stage will have to be looked into. We only need an audience of 3000 from a population of 40,000. If we can't sell these plays, what can we sell?"

The problem for the Civic may have been the alternative entertainment across the road at the Stardust Centre where cabaret was interspersed with bingo sessions. The newly revamped Social Club, with Radio Two DJ David 'diddy" guesting on the opening night, was to became highly popular with stars of the calibre of Del Shannon, Sandie Shaw and The Searchers all gracing the Stardust stage this year.

Steelworker George Bradshaw couldn't believe it. "I used to buy all of Del Shannon's records when I was a teenager, "Runaway," "Hats Off To Larry," and "Swiss Maid". Never thought I'd ever see him, let alone at the Stardust!"

Pipefitter John Kenrick and his wife Marilyn, former vocalist with 60s band The Pacifics recalled, 'the Stardust was always packed out. It was great to see artists we grew up with and who's records we once bought, up on the stage in George Street. Those people were on around a grand a week, it was a lucrative circuit to be on, the bingo circuit. The artists would play for about an hour and that was it, they were off. It was back to "Eyes down!"

The Arts Festival, which was based around the Civic Centre, was under threat once more following a council meeting at the beginning of the year. The result being the Arts Council Committee stating they would resign en bloc unless the council came up with hard cash and answers. They demanded to know why a suggested programme and breakdown of events for the 1976 festival had appeared in the council minutes before any member was consulted and they wanted assurances from the council that cash would become available for spending on the festival by the Arts Council. Unless answers were forthcoming they would resign. Chairman Trevor Wright and Vice Chairman Keith Patrick were adamant with their intentions of resigning immediately but changed their minds when they gained the full backing for a last try at making the Arts Festival a viable and financial success.

Trevor was in sardonic mood, 'the council seems to want to take things out of our hands, I don't know whether they think we are incapable of spending the money properly."

Given the green light with the council donating £2800 to book and pay artists for the five days in July, it was agreed that from the money, the Arts Council would pay back £750 box office returns to the District Council who would also handle all the advertising and other aspects of the festival.

Trevor Wright was appeased, "We are very pleased that the 10th Arts Festival can go ahead."

The Halle Orchestra would kick the week off on the Sunday and The Terry Smith Jazz Band followed on the Monday. The name may not have resonated with fans but guitarist Terry had toured with Scott Walker in the 60s, worked with American soul singer J.J. Jackson and along with saxophonist Dick Morrissey, had formed jazz outfit If.

Bob Kerr's Whoopee Band, an offshoot from the wacky Bonzo Dog Do Dah Band were on Tuesday and Jo Anne Kelly filled the Wednesday night blues slot. Bob Davenport and Five Hand Reel kept the folk enthusiasts happy on Thursday and the week was finished off with Sidewinders"

Saturday night promotion with Bumper who once again drew favourable reports from the man at the *Evening Telegraph*, "Bumper stole the show."

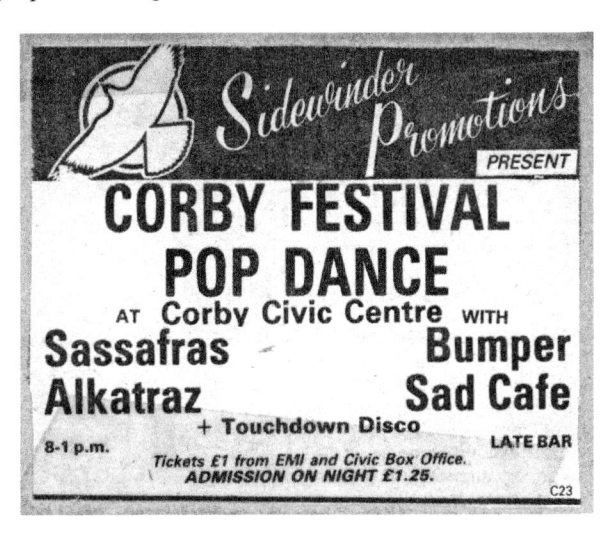

> **Sidewinder Promotions PRESENT**
> **CORBY FESTIVAL POP DANCE**
> AT **Corby Civic Centre** WITH
> **Sassafras — Bumper**
> **Alkatraz   Sad Cafe**
> + Touchdown Disco
> 8-1 p.m.   LATE BAR
> Tickets £1 from EMI and Civic Box Office.
> ADMISSION ON NIGHT £1.25.

"A packed Festival Hall erupted with enthusiasm when the boys gave what was probably their best performance in Corby yet. Sassafras had a hard job to follow the Corby band. About 800 people turned out for the concert, though until Bumper went on stage to the usual infectious acclaim, a large part of the audience was crammed into the bar downstairs. The band's show reached new heights with a phenomenal performance of their piece de resistance "Norwegian Wood Rock Show". And drummer Nigel Hart stunned the audience with a superb drum solo in another number."

Part Three

No More Heroes

1977

The death of Elvis Presley in August overshadowed every event in 1977. The Queen's Jubilee included. As with the deaths of John F. Kennedy and later John Lennon, most people of a certain age recall instantly where they were when they first heard that Elvis had died in Memphis. Val Smith, a member of the Elvis British fan Club based in Leicester was so distraught, she collapsed at home when she turned the radio on and heard the news.

Val was among a group who had travelled to see him just three weeks previously in Las Vegas, "I was stunned, when we saw him, he looked really well. He didn't look 42 and he didn't look fat." Elvis did have a problem with his diet, he couldn't resist the old cheeseburgers and his weight ballooned, whatever Val's eyes saw. Presley's death was a seismic shock to the generation weaned on rock and roll in the post war years. Even more so than the loss of Buddy Holly, Eddie Cochran and Gene Vincent, three of the original rock stars now awaiting the arrival of the biggest of them all to the great stage in the sky. Tributes were paid to the "King" all around the globe.

Over a 1000 people attended the Stardust Centre in Corby to see Elvis impersonator "Rupert," a Scunthorpe steelworker on stage. "He was fantastic" enthused manager Arthur Pitcher, "I don't think anyone left the show and complained that "I Got Stung." Four other members of the rock hierarchy followed in Elvis's footsteps this year. Marc Bolan died in a car accident and three members of Lynard Skynard were killed in a plane crash in Mississippi.

Maybe the Queen's Jubilee was a welcome distraction after all. The Jubilee New Year celebrations were mooted with Britain finding itself engulfed in the grip of the worst weather for fourteen years, snow covering virtually the whole country. A recurring theme at this time of the year throughout the 70s. Rail services, confounded by the irritating leaves on the lines, roads, airports all ground to a halt as paralysis took hold.

The Queen wasn't hanging about though, she departed "Blighty" to embark on a round robin tour of what was left of the Empire. Convenient excuse to get the hell out of it you could ascertain. The miserable weather didn't stop Billy J Kramer from hanging around either. The Merseyside star who had a string of hits in the 60s, 'little Children," "From A Window," 'do You Want To Know A Secret?," made a twelve-hour trek through the snow from Liverpool to appear at Corby Stardust in January. Bill didn't need 'trains and Boats and Planes" to get to Corby, well maybe he did but he did promise "I'll Keep You Satisfied" to the crowd of over 500 who braved the elements.

Top of the *Melody Maker* charts in the first week of the New Year was crooner Johnny Mathis with "When A Child Is Born". Keeping him company was another balladeer, David Soul with "Don't Give Up On Us", Dana with "Fairy Tale" and a seasonal hit by Chris Hill "Bionic Santa". All pretty lame for followers of the Sex Pistols who continued to make front page headlines, being unceremoniously "fired" by their record company EMI in January following their repugnant performance on Bill Grundy TV Show in December.

A vomiting incident at Heathrow Airport proved to be the final straw for EMI who paid them off with a £40,000 cheque. Bassist Glen Matlock quit in February and was replaced by Sid Vicious and the A&M label signed them up in a carefully orchestrated ceremony in front of Buckingham Palace to plug their single "God Save The Queen," complete with the photograph of Her Majesty with a safety pin through her nose on the record sleeve. Just a week later the contract was terminated! Singer Johnny Rotten vented his feelings in a scathing riposte, 'they've given us up through fear and business pressure."

Melody Maker, no fan of the genre, despite the diatribe from their reporter Chris Brazier about the Pistols Copenhagen gig, did its best to ignore the punk phenomena, stuffily proclaiming "it only broke through because of the stagnant climate and mostly as a cultural or fashion statement rather than on musical merit. It is the greatest hype of all time." Be interesting to know what Mr Brazier thought about that comment from one of his peers!

As if to emphasise the point, more coverage was given by *Melody Maker* to past masters of the 'shock, horror" scene, the Rolling Stones. On tour in Canada the Stones were caught up in a drug scandal when the Royal Canadian Mounted Police arrested guitarist Keith Richards for possession of cocaine and heroin. Released on $25,000 bail, Richards was later fined £750. Others making headlines included Fleetwood Mac guitarist Peter Green who was committed to a mental hospital after firing a pistol at a delivery boy bringing him a royalty cheque and Alice Cooper entering a rehab clinic for alcoholism after 10 years of drinking a pack of beer a day. The Pistols were choir boys by comparison!

Also in 1977, Fleetwood Mac released their record-breaking album 'Rumours". The USA's "American Bandstand" celebrated its 25th anniversary with a 'special" hosted by Dick Clark featuring Chuck Berry, Booker T and MG's and Charlie Daniels. Sara Dylan filed for divorce from husband Bob this year and Geno Washington was appearing at Kettering's North Park Club. The soul singer returning to Britain after a sojourn back home in the States, reviving a career which had seen him hogging the album charts in the sixties with "Hand Clappin, Foot Stompin', Funky- Butt ... Live!" and the follow up "Hipster Flipsters Finger Poppin' Daddies". Obviously titles like "Geno at the Palladium" or "Geno at the Talk of the Town" was too boring.

Ten years earlier, October 15th 1967, Geno had appeared at Corby Festival Hall, sharing the bill with John Mayall's Bluesbreakers. Working as an usherette in the Civic that night was Ros Toleman, sister of Rising Sons bass player Dewi.

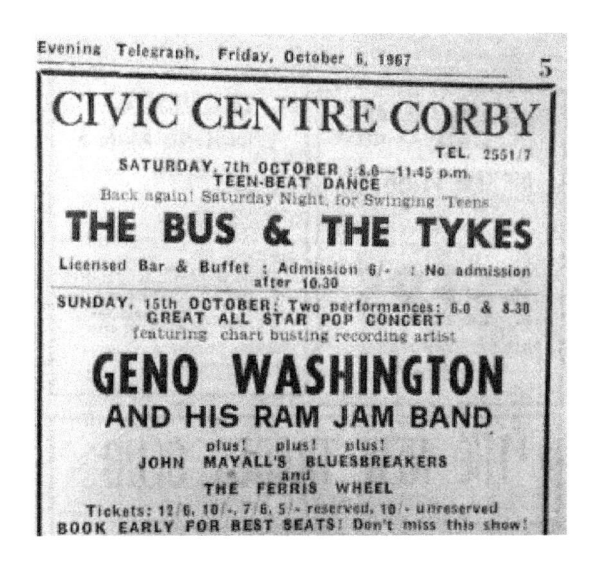

Evening Telegraph, Friday, October 6, 1967

CIVIC CENTRE CORBY
TEL. 2551/7
SATURDAY, 7th OCTOBER : 8.0—11.45 p.m.
TEEN-BEAT DANCE
Back again! Saturday Night for Swinging Teens

THE BUS & THE TYKES

Licensed Bar & Buffet : Admission 6/- : No admission after 10.30

SUNDAY, 15th OCTOBER: Two performances: 6.0 & 8.30
GREAT ALL STAR POP CONCERT
featuring chart busting recording artist

GENO WASHINGTON
AND HIS RAM JAM BAND
plus! plus! plus!
JOHN MAYALL'S BLUESBREAKERS
and
THE FERRIS WHEEL
Tickets: 12/6, 10/-, 7/6, 5/- reserved, 10/- unreserved
BOOK EARLY FOR BEST SEATS! Don't miss this show!

Ros was reminiscing about those days when home for a Grammar School Reunion organised by Bip Wetherell in 2015, "I used to do a bit of 'usheretting' at the Civic" Ros revealed, "wrestling and shows, waitressing at functions and a (pretty disastrous!) attempt at bar work, I was told on more than one occasion (in Scottish accent) 'that must be the worst pint o" beer I've ever had pulled for me hen!!"

"I also worked at the swimming pool as cloakroom attendant handing out baskets in changing rooms, then in the cafe, then in the cash box and eventually as a lifeguard when I came home from college during holidays and had my bronze medallion. At the John Mayall concert, I just showed punters to their seats. I was introduced to Geno Washington afterwards and invited to their after party. I was pretty green at the time so politely declined and told him my dad was picking me up …how rock and roll is that?"

"The Mayall/Geno gig was the first time a show at the Civic had been "all seater, an experiment" the Civic Leisure Committee declared. This was the same committee that turned down the chance to book Pink Floyd at the Civic. "Not worth the money" they said. Well, having to sit down didn't go down too well. Geno had a reputation for stomping around and getting everybody off their feet which with all the seats in the hall made life difficult. It wasn't quite like the days of the Teddy Boys and jiving in the aisles but there was no way I was going to go and tell people to sit down! I didn't get paid enough!"

"The Civic Centre had gained a reputation for being a rowdy venue. Apart from the Geno and Mayall night, when punters were trapped in their seats and voiced their displeasure at a lack of an encore, two more concerts involving The Herd and later John Walker degenerated into near riots. First, when the Herd, featuring Peter Frampton, were late turning up and then John Walker of The Walker Brothers was pulled head first off the stage by screaming teenage girls. Crazy days!"

Bip Wetherell added, "The two things I remember about 1977 was the freezing winter and the explosion of the Sex Pistols. The weather was that bad that one Thursday night, on my regular Country and Western nights at the Nags, I had 'ray and Brett" already to entertain, my wife Elaine on the door, her sister Pam behind the bar with myself compering the evening. We always had a good crowd on a Thursday because it was the night when the workers could go and collect their wages with the next stop being the Nags Head. This night, because of the extreme weather, all the roads were snowed up, we had ONE customer! Can you believe it! Ray and Anne Brett played all night to this one hardy gentleman."

"As for the punk explosion in the music scene, it was desperately needed to replace the glam era when all the bands dressed up in their glitter suits and played pop/rock. There were a few classics, the Rubettes 'Sugar Baby Love' springs to mind but generally the bands concentrated on their image rather than their music. Then the Sex Pistols arrived and changed everything."

"My brother, Stuart, and I started the 'Double D.J. Show" on a Sunday night and would endeavour to begin the evening with something different. Can you imagine the whole pub being in complete darkness when together the strobe lights would be switched on in time to the fantastic opening chords to "Pretty Vacant". The place went nuts with all the Corby punks rushing to the dance floor to start "Pogoing," jumping up and down, spitting at the strobes. It was nuts. I even promoted a "Punk" night booking a London punk band called The Spitfire Boys. They only lasted one number. They couldn't handle the Corby Punks spitting at them and throwing empty beer cans at them. It was absolute chaos! I went into the dressing room to find four very young punks cowering together with the youngest one in tears. So that was the end of me promoting Punk. It was a shame as some of the tracks from the Pistols, The Clash etc were brilliant."

"The one thing that was always a constant in managing Pubs was the requests to help with Charities, Fund Raisers etc. Obviously Elaine and I did the best we could to help people but one of the maddest things I did was a parachute jump. A group of us spent a couple of days training over at Sibson Airfield where the Parachute Centre was and, come the day, I was fairly confident it was something I could do. We had raised a chunk of money so the pressure was on. I was the last to go and remembering my training I practised very slowly and carefully the mantra of "one thousand, two thousand, three thousand pull" and that was when the parachute would open and all would be well."

"I was OK until I put my leg outside of the aeroplane ready to launch myself to infinity and beyond but the wind rush and my own terrible fear of heights kicked in and I turned to the instructor to tell him I wasn't going to do it only to be met by his size 10 boot kicking me in the chest and propelling me into the blue sky with blighty still 2000 feet from safety. Well you can forget the measured professional tones of counting out to 3000, I shouted them out that quick I sounded like one of the chipmunks. I desperately pulled the rip cord, pulled it again, and, wonderfully, the chute opened and I floated down singing "Everyone is going to rule the world" at the top of my voice. The only trouble was I forgot the training in how to land and I ended up landing on my spine which gave me terrible pain for a couple of months until it healed. It goes without saying that was the last time I was going to jump out of a perfectly good aeroplane."

John Grimley said, "Bip had gutted the back room of the Nags to make it an ideal place for live music. Anybody could get up and have a go if they wanted. A regular in the Nags was Dave Stocker, well known for being an enthusiastic music fan who had the cover of the Santana album "Abraxas" emblazoned over the bonnet of his Mark Cortina III car. Big Dave had an aura about him though his looks could be off putting if you didn't know him. He sadly passed away in 2005."

Chrome Molly guitarist Colin 'Fez' Pheasant also shared his memories of Dave Stocker in 2011. "Dave used to work the door for us when we played in Corby. He had a reputation but really he was a great bloke. There was never any trouble when he was on the door that's for sure. People would look at him, he wasn't the friendliest of looking guys, and they decided it was better to keep on the right side of him! He was a massive music fan with a hell of a record collection. I called him the John Peel of Corby. He had albums that you'd never heard of. He'd often say "Hey Colin, take this and listen to it." It'd be anything from the latest Stones album to Kevin Coyne's "Blame It On the Night," one of the earliest releases on Virgin Records and featuring Rick Dodd.

One memorable day, he came to my mum's house with a bag of albums. My dad answered the door and told him I was in the bath. "Go on up," my dad said.

There was I, lying blissfully enjoying a peaceful soak when all of a sudden the door barges open and Dave walks in, "Here, I've brought you some albums!"

I couldn't believe it! "Blimey Dave," I said.

"It's alright," he replied, "your dad told me to come up!"

A compatriot of John Grimley and Colin Pheasant was Mick Ferguson who's musical career spanned four decades, spawned inadvertently following an altercation with the landlord of the George Inn, Cottingham during the summer of 1972.

Mick and his pal Angus McKay rode down to Cottingham on their Lambrettas one early summer evening and parked their scooters up in the pub car park. Revving their engines, 'making a right racket," soon became too much for landlord Butch Lenton who charged out of the pub and chased them off with a mouthful of expletives.

Mick said, "Next time we went down there, we left the scooters parked at the top of the road! The George had an old upright piano at the time and I asked Butch, who clearly didn't realise we were the two guys he had chased a fortnight earlier, if it was alright if I had a tinker on it. 'sure" he said, and I must have impressed him as he asked me if I fancied playing piano for him on Saturday nights for £3 a night."

"The George was only a small pub, forty or fifty punters and it was jam packed. My dad James, who played the accordion, joined us and we soon built up a repertoire and crack. We'd ask the punters what they wanted to sing, I'd find the key and that was it. They were great nights and Butch was more than happy. Two years we did this. I loved it and began to think about the possibility of playing in a band, something I really fancied doing but wasn't sure on how to go about achieving it, until I spotted an advert in the *Evening Telegraph*. A band with the unlikely name of Andreas and the Quantros was looking for an accordion player, with the aside that 'vocals would be an asset, but not essential'."

"I'd never actually sung before but I took the bull by the horns and phoned the Kettering number to arrange an audition. Nervous as hell, I rode over to Kettering on my Lambretta with my dad's accordion in my sidecar. I don't know what they thought when I turned up, probably that I was a right geek! "Come in," Brian Turner said. All the band were there. I was introduced and then asked if I could play a certain number, then another one. This went on for about twenty minutes. I was sweating buckets by this time, my nerves were getting the better of me, the heat in the room was getting unbearable, and then I passed out! Collapsed on the floor."

"Next thing I know, they were picking me up as I was coming round, and saying, 'You've got the job!' Rehearsals were held every Tuesday at Kettering Working Men's Club, running through numbers that were popular in the charts and because none of the other guys were keen on singing, I was thrown in at the deep end and the very first song I sang was Don McLean's "Vincent". I realised then this is what I was meant to be."

Mick made his debut as a Quantro in January 1974, at the Ex-Serviceman's Club in Lloyds Road, Corby where the band were resident every Saturday and Sunday night. Mick said, "The club was packed every weekend and after breaking my duck as a live vocalist my confidence shot through the roof. There was a novelty number by Little Jimmy Osmond called 'long Haired Lover From Liverpool" which I did. It was a piss take really, I'd sing the first half of the number normally then switch to a high-pitched falsetto to finish it off. It brought the house down every time. The crowd loved it."

"Then at the end of May, a record came out by a The Rubettes which went all the way to number one, 'Sugar Baby Love'. Brian Turner got hold of the sheet music, we learnt it and tried it out at the Ex-Serviceman's. The song was so high I had to hit top G in falsetto to accomplish it. The reaction at the end of that first attempt was unbelievable. It was embarrassing! The whole crowd went nuts, standing on chairs, applauding, whistling, cheering. I couldn't understand what the fuss was about. Never seen anything like it. They wouldn't shut up until we did it again. Whether they thought it was a fluke I don't know! It's when I really burst on the scene!!"

"A nice anecdote to this is a signed photograph from the Rubettes which took pride of place in Mick's lounge. John Grimley got it for me. It says, 'I did it first! To Plug, Mick Ferguson, from the boys in the Rubettes.' The Quantros split up this year, 1977. The guys got fed up being in a band and called it a day."

Mick, who sadly passed away in 2022, wasn't at a loose end for long, as the Roy Bishop Sound came calling. The band included two former Size Seven members Billy and Jimmy Geary, both who'd been around since the skiffle days of the mid-fifties. The others were Paul James on organ, Roy on sax and Mark Plant on bass guitar.

Mick Ferguson with the Roy Bishop Sound

Mick, an accomplished accordionist, also played at the retirement party of long-serving Corby police sergeant Brendan McCormack, who was hanging up his truncheon to become the scourge of Corby taxi drivers as the town's Taxi Inspector.

Mick Ferguson with Brendan (Sgt McCormack) 1977

Retiring too this year was resident pianist at Corby Welfare Club, bandleader Johnny Ballantyne. A career coming to a close after 40 years as Johnny had arrived in Corby in 1936. His first dance was on the night of Edward VIII's abdication. Another notable gig was the night his band played at the Welfare Club on V.E. Day May 8th 1945.

It was a gig reported on by the *Evening Telegraph* who stated, "All roads led to the Welfare Club on Tuesday night. Mr. C. L. Benner and the Welfare Entertainments Committee threw the grounds open from 6 pm till - just as long as the people wanted to remain, which was around 2 am. Four bands, George Graham's, Johnny Ballantynes, Corby Silver Band and Eva's Trio were in attendance. The back entrance to the stage was opened and fitted up as a concert platform. Loudspeakers brought the music over the grounds and open-air dancing went merrily on until everyone was satisfied. Over the stage was Hitler - hanged well and good. One onlooker, after seeing the effigy, plagiarised Winston Churchill, and remarked "Some chicken - some neck."

Refreshments were served in the Club until 11 pm. It was floodlighted and well decorated. Many local artistes had volunteered to help to entertain the crowd, yet the compere repeatedly asked for more artistes, and got them. The spontaneity and goodwill was infectious.

Effigies of all the Nazi chiefs were burnt, and the children had a great time. Our reporter stood at the top of Rockingham Road at 12.30am on Wednesday morning. In all directions he could see the glare of bonfires reflected in the skies. To the East, Benefield way, rockets rose and exploded in cascades of brilliant stars. The factories were working with the black-out off. The bleeder was roaring and flaming and from this vantage point the centre of Corby looked like a cauldron of fire surrounded by lesser fires.

Over the years, Johnny Ballantyne would recruit a number of prominent local musicians for his bands, among them, Jackie Wilson on trumpet, Bill 'dozy" Clark on drums, Les Gilbert on tenor sax, Les Watson on alto sax, Arnold Webb string bass and Bob Crawford on tenor sax.

"A gig I remember was at this place in Bedford," Bob recalled. "We were to commence at 8 pm. What was a regular occurrence was the band would stop at the Green Dragon pub at Higham Ferrers on the way, and play Shove a"halfpenny. One summer evening at this establishment in Bedford, no jackets were worn and the array of tattoos and braces on show was amazing. The management were not amused, and the final nail in the coffin was when Les Gilbert dragged a crate of beer across the dance floor knocking some dancers over and this lead to the residency being cancelled."

Support for Johnny Ballantyne on his retirement night came from the latest incarnation of the Billy Mathieson, Derek Cowie, Reggy Knowles, Jim Smith and Ray Haggart quintet, now operating as The Licquorish Allsorts. A handle which encouraged Billy, ever the optimist, to write to Bassett's to enquire if they would be interested in sponsoring the band as he felt they would be getting good value for advertising their confectionary.

"They told us to bog off," Billy admitted.

***

The Annual Haggis Eating Contest at Corby Festival Hall was won this year by Peter Dowdeswell from Earls Barton. The eating machine had built up a reputation for gorging everything put on a plate and had numerous titles to his name. The Guinness Book of Records hailed Peter as the champ for eating eggs, (hard boiled, soft, raw), cheddar cheese, beer, eels, pancakes, spuds, prunes, jam sandwiches (40 in 17 minutes), shrimps, burgers (with buns, 21 in 9 minutes) and Peter revealed he had the gherkins and lemons records in his sights. "It's all done for charity rather than Peter's insatiable hunger," Guinness explained.

Peter had some rivals around the world including two New Yorkers, Donald 'Moses' Lerman, and Charles 'Hungry' Hardy who elucidated, "You don't have to be a big fat slob. I started on French fries and ice cream to get into it." Hardy was the current holder for hot dogs, 23 in 12 minutes.

Peter later returned to Corby for a crack at his own world record for eating pancakes, 61 x 6" scoffed in 7 minutes, at the Stardust Centre. The holder of over 70 eating and drinking records wasn't up for it this night however, managing only a mere 28. "I knew I should have left my dinner" he mused.

His fame spreading, Peter flew out to California to take part in a doughnut commercial, even though he admitted, "I hate them. Last time I ended up in hospital because I ate too many." On his return home Peter was in for a shock when he found that he'd lost his job as a building worker, though he dismissed it with a curt response, "I was looking for a new job anyway, the canteen was crap."

Peter Dowdeswell

The Stardust Centre was the "Talk of the Town" with 60s stars Marty Wilde, Karl Denver, Ricky Valance, Marmalade, Johnny Tillotson, Kathy Kirby and Del Shannon all lined up in 1977, for a modest 20p entrance fee.

P.J. Proby was another star to appear, his claim to fame included making demos for Elvis Presley in the early 60s mainly for those awful films Elvis was trapped into by his manager Tom Parker. Making demos of "There's No Room To Rhumba In A Sports Car" and "Yoga Is As Yoga Does" for "Fun In Acapulco" and "Easy Come Easy" must have been excruciating. P. J. did have a number of big selling singles to his name, "Maria," "Somewhere," "Hold Me" which improved his street cred.

Bass guitarist Roger Nicholas who lives in Desborough has played with a host of star names over the years and recalled in Tornados drummer Clem Cattini's autobiography "Thru the Eye of a Tornado" his experiences of playing with the American star. "P. J. Proby was a strange fellow. Often a nightmare. One minute he'd talk to you as if he's your closest friend then next time he sees you he'll blank you or be as ignorant as sin. He was always telling everyone he was a better singer than Elvis. He used to record demos for the King and said his version was always better. Elvis ruined them! He made demos for about a dozen Elvis films which if to be honest, many were far from memorable. He did have a great talent for imitation though. He could mimic any singer, women as well."

Clem said, "I was working with P. J. Proby at EMI when he collapsed in the studio. I played a few gigs with him too. One in Bournemouth when I insisted on staying in the same hotel as him. I was asked with incredulity, "Why do you think you should stay in the same hotel as the star? My reply was blunt, "I've travelled down from London to play for him. Left my wife and the comfort of my home to stay in this place! Don't think so!" That's what it was like, unbelievable."

Edison Lighthouse drummer Simon Aldridge and friend of Roger and Clem recalls a gig he played with P. J. Proby, "We were playing one night when I had provided most of the gear, including the PA. Suddenly in the middle of a song he threw the mic, my mic, up in the air, and did a cartwheel! The mic went through the canopy above the stage and that was that! It was knackered! Proby retrieved it, went to sing again and you couldn't hear a thing. He stood there like a goldfish looking as if he was miming! He turned round to me behind the drums and mouthed something indiscernible. Pissed me right off! 'that was my mic you've just broke!" I shouted back at him. He didn't give a toss..."

By the late 70s. drink had become a problem for the American singer and he was now reduced to playing Working Men's Clubs. Taking the Stardust stage in Corby obviously the worse for wear his performance was reported as a shambles from start to finish. The punters, who numbered nearly a thousand, showed their disgust and began booing and shouting "get off!!" "Proby responded by shouting back and within minutes the scene degenerated into total farce with the audience and the star trading insults. Standing in the wings, Stardust manager Arthur Pitcher was dismayed. Fifteen minutes into the set, with the abuse and howling growing in intensity, Arthur walked on to the stage and dragged P. J. off, apologising to the audience, later explaining, "Proby's act was so unbelievably bad, the management had to stop him."

Postman Willy McCowatt and his wife May were two who witnessed the Proby show and had joined in the booing, 'may said to me, blimey Willy, he's bladdered! Then a few started hissing and hurling insults at Proby. "Rubbish. You're crap!" Proby retaliated, he was steaming. Danny Quinn sitting near us was going to stick one on him! What a laugh! It was just as well Arthur took him off."

Despite hiccoughs like the P. J. Proby night, Arthur Pitcher showed his ambitions and announced his intent on gaining a higher profile for the Stardust, including the late-night venue Shafts which was reverting to its former name of the Exclusive Club and insisting on "gentlemen wearing collar and tie at the weekends."

Shafts has assumed legendary status over the years for its notoriety, a shameless den of iniquity. Late night drinking with live music from local bands, Shafts was the place to go… and if you were looking for some company…

Arthur Pitcher said, "We felt it was about time to improve the image and no member would be admitted unless we considered them to be properly dressed."

Falling foul of the new rules on the opening night was a friend of guitarist John Grimley, Mick Dickson, who recalled the event during a Sunday dinnertime session with myself and John at the Labour Club in 2016. He was still angry. "I was sitting in an alcove with a girlfriend, having a quiet drink when a bouncer asked me where my tie was. I told him I didn't have one. "You'll have to get out then!" he said.

"Look, I'm not doing any harm," I replied.

I was minding my own business, and the thing was, I was dressed quite smart and there was a right load of scruffy gets in that night, wearing torn jeans and crappy jumpers to hide their tie. You could see the ties just sticking out of the neck like a wee bob. The bouncer ignored them and told me to get out! I told him politely to go away.

Next thing, a fist smashed into my face, knocking me flying. I jumped back up and booted the guy. He went down. Then his mates piled in, gave me a few whacks and tossed me out. I was well unhappy. Next day it was preying on my mind and I was thinking, "I'm not letting that go, I'm gonna have that guy." So I went back up to Shafts the next night, knocked on the door and they opened the little hatch and looked out. "What do you want?" a voice asked.

"I want that big guy, that's what I want," I said.

"Too bad," the voice said, "he's in hospital."

"How?" I asked.

"You broke his kneecap when you booted him last night!"

Bands providing the soundtrack for the shenanigans that became legendary in Shafts included Knobbs, Edition and Sweet Wine featuring Dave Martin on keyboards, guitarists Dave Dean and Ian Smith and drummer Alan Booth.

Shafts regulars Knobbs

Dave Martin gave an interview which was amusing and enlightening shortly before he sadly passed away in 2008 after a long illness. "Sweet Wine worked all over the Midlands at nightspots, including Shafts, playing cabaret soft country rock stuff. Some were more memorable than others. We played a venue called The Paddocks in Daventry where a pool match was going on. The table was right in front of us by the stage, it was ridiculous. After a while, we realised nobody was paying any attention to us and we said to the manager, 'We'll take the money and call it a day!' I doubt if anybody realised we'd gone."

"A Young Farmers Ball in Towcester was interesting too with us performing on the back of a trailer in a barn. When the bevy started taking hold of the punters, it got even more bizarre. The women started taking their bras off and waving them in the air! Maybe they thought we were St Cecilia or something! "Leap Up and Down" and all that. Then everybody disappeared outside, left us playing on our own. Weird."

"Another strange night was at Corby's Exeter Club which erupted into an almighty battle. Everybody was fighting. We asked them to stop fighting while we got our gear out of the way and couldn't believe it when they did. Then they started fighting again!"

"We made a lot of money with Sweet Wine and decided to invest it in a music shop. It turned into a disaster. We bought Warren Eagle's shop in Rockingham Road and somebody mislaid all our tax assessment forms. We should have been more aware and diligent but trusted the guy who assumed control of this side of things. Consequently, threatening letters arrived from the tax people, with ever increasing penalties and finally we were forced to close down. Cost me my life savings, which didn't amount to much but all the same, it went."

Dave also recalled adventures when backing or supporting famous acts which included Ricky Valance, Dave Berry and Tommy Bruce. "Our association with Ricky Valance started in the Music Shop. He came in one day and Dave Dean got talking to him and next thing I know, he was arranging for us to back him on tour."

John Proctor was in Dave Dean's shop when Valance turned up and remembers the occasion very well. "What a tit he was, loved himself.

He asked me, "Do you know who I am?"

I said, "No."

"Have you heard of "Tell Laura I Love Her?" he asked.

"Oh yes, by Frank Ifield." I said.

"No, listen," and he started singing.

I had to admit, "Have to say, you're a good singer."

To which he replied, "Thank you, that's good. You clearly know a good singer when you hear one! Even if you didn't know the song."

After he'd gone, Dave Dean said to me, "Frank Ifield sang "I Remember You!"

"Oh yeah!" I said. I did know. I was winding him up.

Dave Martin said, "A most memorable gig was at the Dominion Theatre, London, a "Heroes and Villains" charity concert with Herman's Hermits and Dave Berry. Billy Mathieson sat in on drums with Dave Dean on bass and me on guitar. This was the gig when Valance fell off the stage. What a laugh that was. Billy told him that was the best he'd ever gone down! He didn't see the joke. Poor guy had to wear a neck brace for months afterwards."

Billy Mathieson added, "Valance was a right poser. For some reason he decided to walk sideways along the stage to take a bow, and fell head first into the orchestra pit! The place was in uproar, everybody was laughing their heads off. Tears were streaming down my face. He reckoned he was fit, been a bit of a boxer in the army. He tried to haul himself back out of the pit and got stuck three times. Each time the audience went mad. It was a scream. We took the piss out of him for ages after that. Even drew a cartoon with Valance in stage gear and a parachute. He didn't laugh, no sense of humour at all!"

"He was also a tight-fisted git. We did a tour of Scotland one time when our 'roadie' let us down at the last minute and we had to hire a transit van for £100 from B.B. Motors. It skint us. After the first show in Fife, we asked Valance for some money, and he told us he didn't have any. The three of us sat their drinking pints of water. A comedian, Andy Cameron came over to us, "I don't believe it, a rock and roll band drinking pints of water!" No choice we said and told him the story."

"You not paying them?" Cameron asked Valance.

"No money till the end of the week," was his reply.

"Cameron went to see the agent who'd booked us and was told he had paid Valance. The agent went to Valance, called him everything. He bought us all a round of drinks, cigarettes, some food. Then he told Valance he'd make sure he wouldn't play in Scotland again!"

Dave Dean said, "Valance used to make us laugh when he put on his phoney American accent. We played with Jerry Lee Lewis and Carl Perkins in Newport, South Wales another time. This was a place where there was a big star on one of the dressing room doors and Valance thought it was for him. He swaggered on through and was promptly kicked out!"

He used to pay us and deduct the price of drinks out of our wages. We stayed at a hotel and were asked what we wanted to eat, all free. Valance said, "Steak, the rest will have sandwiches!"

I said, "Hoy! we'll have four steaks here as well." He turned and glowered at us. That was the sort of bloke he was."

Dave Martin added, "We also backed Tommy Bruce who had a minor hit way back when with "Ain't Misbehavin". He was arrogant as well. Hardly talked to us all day. I don't know who he thought he was, he was rubbish. And he had some guy hanging around him all the time, carrying a brief case. Silly. Made us laugh really. We spent all day rehearsing to perform two numbers! Dave Dee, Dozy, Beaky, Mick and Tich, the Nashville Teens, Marmalade and the Tremeloes were all on the show. It was a great experience, filmed by a TV company and released on video. It took me years to get a copy though. Playing with all these artists, I couldn't help thinking it was a bit weird, I used to buy all their records and here I was playing on the same show as them."

***

On the back of achieving third place at the Roundhouse, Bumper were signed up by the Barry Collins Agency in Southend who's clients included hitmakers Pilot (Magic 1975) and Love Affair (Everlasting Love 1968).

Collins soon had Bumper playing all-round the country, week-long residencies, one-night stands, a grind which had to take its toll, and eventually would do. Driving duties for these treks was designated to the youngest member of the group, Nigel Hart, "as the Irving brothers Stewart and Jimmy couldn't drive and Bob Grimley and Mick Haselip liked a drink."

Stewart said, "We did put a lot on Nidge, which to this day I do regret. We took advantage of him. He was a very sensitive guy. With Barry Collins we were playing tours which were ridiculous. One occasion we were playing in Whitley Bay and the next day in Dorchester, and Nidge did most of the driving. We had a transit van with our gear in which our roadies drove while the rest of us travelled by car. John Dolby, a mechanic and veteran of the Corby music scene lent us his car for the Whitley Bay trip and on the way down to Dorchester we were pulled over on the A1 by the police near Worksop. We were all knackered, we hadn't been drinking so that wasn't a worry, but the police asked Nidge for his driving licence and he didn't have it."

"Bob Grimley had John's licence and passed it to him, 'tell them your John Dolby" Bob said. Nidge handed it over, the police looked at it, and asked, "John L Dolby, what does the L stand for?"

Nidge panicked and then blurted out "Lenny!" Which had all of us pissing ourselves laughing.

"Right, get out!" the police officer growled. And apart from being done for having no driving licence, Nidge was also done for having a dodgy tyre!"

Nidge said, "For all that, it was a treat to sit behind those boys and watch as they stirred everything up. Stewart Irving was arguably one of the most underrated vocalists around. He could really bump the audience up, had great stage presence and personality."

"I didn't mind the driving at first. I was a non-drinker anyway, but I have to admit to feeling put on at times. I did around 90% of the driving. Bob would give me a break occasionally. The Whitley Bay to Dorchester affair was typical. Another was when we played in Barrow-In-Furness, where we were on stage from 1 till 2.30am, and then I had to drive back down to Northamptonshire right after. It was absolutely knackering! This was a normal sort of schedule and arduous. I had dreamt of the lifestyle but soon the reality was not what I expected. It gradually wore me out and in the end I quit."

"I moved to Cambridge in 1981 after splitting with my girlfriend, gained my HGV licence and continued to play around the Cambridge area in all kinds of outfits, pub rock bands and dance bands complete with a dickie bow!"

"The rock band was called Private Line and featured at a number of top class and well-known rock musicians. Rick Wills had played with Cochise and Foreigner. Guitarist Mick Grabham was another ex-Cochise man who was known for his work with Procol Harum. Don Airey ex Whitesnake keyboards. Dick Parry, sax player on Pink Floyd albums. I can still recall sitting on the drums, looking at Dick play and thinking this was the guy who had played on "Dark Side of the Moon" and other Floyd albums. It knocked me out!"

"We had a residency at the Crown and Cushion in Great Granstead each Tuesday. It was mobbed every week for nearly five years. We eventually became Los Amigos and played as a trio before I moved to Thrapston in the early 90s. My next band had a quite appropriate name, High Mileage!"

Following the departure of Nigel Hart and bassist Mick Haselip who left to join up with his brother, Tony, in Chrome Molly, Bumper changed their name to Scene Stealer and hit the road again with new recruits found after placing an advert in the *Melody Maker*.

SCENE STEALER

Bob Grimley said, "There seemed to be hundreds interested in the job, the phone never stopped. Norman Hickens stepped in for Mick and Tony Norris from Derby took over from Nidge on drums."

As time rolled on, having recorded their debut album "First Offence" and with no news of a release date, plus a cancellation of a proposed tour to Germany, the boys started to get restless.

Gavin Dare (Rebel Records) picked up the vibes in December, and in an attempt to placate them, sent them an update on what was occurring. "We thought it was time we wrote to let you all know what is happening with Scene Stealer around the world, but firstly to look back over the past few months. From the time of recording the album until now has probably been the hardest for all concerned. At the end of August the album was mixed and ready for presentation. The UK reaction was not favourable but nevertheless acceptable and owing to heavy commitments of EMI the release date was constantly being changed. This position now seems to be rectified and a release is promised for early in the New Year (1978).

The gig situation has gone from bad to worse and with the latest episode regarding the German booking we can understand your reactions. With reference to the German tour Barry Collins informs me that he is trying to recover this work by directly booking you as opposed to subcontracting the work. Failing this he assures me that he will make sure there is a minimum of £500 worth of gigs for December. Well, how do we stand now? What is there to look forward to? Let us explain. With a highly professional album in the can we can look forward with confidence to a fast moving, star making, and highly profitable 1978 but this is going to require a concentrated effort on all sides. Why? Because of the phenomenal reaction to the album throughout Europe.

We have just returned from Germany where they think you are one of the best bands they have heard in a long, long time and are planning to back up this statement by arranging TV, radio and personal appearances for you, to coincide with the release. They assure me that the release will be in early January and we have no reason to doubt them. There is a marvellous team operating in Germany, and they are 100% behind you, so if we can give them the same sort of co-operation, there is no problems at all. We had the same reaction from Holland and at the time of writing, have planned to visit them on Monday the 12th December to discuss Scene Stealer further and they also have a fantastic team that are behind you 100%. We feel sure that you will agree with us that we are now on the threshold of something big and only by giving all of our support can we obtain the success that we all so richly deserve. We have no doubt that you will play your part and you know us well enough to play ours.

Don't be despondent lads, there's not much longer to wait. We take this moment to wish you all and your families a very merry Christmas and a real REBELious New Year! Rock On!

Signed,

Gavin and Dave"

Jim Fotheringham

There have been many local lads to have broken into the big time but not many will be aware of who was the first. Back in the 1950s, former Corby Boys School player Jim Fotheringham was making a name for himself at centre half playing for Arsenal. He did in fact play for Arsenal against Manchester United the Saturday before United's ill-fated trip to Yugoslavia and the Munich air crash in 1958.

Jim Fotheringham playing for Arsenal 1950s

In 1955 Jim was featured in the July edition of the *Charles Buchan Football Monthly*. Re-produced here:

"My Arsenal pals who have more soccer service in years than I have in months have often told me that the game a player never forgets is his first league match. I fully endorse that now, especially as in my case the first league problem that I had as a centre half, I had to deal with a fellow in a number 9 shirt named Nat Lofthouse. My second senior outing was against a Russian side in a match that had been lifted from the sports page to the front page - with the knowledge that millions were looking on through TV."

It all added up to quite an opening for a teenage Scot. "That was some week for me, last November. It began with a message to report to Mr. Whittaker's office on the Wednesday before our game with Bolton at Burnden Park. The boss told me I would be playing, also that I was being given early notice to get used to the idea and so stave off last minute nerves. But only when he wished me luck did the news really sink in. Nervous? I took it all very calmly - on Wednesday.

On Thursday, thinking about the coming ordeal, I hardly ate anything! But by Saturday I felt quite composed. Nat Lofthouse was a great sport and I thoroughly enjoyed our first meeting. We got a much-needed point in a 2-2 draw. Nat didn't score and it was this as much as anything that brought me to the end of the match very much relieved. I don't claim to be without nerves and I suppose the thoughts of playing against Spartak three days later should have been enough to worry anybody. But I kidded myself into thinking that it was just another game, despite the trimmings that were being woven around it. Honestly, I couldn't get over excited about the match. I suppose that is why I went out to have what I feel is my best game so far.

We Arsenal players tried all we knew to wipe out the memory of that 5-0 beating by Moscow Dynamo a month earlier. Maybe if we had got that second half penalty for a foul on Arthur Milton our right winger, we would have made it a draw. But though we went down 2-1, we all knew that we had done something to atone partially at least, for the Moscow beating.

For Arsenal was a grand team that night. In all modesty, we can claim to have blown up the theories that Spartak were world beaters - Wolves later confirmed the point. That first week of mine is, naturally, the high spot in a modest career that has yet to stretch to a full season. But there was another week when it seemed that things might work out in rather hectic fashion for me. Looking back now I am rather frightened at the thought that my first big game might have been at Wembley in the Cup Final.

Here are the facts, Three years ago Arsenal, due to meet Newcastle at Wembley, had the unluckiest bunch of injuries a club could have. Jimmy Logie and Doug Lishman were hospital cases and Ray Daniel our centre half, had a broken wrist in plaster and was very doubtful. I was reserve centre half, but right half Arthur Shaw-with much more experience- was given a game at centre half I case he had to take Ray's place. And Arthur also broke an arm.

I had read in the newspapers that Arsenal might have to call on a young unknown in the Final. His name was Jim Fotheringham, and those reports made me very nervous. I doubt if I was seriously considered at the time, but Arthur's injury made the situation even more desperate. Perhaps I solved it. That Saturday before the Cup Final I fell against our goalpost in trying to head away a corner. I caught the bottom of my spine and my legs became paralysed. They had to carry me off and I spent the next week in hospital.

But for my football I would have followed father into his trade as an engineer. My father came to Corby, Northants - 'little Scotland" they call it, when I was eighteen months old. Many people are surprised at my Scottish accent when I tell them I have been in England so long - but Corby and thousands of exiled Scots explains that. Like most kids it was Rangers for me in the early days - even at some 400 miles range. Too busy playing, I saw little senior football as a youngster. But in Scotland on holidays I usually managed to see a game or two there, and big Frank Brennan was my favourite. He was then playing for Airdrie.

My school games were played in the Samuel Lloyd School side, I was a left back then. Then came a move on to Corby Technical College and a change to centre half. I also represented Northampton Youth and was thrilled at the news that Sunderland and Leicester scouts were watching me. But before then came a chance for me, a Scot, to play for England schoolboys. I was picked for the South team to meet the North in a trial at Oxford.

A few days before the game I went down with flu, but scared that I would miss my chance, I pretended to be better on the day. I made a real hash of things and bang went my cap. Strange, something like that almost happened to me on another occasion when I had my heart set on a game. I got the chance to play for the Army against Scotland at Hampden Park, during my service days. It was a wonderful thrill until a troublesome boil on the face almost closed my left eye. I had daily penicillin injections, but it was nowhere near right on the day and again I had to pretend that I was much better than I really was. But who wouldn't have done the same in my place? We lost 2-1, but I had the privilege and pleasure of meeting fellows like George Young, Tommy Ring and Bobby Johnstone that afternoon.

My father, to my surprise, would not hear of trials at either Sunderland or Leicester for me. Much later I found out that he had his eyes and his hopes on a London club for me. An Arsenal scout was the first to enter our sitting room, and, in 1949, I was off to Highbury.

So keen was I, to make good that I spent a fortnight's holiday there in order to be really fit for my test. I was determined not to let my father or myself down. My first game was against Leyton Orient in the London Mid-Week League. I was then 16. Now, at 6' 3", they tell me I'm the tallest player in the game. Well, it's handy, to say the least, when the ball is in the air. I have had the best coaching from great players and great colleagues like Alf Field and Leslie Compton - and Tommy Lawton has been long suffering and a model of patience in teaching me how best to head a ball. And Arsenal? Even to a football rookie like me it is so obviously the best club in the world!"

Jim Fotheringham was selected for the Scotland World Cup squad in 1958 and later signed for Hearts for £12,000. Returning south he joined Northampton Town and broke his leg which sadly, was the end of his career. Jim spent three months coaching the Libyan national side in 1961 for the Arab Olympic Games. Turning his back of football, Jim took a job in the steelworks and passed away in Corby at the age of 44 in 1977.

Don't Leave Me This Way

Celebrations were reaching fever pitch by the time festivities kicked off in June with street parties, fetes and a general ballyhoo sweeping the country to commemorate the Queen's Jubilee. Whilst most of us were enjoying ourselves, discounting members of the Punk fraternity where Dead Kennedy's vocalist Jello Biafra miserably complained 'the Jubilee is an absurd, pompous self-celebration," it was ironic that the country was simultaneously almost drowning in a sea of anarchy.

Jim Callaghan's government was immersed in a series of battles with unions that culminated with Labour embracing the Liberals who had offered their support to defeat a Conservative vote of no confidence, avoiding the likelihood of an immediate general election.

Disputes were becoming endemic. British Leyland threatened a shutdown of all their car plants to put an end to the strikes. The British Steel Corporation was dogged by 'local" strikes, the miners demanded £135 for a four-day working week. Undertakers in London walked out, leaving a backlog of 800 corpses unburied. Industrial action blacked out the state opening of Parliament. Firemen went on strike for a 30% wage increase. Bakers and bread deliverymen joined in, prompting one wag to scrawl graffiti on Hammersmith Bridge, "let them eat Corgi" during the Queens celebrations. The bread delivery men had a "cob" on when supermarkets began to undercut them with cheaper prices and threatened to boycott all stores who sold their bread at less than 18p a loaf. Their cause not helped by the caustic response of an MP who urged housewives to bake their own bread, "shop bread is tasteless anyway."

Panic ensued, dawn queues formed with people stocking up fridge freezers with all the loaves they could get hold of. The black market saw the cost of a loaf go up to 47p from 27p. The General Sec. of Bakers and Food Allied Workers Union explained, "The row is over pay for time off and holidays. Bread workers earn £28.50 a week. But many work long hours, work Sundays, six days a week and with very little leisure time." Never was the term "on the breadline" more appropriate.

As it happened, on October 19th, the Bakers strike crumbled and they went back to work. Corby bin men had three weeks off when a refuse collector was suspended for riding on the back of a lorry. "It was Hughie Mellows riding the dustcart," Union official John Black recalled. "Hughie was a stocky wee guy with one eye. The problem was down to a stroppy new manager. On his first day down at the yard, he came into the changing room and started barking orders out. He had a terrible manner, no man management skills whatsoever.

Most of these bin men were hard cases. Their response was an abrupt "up yours!" and we all walked out. We played football all day. He got the message. The dispute became even deeper over proposals for clearing the backlog of rubbish. Garbage was piling up in the streets. The men asked me to be the union official, so I went in with the bosses and came back out with what I thought was a good deal. Then this big Kettering guy standing at the back piped up, "Call that a deal?" he said, "you're hopeless!"

I looked right at him, "Hopeless? there's a big car park over there, I'll show you who's hopeless! A row erupted and everybody started shouting and arguing. The Kettering guy backed down and agreed with the rest of us that we should settle for £50 each.

With strikes consuming the country, Corby steelworkers were given cause for optimism with an announcement that an order from BSC's Tubes Division, worth £3 million was in the pipeline for a massive new 2000 ton walking Dragline. Work on the construction of the giant ore quarrying machine was scheduled to begin in 1980 and erected on the site in 1981. A 279 feet boom would also be fabricated on site. The capacity of the bucket, 36 cubic yards, was large enough to hold three mini cars and able to lift 50 tons at a time. It would be the first new Dragline at Corby since 1963 and join four others in operation.

Following this came news of BSC winning a £21million order for oil-well casing and tubing placed by Chevron who were developing Ninian Field, the third largest in the North Sea. Though the 50,000 tons of high-grade equipment was to be produced largely at Clydesdale, Scotland, significant tonnages would be made at Corby, Stockton and Llanwern.

For all the good vibes, dark rumours continued about the future of Corby steelworks. A meeting of the East Midlands Economic Planning Committee and representatives of Corby District Council led to this appraisal, "New jobs are essential to the town's survival unless there is government action. Without government support the town will become an industrial wasteland. The town badly needs new roads and control over its own land to attract industrialists and vital jobs. The unemployment rate standing at 7.5% is among the highest in the country. Not only must steelmaking remain in the town operating at present levels at least, but we have got to attract new industry to Corby. The long-term fear is Corby will not have the ability to control its own land once the Corby Development Corporation is absorbed by the New Towns Commission."

Shortly after this, it appeared as if prayers had been answered when the *Evening Telegraph* ran a frontpage story with the headline "Bonanza for Town". The feature announced news of a 'massive £60m investment programme set to confirm the town's place as one of the most important steel producing centres in Europe. "Work has already started on a new plant and installation of machinery that will help push Corby into the forefront of BSC's strategy for the 1980s. A £50m scheme to build a new electric weld stretch reducing mill plus upgrading of existing mill is expected to increase production of round and rectangular tubes. The new mill should start production in 1980. £6.5million will also be spent on a new dragline."

Good vibes it all was but a dispute which caused thousands of steelworkers to go without meals occurred when 260 BSC canteen workers at Corby walked out over a "heat wave" argument that came to a head when a woman fainted. The women claimed a weekend hot spell had sent temperatures soaring to 120o inside the Works" canteens. "We asked for cooling systems last summer but nothing was done. We'll go back when the weather changes" the irate manageress of the EWSR canteen stated. "Flat banger" (square sausage) fans weren't amused.

Minor disputes were not unusual in a complex as vast as the steelworks. I was witness when Tubeworker George

Magee's late return from the EWSR canteen one backshift epitomised the poor industrial relations between workers and management. George was on overtime, 'twelve hours" in the EWSR, as I was, helping out the backshift by agreeing to operate a tube straightening machine. Arriving on the job ten minutes later than scheduled, George, a Dunkirk veteran was met by the foreman, John Flood, foaming at the mouth. Pointing to his watch, Flood growled, "What time do you call this? You're supposed to be on the job at 3.20! Twenty minutes is all you get for your break!"

Looking at the two and a half ton of tubes on the table waiting to get straightened, Flood barked at George, "You won't leave here until you've finished this lot!"

George puffed on his pipe, taking his time while considering his response. "Can I borrow your phone?" he finally asked Flood.

"What for?" Flood replied.

"To phone my wife, to tell her to bring my shaving gear down. I'll be here all night!" said Flood.

Another dispute occurred over the maintenance of a toilet seat. Most of the ablutions in the older plants of the Works had a hole in the ground with two footprints either side to do the business but the modern ultra tech toilet blocks were grander, i.e. the introduction of the pan. Albeit minus the seat. Instead, two wooden slats screwed to the sides acted as a buffer. Mick Ferguson's pal Angus McKay, a welder in the Wagon Shops caused a row after reporting to his foreman that one of the slats was broken and splintered his arse. The information was passed on and thus began a dispute which lasted for months as departments argued as to who was responsible for repairing the toilet. "Not us," said the plumbers and "Not us," said the carpenters. Angus said, "The toilet was out of action for months with tape tied around the block like it was a murder scene!"

All these arguments aside, BSC Chairman Charles de Villiers was cautious regarding the prospects for Corby. "We have a marvellous complex at Corby. But tubes are a difficult business and has been bad throughout the world. We need investment at Corby very badly. A massive wage explosion could kill the industry, it could be catastrophic."

Just a month later a bombshell hit the town. "A major decision is expected soon on the future of steelmaking at Corby. It could mean loss of jobs. BSC chiefs at Corby have been ordered to economise all plants in a desperate attempt to cut back expected losses which could be as much as £250m in 1978."

The plan to axe 1200 jobs at Corby, 10% of the workforce, was announced was on September 20th, confirming everyone's worst fears. Cuts across the board in management and production workers would be through natural wastage, early retirement and voluntary redundancies. The report revealed, "Corby ended a disastrous run of three years in the red last year with a £6.3m deficit. Meanwhile, at four other groups in the Tubes division, profits were up to £2.7m. The consequences for Corby could be dire. School leavers are joining the dole queue in their dozens every year in Corby."

Union leader John Cowling spoke out, "Corby could become one of the most depressed areas in Britain unless a bid is made to save the 1200 jobs at BSC. It is time the people of Corby woke up to the fact that their town is crumbling around them."

On October 8th a mass rally, called by the Iron and Steel Trades Confederation was held in the town. Speakers included Sir Geoffrey DeFreitas who shortly afterwards announced his decision to retire as an MP at the next election, and Bill Homewood, ISTC Senior Divisional Officer who pledged to form an Action Committee, "There's an urgent need for action. Corby will suffer deprivation and decadence unless we close ranks." The rally only attracted around 60 people. Mick Skelton, ISTC joint Branch Secretary, admitted he was disappointed with the turn out, "Everybody knows about the apathy in this town. People in Corby only put up the umbrella when it starts to rain. I've had my umbrella up for eight years now and I certainly don't want to get caught in the storm that is going to break in this town." Alec Nimmo, ISTC Branch Chairman, was far from optimistic, "It is BSC's intention to close Corby steelworks. The 1200 jobs are just a start."

Apathy prevailed and another meeting, held in the Labour Club attracted just 30 people, causing Bill Homewood to slam Corby workers and public alike, "I am very disappointed, Corby doesn't seem to be taking this seriously."

Blowin' In the Wind

Corby's Rick Dodd had retired from the full-time music business and in 1976 was playing sax with a band that featured guitarist Barry Monk called Big Licks. Barry, who moved to Surrey in 1977, recalled those days and his time playing with Rick in 2020.

"I was with the Lykes of Witch in the early 70's and then formed Supalik with Mick Haselip. I played my 6 and 12 string Jimmy Page double neck at the Rugby Club marquee gig, after which Stewart Irving approached us to form a new group, Hard Road, which later turned into Bumper. Unfortunately I had to go into hospital for a short while and was replaced by Bob Grimley, and the Irvings decided they couldn't let me back in! When Ned McGuigan left Hard Road we then got together with Ricky Dodd and formed Big Licks in '77. For our debut gig we took over the White Swan at Harringworth, the upstairs room, and I kid you not, every musician in Corby turned up out of curiosity. Needless to say we went down a storm, but unfortunately we didn't last long because of Rick's "habits. When I moved to Surrey, I carried on playing, right to this day, but I look back with fond memories on my Corby days."

Rick Dodd had been on the road, to use a well-worn rock anecdote, since he went to Ronnie Scott's Soho club in 1965 as a sixteen year-old prodigy. Scott became something of a mentor, arranging for Rick to meet and play at the Bulls Head in Barnes with such jazz luminaries as Dick Morrissey, Phil Seaman, Roland Kirk and Ben Webster. In the 1970's Rick enjoyed two years with the Roy Young Band where he found himself in the company of rock royalty like Chuck Berry and Pink Floyd.

When Young called it a day Rick joined up with blues/rock guitarist Kevin Coyne, described by BBC disc jockey Andy Kershaw as "a national treasure, one of the great British blues voices."

"Formerly a therapist in a psychiatric hospital, Coyne had a reputation for being an uncompromising and unorthodox artist blessed with one of the most individual voices in rock. His 1973 album "Marjory Razorblade" won critical acclaim for its variety of disturbingly accurate character studies, delivered with a voice of astonishing range and volume. Coyne was notable for his unorthodox style of blues-influenced guitar composition, the intense quality of his vocal delivery, and his bold treatment, in his lyrics, of injustice to the mentally ill." *Wikipedia*

Coyne had advertised for a sax player in the *Melody Maker* "….to fill out his sound for a forthcoming European tour with John Mayall's Bluesbreakers."

Rick followed it up and was invited along for an audition which he recalled over a beer in the White Hart, Corby in 2004.

"I turned up at a rehearsal room in Chelsea which was booked from 8pm till 1am to find no one around, except the roadie. "Where is everybody?" I asked. "In the pub," came the reply. That was my introduction to Kevin Coyne. I went over and found the rest of the band well into a drinking session. Kevin greeted me and bought me a pint, then introduced me to the rest of the band and that was it. We concentrated on getting blotto before managing to get in about an hour of rehearsal at the end of the night."

The tour with John Mayall's Bluesbreakers promised to be exciting. Mayall was a British blues icon. Many legendary British blues legends passed through his ranks. Eric Clapton, Peter Green, Mick Taylor, Mick Fleetwood, John McVie, Jon Hiseman, Colin Allen… an endless list.

The '74 Bluesbreakers was featuring session guitarist Jesse Ed Davis who had played on albums by George Harrison, Eric Clapton, Ringo Starr and Rod Stewart. He also played at George Harrison's 1971 Bangladesh Concert in New York. Former Canned Heat bassist Larry Taylor was also in the Bluesbreakers so Rick was in the company of some elitist musicians.

Rick's memory of the tour however wasn't John Mayall's stage presence or musicianship but that Mayall couldn't speak a word of French.

"Mayall was a renowned hard taskmaster but the tour did have its lighter moments. My main memory of John is watching him trying to order some food when we were in Paris, that was very funny. John was very articulate and thought the locals would understand his efforts with both tongue and sign language no bother. He eventually gave up and asked me if I could help him out."

Life on the road with Coyne and Rick was rarely dull, as keyboard player Tim Penn and bass player Tony Cousins recalled when interviewed in 2007.

Tim Penn said, "Rick was a really good sax player and had a bizarre sense of humour. I remember two things in particular. On tour sitting in a restaurant, Rick placed a pizza on his head like a beret, with a little olive sitting in the middle. He had us in stitches. I also remember him telling a story about the soul band he used to play in, called the New Formula. How all the musicians had invented a catheter like apparatus, using a condom and plastic tubing, going down to a bag strapped to the leg, so that they could drink and urinate without having to leave the stage. Whether that was true or just a musician's "urban tale" I don't know! I played with Kevin from May 1974 until Dec 74, at which point Rick, Terry Slade and Tony Cousins were unceremoniously sacked as Virgin (Coyne's Record Label) wanted to "commercialise" the band. I lost contact with Rick after Dec 74 and I understand he gave up the life of a professional musician after Coyne. I think he was quite a bit older than some of us and the break-up of the band was pretty upsetting to him - but I'm not sure."

Tony Cousins added, "Rick took that Virgin rebuff worse than everyone else, and as far as I know quit the music business in disgust. In a way it was understandable because he was bitter about the way he had been treated before he joined the band. It would have consisted of the usual hazards involved in being a musician - failed promises, rip offs and sordid living conditions. Rick could be very inspiring to play with. My main memories are to do with his extraordinary appetite for drink and drugs. I saw him more than once, vomit before he went on stage and then play as if nothing had happened. He was not a big man but his constitution must have been iron. I suppose he was more used to it than anyone else because of being schooled from an early age, playing in Germany etc.

Rick used to call Kevin "Ken" which irritated him. Used to wind him up. Coyne tried very hard to like Rick and make him welcome into the band, he did this with everybody as you might expect but he always found Rick difficult. Rick had us thrown off the bus on the John Mayall tour because he was continually winding Larry Taylor up. Rick didn't know when to stop and Taylor, who was a well-respected musician, refused to put up with it. The Mayall tour was not very long, possibly ten days or even a week but it was certainly eventful. In Rome we were booed because the audience couldn't hear us properly, this was in the days before everything was fed through a mixing desk. In Naples there was a riot and the glass front of the club was demolished. I remember sitting in the dressing room after our set and three guys walked in, turned a table upside down, broke the legs off and went off to battle.

The worst gig was in Bari, in the Opera House where we were all so drunk we couldn't tune up let alone play. We were booed off stage again. Very ignominious. Even though Kevin had obviously quaffed a few he always managed to hold himself together so he was livid and rightly so. The Coyne band played quite a lot in Europe, always short tours of a week or two. Outside of the gigging life of that band we didn't socialise that much, possibly because our encounters were intense but I'm only guessing. Kevin had a huge appetite for life and was as demanding as he was compassionate. Our guitarist Gordon Smith was in some ways just as bad as Rick except that he kept quiet. He says he has virtually no memory of any of it because he was perpetually drunk."

Rick adds, "Gordon Smith was an oddball. He was a familiar face around London as a busker. At times he would go days without speaking to anyone. You'd ask him if he was ok and he'd just nod his head as he sat there grinning! I think a lot of it was the boredom when we were driving miles sitting in the back of the bus. That used to get me too. People think it's a glamorous life and to a certain extent it is but when you consider that a lot of time is spent travelling miles in the back of a van and hanging around, it does your head in."

Rick Dodd seated on left with the Kevin Coyne Band at Hyde Park

During his time with Roy Young and Kevin Coyne, Rick appeared on TV's "Old Grey Whistle Test," which you can find on Youtube. With Young they were playing "Wild Cherry Wine" in the studio, the Coyne clip is from the 1974 Hyde Park gig with Rick prominent on the song "Poor Swine".

Before returning to Corby in April '75, Rick and some buddies from the Roy Young Band, and also Elton John, played a benefit gig at the Marquee for the Average White Band's deceased drummer Ronnie McIntosh. Then, Rick was offered chances to join both the Averages, and also Ted

Nugent's band who were scheduled for a U.S. tour with Steely Dan. Nugent's band included Rick's brother-in-law Cliff Davis on drums and Ted asked Cliff to phone Rick to ask him to come to a rehearsal.

Rick said, "Cliff gave me directions which I wrote on the back of a packet of cigarettes. I came out of the Underground, blinking in the sunlight, looking to get my bearings. The instructions said turn right, first left, then right again. Opposite The Duke's Arms was the rehearsal room. I arrived at the spot on the fag packet marked with an X and looked around, no Duke's Arms. Thinking I must have taken a wrong turn, I backtracked to the Tube Station and tried again, and ended up in the same spot so I headed for the nearest phone box to contact Cliff.

"Have you followed the instructions?" Cliff asked me.

"Yes, all I can see are Greek restaurants and Launderettes."

"Stay by the phone box and I'll come and get you."

Twenty minutes later, I was still leaning against a wall and waiting for Cliff. I phoned him again. To my surprise he asked, "Where are you, I've been down there twice and there's no sign of you."

"Well, I haven't moved, I can assure you of that."

Cliff asked me to read out the instructions on the fag packet. "Turn right out of Shepherd's Bush Tube Station...."

"Shepherd's Bush!" Cliff shouted down the line, "You should be in Hammersmith, you dipstick!"

Rick eventually made the rehearsal/audition but admitted he wasn't really interested. Pity really. One of the Ted Nugent gigs was in Central Park, New York.

Rick passed away in 2006 in Fleetwood, England, after a short illness.

Kevin Coyne died in 2004 in Nuremberg, Germany.

Following in Rick's footsteps was saxophonist Bob Clark who in 2010 agreed to be interviewed in the Wayfarers pub in Kettering. "I was brought up listening to the radio. We didn't have a television 'till I was around 10! My dad didn't like TV, he preferred the radio. The Light Programme was the main station but when I could I would tune in to AFN or Radio Luxembourg. Dad had a great collection of Big Band records, Stan Kenton, Benny Goodman type stuff. My older sisters were into rock and roll, Buddy Holly and Elvis, but it was predominantly jazz that resounded around the house and made the bigger impact on me. Then my sister Iris started going out with Alan, a guy who was in the RAF and happened to play sax in the force band and I was hooked. Iris took up playing the euphonium and to this day the two of them are playing for their local Broadstairs Silver Band.

With my friends Alan Murphy and John Wilson, I used to hang out around the back of the Welfare Club when the "big" names played there. Lulu, The Four Pennies, The Nashville Teens. It was a great thrill asking if they wanted a hand with their equipment from their vans at the back of the hall. You could hear and sense the atmosphere standing at the back of the stage door. It was brilliant."

Pat Casey, sax player with the Midnighters tells a story of when they were support to Lulu and the Luvvers, then in the charts with 'shout," at the Welfare Club in 1964. Pat's sister, Cathy was excited to meet Lulu in the dressing room before the show. And even more thrilled when Lulu asked her if she could borrow her hair spray. Something to brag about! It all turned sour after the show though when Cathy went back to ask Lulu for her hairspray back. Lulu, obviously still full of adrenaline called her out, "What! I've used it all, you can't be that hard up!" Or words to that effect. Cathy responded by calling her everything and a right barney ensued with the two of them shouting abuse and insults at each other. Over a can of hair spray!

Bob Clark adds, "Next best thing for us young teenagers was the Corby Boys School dances or the ones at Nellie's Bin at the Our Lady's School. A lasting memory I have of the Boys School dance in James Watt Avenue is of Ian Eccles" band The Sensitive Set playing Joe Tex's 'show Me" and the Tremeloes "Here Comes My Baby". Then a boy playing the clarinet appeared and gave a good rendition of Acker Bilk's 'stranger On The Shore". I was amazed. Don't know who he was and it seemed so out of place.

At an early age, I remember saying to my dad that I wanted to play an instrument, preferably a clarinet, or anything! He wouldn't listen though, kept saying it was only a passing phase, "You'll move onto something else next week!" But I was determined and badgered him relentlessly, to no avail. Until I got myself a paper job and persuaded him to lend me the money and I would pay him back every week. He gave in eventually and it was with great excitement we trudged off to the Warren Eagle Music shop to buy my first sax, a Selmer Pennsylvania. It cost £105.

Six months tuition with Bob Crawford and I was confident enough to join my first band, The Unadopted Society.

Another sax player at the time was Tony "soggy" South. He was a Kettering schoolteacher who had served time in the early 60s playing with bands in Germany and later took up the piano. Tony suggested we should get ourselves more education on jazz improvisation with Peter Ind, a London guy who was the first jazz bass player to emerge after the war. Ind had moved to the USA for a few years after working on the Queen Mary and played with Buddy Rich, Lee Konitz and Lennie Tristano in New York.

On his return to London, he started teaching jazz and in the 1980s had his own club, the Bass Clef in the East End. It was on his advice I traded in my sax which was really only a basic model, and purchased a Selmer Mark II, 'the Rolls Royce of saxophones" Peter called it. It was a Rolls Royce price too, £205!

Soggy and I travelled down to London every weekend for over a year, usually by train if his car wasn't up to it. In between times, jam sessions at the Corinthian pub enabled you to get some practice. There was virtually a "house" band of regulars, all under the generalship of Bob Crawford."

Bob Crawford remembered it well, "The Corinthian jam band began with myself playing solo saxophone then over a period of a couple of months I was joined by Bob Clark, Dave Johnson, the Grimley Brothers (Bob and John) and Johnny Heron on drums. It became so successful that the police shut it down because it had no adequate fire exits. The first Christmas the pub was open, was I believe the day the Corinthian was flooded. The landlord had decided to have a special event by having the jam band play on Christmas Eve. However that dinnertime the pub was heaving and a friend of ours, Joe Doran, suddenly, for no apparent reason, stood on a table and lit a match. This set off the water sprinklers which resulted in the pub being flooded and the 'jam" was cancelled."

Bob Clark

Bob Clark explains, "I first came into contact with keyboard player Dave Johnson in 1970. We became great friends and remain so to this day. Dave had this band called Eve, with Phil Daltrey on drums and Chris Jones on guitar, playing what they called "Progressive" music. Black Sabbath, The Nice type material. It was trendy at the time. This genre with the tag "Progressive" or "Underground" gave you a different identity to the average pub band. We thought people might take us more seriously. With hindsight, maybe they didn't. The band only lasted about six months!

Dave and I then formed a five piece, what we called a function band, and found ourselves inundated with work. If we worked it right, we could be playing every night of the week. As The Clark Johnson Set we travelled the country playing the clubs most weekends which was a great learning curve. A thing I happened to notice was that many of these working men's clubs all looked the same. We played in Hartlepool one time and I couldn't believe how alike the club was to Corby's Welfare. There must have been a template for this type of building or something.

My memory of Hartlepool though was us turning up late and the entertainments officer telling us our pay was being docked! Those northern clubs were a world of their own. Arriving at another venue, in Consett, we were told by a committeeman "if the audience boo you, we'll throw them out!" It was an education playing those joints!"

In 1977 The Clark Johnson Set joined forces with another local combo, the Alan Howard Band, recruited singer Kathy Lee, and became the Steve Wheeler Band. The line up reading, Dave Johnson on keyboards, Chris Jones guitar, Jack Thomas bass, Brent Webb drums, Mark Webb trumpet and Bob Clark sax.

Bob explains, "We diversified to a certain extent, playing more contemporary material like Manhattan Transfer rather than modern jazz and found ourselves playing the cabaret circuits. This lasted a couple of years and it was back to the Dave Johnson Band, playing up and down the country again.

One day our bass player let us down and Dave phoned up Jack Murphy to see if he could sit in.

"Where's the gig?" Jack asked.

"Up the A1," Dave told him, intentionally giving him only the bare truth. It was way past York! Jack was alright about it though, he was always game for a crack anyway. He stayed with us for years!

Sunday dinnertime sessions at the Kings Arms in Kettering were also a regular stint until we fell out with the landlord. Dave uprooted us and we moved to the Royal Hotel in Kettering instead. This was a great success, enhanced by guests of the calibre of Dick Morrissey, Pete King, Tommy Whittle from London."

During the 1980s and 90s, Bob Clark continued to play wherever there was a gig going. For a spell he teamed up with guitarist Tommy Hall. As the Blues Cruisers, with Jack Thomas on bass and Ronnie Ball on drums they played "a mixture of jazz and blues" and were soon re-christened the Booze Cruisers!

The Cruisers joined forces with Wellingborough band Zoom Club and became an eight piece, with Clark back playing his first love, soul music. "We had some good gigs, Car Shows, Corporate Shows. We had a big following. I met Barry Fletcher here, he was a Hammond organ player who had been around for years. Played in backing groups for people like Edwin Starr in the 60s. Barry wanted to break away from Zoom and asked me to go with him. Not one for laying down too many roots, I did!

We became the St Louis Union, not to be confused with the 60s band that had a hit with Beatles song "Girl," and worked the London clubs for a few years. When that ran its course, I came back and rejoined my old mate Dave Johnson again. Talk about going full circle. Nowadays, I just play when Dave wants me. He has a bank of musicians he can call on for any type of gig he takes on. Suits everybody down to the ground."

Part Four

Stayin' Alive

1978

Unemployment figures published at the beginning of 1978 saw Corby at the highest level in the county, which didn't bode well with the threat of the steelworks closure hanging like a cloud over the town. It was to this backdrop that the Chairman of Corby Council, Harold Lear, delivered a New Year message to update everyone regarding developments in the council's quest to attract new industry. "The problems will be the major issue with which the District Council will have to deal with in 1978. Active deliberations have already commenced with delegates from Corby visiting the responsible ministries in London. The council, working with the Development Corporation, will do their utmost to attract new industries to the town and to alleviate the distress which has now been caused to many families hit by unemployment."

The future for Corby was highlighted in a report by the *Evening Telegraph*. "A cloud of gloom hangs over Corby and it is not surprising. Every day brings stories of vandalism in the town, job losses, and crisis in the town's biggest industry - steel. Travel the country and discover that opinions define Corby as dirty, tough, drunken and thoroughly disagreeable. Little wonder ordinary men, women and children who make up Corby's population are sick to their back teeth of their reputation and edicts that tell them they have no future. Prophets of doom have always had plenty of scope for extending their craft in a town that has felt every hiccough on the economic graph. But their field day had just started when the area's biggest employer, the BSC, announced it was to axe a tenth of its Corby workforce, totalling 1200 jobs.

The effects of the bombshell have rippled through the town ever since, encouraging more prophesies of the tragedy to come. But little has been said about the fighting spirit being shown at grass roots level by the Corby people. One of the biggest campaigns to bring work to Corby has been mounted by trade unionists that formed their own organisation, Corby Action Committee for future employment.

The organisation got off to a shaky start with a series poorly attended meetings but Councillor Jimmy Kane remains optimistic if not defiant, "People in Corby have lived and breathed steel ever since the town was started in the 1920s and 30s. That wasn't a bad thing when there was prosperity in Britain, but the full effect of neglecting to broaden Corby's industrial base is being felt now when there is no boom and jobs in heavy industry are just not wanted. We have a good town with many excellent facilities and excellent housing, despite what people may say, and the potential for a great future."

Sir Geoffrey DeFrietas came under fire from Tory councillor and Stardust manager Arthur Pitcher who condemned him for his lack of support and for failing the town over the jobs crisis. "Corby is in need of a champion to help solve the urgent problem of unemployment. There is no doubt that Corby needs a strong voice in parliament to fight for the town's very survival. Our MP is doing very little to help in the fight for jobs. It would help if we had an MP with guts. The sooner he resigns the better."

Depressing as this was, union boss Bill Sirs claimed Corby's future was assured as one of Britain's major steel towns. "The Corby complex will maintain its position as a top steel producing centre. People in the BSC and government are in a very negative state of mind because of the total orders situation."

Sirs was burying his head in the sand. As an economic report published some years later revealed. "It's true there was plenty of money to be made in steel until the mid-seventies. Towns with steel plants were among the most prosperous in the country. By 1975, however, some of the threshold countries emerged from the so-called 'Third World' and built up their own production facilities. Not only did these countries cease to be importers of steel, they were increasingly gaining a bigger share as competitors on the world market. What's more, steel was being progressively substituted by other materials in manufacturing that were easier to process. The forces that shook the coal industry were now hitting steel. The once affluent steel towns found themselves relying on government job creation schemes to generate alternative employment."

Unemployment was the major issue and whatever one thought of the punk movement, the music provided the soundtrack for legions of young unemployed in the late 1970s. Corby punk Kelvin Woods tells it like this, "Punk was predominantly a working-class movement. A whole generation was suffering with the decline of manufacturing in the country, the coal mines, steelworks, shipyards were all closing down. Even the shoe factories were no longer guaranteeing jobs. We were all skint most of the time. Many, on leaving school, were scratching around for a job, shop work with menial pay, factory work with very little prospects and low wages. It was depressing and it was the same story all 'round the country.

Dressing up the way we did was like a two-fingered salute to the establishment, our rebellion. It was as if we had nothing to lose. The music may have been on the wane by 1978 but the fashion still remained. Spiky hair, bondage trousers, T-shirts with anarchist slogans. People were just fed up of the whole scene. If you wanted to see any of the major acts like the Stones or Bruce Springsteen or whoever, your only opportunity was to catch them at a big stadium and pay the extortionate prices for tickets. Then you would find the stage so far away, it could have been anyone up there playing. It was rubbish.

When the punk bands emerged, they gave the music back to the youngsters. The Pistols, Clash, Stranglers and the rest, they played the pubs and small venues for a token entrance fee. Franny Lagan used to book some great bands, and not so great, at the Nags Head. Eater, a London band making a name for themselves with a young drummer called Dee Generate were booed off! Apparently, they were supposed to be the next big thing but they were crap. Fran also put on the UK Subs at the Youth Centre, which was a far-better gig. We went to see XTC who had a big hit with "Making Plans For Nigel" at Kettering Central which was one of the first punk gigs in the area."

Kelvin would later shed the punk gear, grow his hair back and conform, going as far to enlist as a Special Constable with Corby Police Force. Which was something of a surprise for his friends who helped him turn over a police car during a riot at a Corby v Kettering football match!

Corby punk and Special Police Constable Kelvin Woods pointing the way ahead to his brother

Appearing at Corby Festival Hall, just as the town was rocked with the news of the impending steel closure, was The Tom Robinson Band who had a hit with "2-4-6-8 Motorway" in 1977.

Recalled by punk Stuart Allen, "At the time, I was lucky, I was working at the Department for Social Security as it happened, making tea for security man and jazz musician Bob Crawford. Tom Robinson was a leading activist and campaigner for Rock Against Racism and a lifelong supporter of Amnesty International and LGBT (lesbian, gay, bisexual, and transgender) rights. He achieved notoriety with the hit "Glad To Be Gay". Tom produced leaflets and fliers about their political views and handed them out to everyone who attended their gigs. They also gave away badges and T-shirts emblazoned with the band's logo. The punters at the Festival Hall thought Tom Robinson was a punk band in the mode of the Pistols and began spitting at them. Which in their eyes was deemed the thing to do, disgusting as it sounds. Tom stopped the show and told the audience to cut it out or they wouldn't continue."

The Festival hall was also the scene of more angst during the annual haggis eating contest which erupted in controversy when the world record was smashed by "pocket-sized" 20 year-old John Kenmuir. Standing at 5' 3", John stuffed the master Peter Dowdeswell who was odds on favourite. "I only entered because I didn't like the idea of an Englishman holding the haggis record" said John.

A week later, a pumped-up Peter regained his title and claimed he only lost the title in the first place because the haggis served up at the Civic was cold. Still having the hump he explained, "Haggis should be piping hot. It was stone cold and I don't think I'll be entering next year if it's not served up properly."

A full-scale row erupted with other contestants also claiming the haggis was cold. Defeated Pat McMahon said, "It wasn't a fair contest and we have asked the Livingston Athletic Club in Edinburgh if they are interested in organising a British Haggis eating championship next year."

David Lang, entertainments secretary of Corby Town Supporters Club who organised the event, hit back, "I refute there was any complaints that the haggis was cold. That's a ridiculous statement, I remember Peter Dowdeswell complaining last year that the haggis was too hot!"

The Road to Argentina

The Haggis controversy was soon forgotten by exiles who were getting more excited about Scotland's participation in this year's World Cup in South America. There was more than a whiff of interest in Corby. Coach loads of supporters left the town to witness Scotland welcoming England to Hampden Park a month prior to the tournament in Argentina for a "warm up" friendly, and despite the "Auld Enemy" winning 1-0 the Scots were in joyous mood, especially as England had failed to qualify.

On the Raven coach was Steelworker George Bradshaw, one of the few England supporters on board, who said, "What a weekend that was. We were staying in Motherwell and had to walk through a gauntlet of abuse and vitriol from housewives as we made our way to Hampden. Walking down a terraced street, all the women came out of their houses, banging pots and pans with spoons, dustbin lids, anything that made a din, chanting, "kill the bastards!" It was hilarious. Mad. Hampden was jam packed. They say it held over 90,000. I reckoned the figure was more like 100,000. The police didn't bother about segregation or anything like that, they just wanted you off the streets, and they herded everybody into what gate they were nearest to. Nobody even bothered to check your ticket."

The World Cup in Argentina turned out to be embarrassing with some dismal performances from a Scotland team that included Kenny Dalglish, Graeme Souness, Joe Jordan and Don Masson. The arrogance and over-excitement of manager Ally McLeod didn't help, telling everyone before the squad left these shores that Scotland weren't just going to South America for the ride, "We're going to win it, nae bother!"

They all believed him and hundreds if not more, made their way to South America, by boat, overland, hitch-hiking, plane, and according to a book published in 2019 "Scotland In the Seventies," even a submarine, convinced the Jules Rimet Trophy was Scotland bound. It was going to be one big party.

Unfortunately, the team didn't live up to the expectations and hype and the opening two games against Peru and Iran was one big let-down. Losing 3-1 to Peru on the face of it wasn't that bad, they could have still qualified out of their group if they stuffed rank outsiders Iran and got a draw against Holland.

It didn't go to plan. The biggest embarrassment came when the minnows of Iran held Scotland to a draw and thus ended their participation in the Finals. However, Scotland still had to face Holland who were among the favourites to win the competition and typically, Scotland stunned the Dutch by winning 3-2 with the "goal of the tournament" from Archie Gemmill!

DJ Ian Bateman has his own memory of that World Cup tournament having received a phone call from the entertainment secretary of Corby Rangers Club, asking if he could work on the night of the Scotland v Iran game. "He told me it would be a quiet night so they would rather have a DJ than a band. Ok, I said. Eight people turned up. Everyone must have been at home watching the game on TV. A dismal draw it turned out to be apparently. I'm not a football fan. Anyhow, the few who were at the Rangers Club enjoyed themselves, dancing, singing along, getting drunk. Lo and behold, at the end of the night, two of them started fighting! Whether one was taking the piss over Scotland failing to beat Iran, which was a 1-1 draw, I don't know."

In Bateman

Scotland fan Derek Cowie, though disappointed with his country's efforts in Argentina, wrote a song called "Braveheart" for the Scotland World Cup team in France 1998, explained, "I asked the Grampian Club if they would sponsor me and let their pipe band play on the recording at Iain Wetherell's studio in Occupation Road. Somehow, Anglia Television got to hear about it and then Central TV and we ended up with an invitation to appear on Channel 4's Big Breakfast Show with Deniece Van Hueton and Johnny Vaughan. They asked me if I could get the pipe band down to London to appear as well. They put us all up in the Big

Breakfast Guest House overnight where next door was a pub. We had a lock in and got wrecked.

Next morning, the smell of whisky in the studio was enough to knock you out! A lasting memory is of Deniece Van Hueton coming in and surprising us with her language! We thought it would be all correct and proper, "good morning gentlemen etc" and she came in complaining about her "effing shoes!" They were too tight apparently and crippling her. Whatever, I thought to myself "Ah, it's like home from home!" Johnny Vaughan also used to be a pupil at Uppingham School and taught the kids at Firdale School in Cottingham Road how to swim. He introduced us as "All the way from Corby in SCOTLAND!"

The '98 adventure was to end in disappointment too with Scotland being knocked out again in the group stages. A 1-1 draw with Norway and defeats by Morocco 3-0 and 2-1 by one of the favourites, the current World Champions Brazil ending their interest. Like his predecessor Ally McLeod, Scotland manager Craig Brown wasn't shy in over estimating his teams" chances. His rallying call from the bowels of the Stade de France in Paris going down into folklore, "Guys, I've just seen Brazil holding hands. They're crapping themselves!"

***

Kettering, like Corby, was facing an uncertain future with fears growing over its shoe industry. Multi-millionaire Charles Clore was building up the British Shoe Corporation through his acquisition of Saxone, Lilly & Skinner, Curtess, Trueform, Freeman Hardy Willis and the introduction of cheap shoes by Marks & Spencer, British Home Stores and

Littlewoods. The trend away from conventional footwear to trainers was the beginning of the end for Kettering as a major boot and shoe town. Timpson's North Park Factory, which opened in 1923 was closing down and Dolcis, Wrights, John White were all under threat.

In 2008, Lucy Wenham who worked at Timpsons in the 60s, wrote, "When I was a child living in Primrose Close, I lived about half a mile from the huge monolithic factory building which was I believe four storeys high. In the winter with early dark nights and late mornings, the light from the factory would illuminate the whole of North Park recreation ground which extended from Bath Road to where Dhalia and Weekley Glebe Road are now. The working morning began then at 7.30 and a siren would sound from the factory at 7.20. This was followed by another siren blast at a different pitch at 7.25.

When I heard the last siren I knew my dad would call me to get up for school. From my bedroom window I could see lines of workers hurrying along the well-trodden path in the North Park field to emerge into Bath Road for the factory gates. If a worker was more than 3 minutes late, they would have a quarter of an hour docked off their wages. They were still expected to work the other twelve minutes free. For many years I considered the huge factory as a terrible place to work especially with all those windows in the summer months. However, I worked there for five years and was surprised how comfortable it was to work in. Warm in the winter and cool in the summer. One of the better shoe factory conditions I had experienced. Of course, the sirens had long since gone silent and the mornings began at 8am. Fond memories."

On the heels of the Timpson announcement was that one of Kettering's oldest venues, the Central Hall in Montagu Street was closing its doors for the final time. Opened in October 1929 the Central was a popular venue for dinners, dances and shows with seating for over 850 people. It also hosted the 1934 World Snooker Final won by the legendary Joe Davis. Which, as actor Michael Caine might say, "Not a lot of people know that!"

Clive Smith adds, "I saw Thin Lizzy at the Central in 1973 just when "Whisky In the Jar" was entering the charts. Four of us, Pat Devlin, Tony 'Smythe' Smith and Alan 'Scouse' McGahey travelled over from Corby. The gig was a sell-out. We actually ended up watching the show from what we jokingly called the 'Royal Box'. We'd walked through the wrong door! It was a great view overlooking the stage and we enjoyed ourselves, drinking bottles of beer from the makeshift bar in the corridor, and, of course, giving the occasional 'royal' wave to those below us. All good fun. And Phil Lynott and the Lizzy boys were brilliant."

Next to close down in Kettering was the Savoy Cinema and Bingo Hall in Russell Street, which was briefly resurrected in the late 1980s by which time it was a ramshackle excuse for a picture house, giving the term "flea pit" a whole new dimension.

Savoy

Clive added, "I went over to the Savoy when Oliver Stone's film "The Doors" was shown and was far from impressed. I hadn't been to the Savoy since the 1960s when the cinema had been revamped and was a real pleasure to visit. Seem to remember a new era was opened back then with a German film "Helga," which had an opening scene of the birth of a baby. Much to the amusement of many, men apparently were fainting in their seats! All this was reported in the *Evening Telegraph*.

This Oliver Stone film was based around the American rock group who I was a big fan of, and what I discovered was equally disappointing as it was disgusting. The person behind the Box Office seemed totally disinterested. Two old guys were sitting on chairs in the foyer sheltering from the rain and having a cigarette. Like a pair of vagrants. Half the lights on the stairway were missing light bulbs.

Once inside the cinema and adjusting my eyes to the darkness, I shuffled around to find row upon row with most of the seats missing A couple of punters who had obviously faced the same problem started laughing! A plank of wood was even stretched right across one row! Thick with dust, where once, the state of art "Floating Screen" proudly presented the latest Blockbuster and "Look At Life" commercials, the stage was littered with debris, including an upturned bucket and a set of stepladders! Refreshments were nil. Overall, it was a very sad and perplexing experience. And I have to say, even though I was a massive Jim Morrison and Doors fan, I thought the film was crap."

A shining light amongst all the gloom was the success of a company set up by Tim Harrison and his father-in-law Bill Osbourne with a small office in Pytchley Road called Harborne Rentals Ltd. Tim and Bill had started the business by hiring out two large lorries and were now in possession of eleven and acquiring the nickname, "Tim's Rock Lorries" after linking up with London haulier Edwin Shirley who supplied the transport for most of the big names in the rock business.

"Edwin Shirley Trucking became indelibly associated with live music tours. He died in 2013, an obituary on Planet Rock Radio by Bernard Doherty referred to the apocryphal notion that "You haven't really made it until Edwin Shirley is moving your gear around." Brian May of Queen, noted Shirley's importance to their touring operation: "Edwin was at the head of Queen's vehicle convoy for so many years I can't begin to remember how many..." (*Wikipedia*)

Tim said, "The lorries are able to haul over 30 tons of PA stacks, lighting equipment and fancy props. Pink Floyd carried a giant inflatable pig, ELO a flying saucer, Abba had their name emblazoned on three of our lorries. Four have just returned from a 9000-mile round trip on the continent with Genesis. Four more trucks are hired out to Yes. The music business nowadays is no longer a simple case of rolling up at a gig, getting the gear off and plugging in. It's a complete theatrical production with giant workshops and lights turrets to be transported everywhere. Bob Dylan used twelve lorries to take his gear to Blackbushe. And you'd be amazed at the amount of parking tickets we get sent from abroad. We average four a week. Only other problem is when the lorries come back covered in graffiti. 'I love Billy' sort of stuff. Don't think that was intended for my father-in-law but you never know!"

Dylan's Blackbushe gig was one of the music highlights of a year that saw the passing of The Who's drummer Keith Moon, jazz legend Louis Prima and Fairport Convention songstress Sandy Denny. Blackbushe was organised after advance ticket sales for Bob Dylan's six nights at Earls Court sold out in hours prompting promoter Harvey Goldsmith to hire the aerodrome near Camberley for an open-air concert, which was described somewhat incongruously as The Picnic.

Eric Clapton, Joan Armatrading, Graham Parker and the Rumour were added to the menu and an estimated 100,000 people turned up. A massive crowd swelled by Franny Lagan's Corby bus.

Dylan fan Stuart Allen recalled, "I was on Fran's coach, we arrived at about 5.00pm. Some guy on the bus was singing all the way down, telling everyone how big a Bob Dylan fan he was. When he got off the bus he hit someone, and was arrested and never saw the concert!"

Another Dylan fan on Franny's bus was musician Steve Everitt, who adds, "I had recently bought Dylan's latest album 'Street Legal' and had played it nonstop. Dylan played a large selection from it which left a few people bemused because they didn't know the songs. "That's crap," somebody shouted, "give us Like a Rolling Stone." I was with Tom Farley and my brother Brian who had his acoustic guitar and we were singing Dylan songs on the bus all the way to the festival. It was brilliant… until the next morning when Brian and Tom were arrested by the police!

It was around five in the morning and we were all tanked up sitting around a campfire. A string snapped on Brian's guitar and he flew into a rage and started smashing it up! Next thing, the police were over and lifting him for causing a disturbance. They must have thought he was a hooligan. Tom stood up and shouted at the coppers, "if you're taking my mate, you've gotta take me as well!" That was no problem and Tom was lifted too. The pair of them were taken to Aldershot police station and flung in a cell for a few hours to calm down. It was only when Brian explained that it was his guitar he was smashing up that the two of them were released."

Knickers and Knobbs

St Cecilia bass player Keith Hancock produced an album featuring Corby's finest at Derek Tompkins" Beck Studios in Wellingborough. Ray and Ann Brett, Alias Smith and Jones, Tartan Combo, Sweet Wine, Ray Ritchie and Peter MacLachlan, all regular attractions at the town's Stardust Club, spent the weekend working on the LP which was due to go on sale in December to catch the Christmas market. Backing vocals was supplied by the Hughie James Sound.

St. Cecilia

St Cecilia were the only Corby band to have a top twenty hit with "Leap Up and Down (wave you knickers in the air)" in 1971. The success of the Stardust LP prompted Keith to contact Bip Wetherell who was playing with a group called Knobbs, with a view to assembling a line up to go out on the road as St Cecilia on 'revival" tour. Keith and Bip had been bandmates in the 60's with The Rhubarb Tree. It would be fair to say that this band of minstrels masquerading as St Cecilia could go down as the first of the 'tribute" groups. Prior to this, unless the musicians actually wrote their own material, they were regarded as "covers" bands. Thus along came the Bootleg Beatles, Counterfeit Stones, Fleetwood Bac and so on. Bip and the boys rejected the idea of going out as St Cecil and went out brazenly as St Cecilia and who was going to complain?

In the 2000s with so many of the original 1960s band members of the most popular groups giving up or passing to the great gig in the sky, the names of the bands continued to travel, some with no original members. Marmalade, Swinging Blue Jeans to name just two. It didn't appear to bother many, after all it was the music they wanted to hear. If they could replicate the hits, who cared? Much to the ire of Keith Hancock though, a St Cecilia WAS touring in the 2000s, with some of the members claiming they WERE in the original line up. Which was not so, and Keith fought the case vigorously."

Bip added, "All we had to do was learn "Leap Up and Down," add it to our Knobbs set and, hey presto, the money was doubled and the gigs were a lot better. Keith's agency Keri Enterprises took their commission from the gigs. It never seemed to bother the audiences that we weren't the originals as we always went down well and I assume it never bothered Keri Enterprises that we weren't the originals when the cheques came in. So, after we had some 10 x 8 promotion photographs taken, off we went. Myself on vocals, Roly Wolstenholme on bass and vocals, Bob Burliston on Lead Guitar and vocals with Charlie Parr on rhythm guitar and vocals, and a drummer of whom I can't remember his name!

Looking back, some musicians would tend to forget you spent some time singing a song about knickers but I really enjoyed it. It got the crowd going, the ladies would twirl imaginary knickers in the air, and it always went down brilliant. In fact on a couple of gigs one or two of the ladies were twirling actual underwear. I like to think that they were spare pairs they kept in their handbags. It only lasted a few months but it gave me a taste of playing in a "name band," the gigs were better, there was drinks, sandwiches, in the dressing room, and the promotors treated you as though you were someone.

Not all the gigs were brilliant though. I remember we were supporting comedian Norman Vaughan who was rubbish! All he did after he told a crap gag was come out with his catchphrases, 'swinging', or 'dodgy'. I didn't mind as he made us look good when we went on and saved the night." Norman Vaughan made his name as compere on Sunday Night at the London Palladium in the early 60s and later on the TV Game show The Golden Shot.

Bip was still pulling the crowds in at the Nags Head. "I booked most of my acts through the Barry Collins Agency. The Tymes, Detroit Emeralds, Anne Peebles, Jimmy James and the Vagabonds, Edwin Starr, The Real Thing. Everything usually went well but on occasion there was a hiccough. I booked 60s band Freddie and the Dreamers and paid the agent the fee, because Fred didn't know who I was. The agent wanted £1500. I sent the cheque off, the Dreamers arrived in the afternoon, sorted their gear out etc and then Freddie Garrity turned up and asked "Who's the boss?"

"I told him I was and he asked me for his money. I told him I'd paid the agent. He said as far as he was concerned I hadn't paid anybody. And if I didn't pay him there'd be no show. I had to go to the cash office and get £1500 quick before the idiot would go on. It took me about a month to get my money back. I suppose he'd probably been ripped off so many times in his career, I don't know but I was upset about the whole thing. I hired the Welfare Club for bigger acts like KC and the Sunshine Band.

I've always been a massive fan of the Beatles and a nice story was told me by Swinging Blue Jean's bass player Les Braid when we were having a drink after a gig at the Nags. The Blue Jeans were invited to the satellite screening of the Beatles" performing "All You Need Is Love," and Les was chatting to John Lennon just before the cameras started to roll. John told him "I'd better go and finish off the lyrics." When Les asked him what he meant, John said he hadn't written the second verse yet and if you ever watch the video of the song you can see Lennon reading the words from a scrap of paper in front of him. That was the genius of John Lennon."

"All You Need Is Love" was Britain's contribution to "Our World", the first live global television link. The Beatles were filmed performing it at EMI Studios in London on 25 June 1967. The programme was broadcast via satellite and seen by an audience of over 400 million in 25 countries. Lennon's lyrics were deliberately simplistic, to allow for the show's international audience, and captured the utopian ideals associated with the Summer of Love. The single topped sales charts in Britain, the United States and many other countries, and became an anthem for the counterculture's embrace of flower power philosophy."

Nostalgia was the theme at Corby Civic Centre when two of the biggest legends of the 1950s, Johnnie Ray and The Platters appeared. Johnnie Ray is regarded by many as the first legitimate rock and roll singer, due to women swooning over him when he first came to Britain in 1953, on the back of his hit record "Cry". Sadly in 1978 the Civic management were ready to cry when his appearance failed to attract the punters through the door. A disappointing turn out of around 500 forced them to cancel a second show scheduled for the following night. 150 paying customers were given their money back.

Three weeks after the Johnny Ray disappointment, The Platters (My Prayer, Smoke Gets In Your Eyes, Harbour Lights) arrived and were given a much warmer reception, their performance received with great enthusiasm. So much so that the audience was loathe to let them leave the stage.

"My Prayer" had been answered, a Civic official might have thought. Head barman Hughie Murphy summed things up succinctly, "Corby people have a reputation for being hard to please, if they are in the mood, they can be the greatest audience anyone could wish to have, if not, the opposite is true."

***

Industrial disputes and strikes that had crippled the country throughout the 1970s would culminate this year in the so-called "winter of discontent," which for the uninitiated was a line borrowed from Shakespeare's "Richard III". Or as the swats may tell you, was also the title of American John Steinback's final novel, published in 1961.

1978 witnessed the largest stoppage of labour since the 1926 General Strike. Industrial action started at Ford Motors when 15,000 workers walked out on and were joined by 57,000 others a week later. A threatened bread strike caused the good old British trait of panic buying once more. A spokesman for Pipes Bakers in Corby was gobsmacked, "People are buying up to six and seven loaves a time, it's ridiculous, we've had to introduce a limit on how many each individual can have.

By Christmas, strikes were commonplace. Journalists went on strike, gravediggers and petrol tanker drivers followed. Rubbish piled up in the streets, schools closed, candles were lit during power cuts and people stocked up on tinned foods, and bread from Pipes.

Scene Stealer's "First Offence"

After almost two years of waiting, Scene Stealer's long-awaited album was released. Re-mixed during the interim period the recording included backing from the Barnet Youth Opera Group and Strings arranged and conducted by Phyllidia Hearn.

The track listing for First Offence was "I Ain't No Angel," "High and Dry," "Loser," "Flying," "White Angel," "Ballerina," "Say It Ain't Nice," "American Lady," "Just The Other Day," "Rolling Man" and "Sunshine Brightly".

Scene Stealer's "First Offence"

Prior to the release, Scene Stealer were booked for a three-week tour of Holland, playing fifteen concerts in Amsterdam, Paradiso and an open-air festival in Rotterdam.

The *Evening Telegraph* followed their progress, "Back in 1962, an unknown British band called The Beatles were making a big name for themselves in Germany. Now 16 years later, another comparatively unknown British band has found fame in Germany while still searching for success on this side of the channel. I'm not saying our continental cousins have a better developed musical taste, but they have the sense to buy more than 6000 copies of the debut album by Corby band Scene Stealer.

Released over there on the EMI distributed Crystal label, "First Offence" is a remarkably strong and mature set by the five-strong group. Bob Grimley, Stewart and Jimmy Irving share the composing credits. I don't know if it's a tribute to the German pressing plant or the London recording studio, but the sound throughout is clean and sharp on the eleven-track album - and there's a nice diversity in style from the west coast like harmony work on "Rolling Man" and "High And Dry" through to the gutsy "I Ain't No Angel" to the more straightforward - a fine showcase for the instrumental talents of the band.

They hope to have the album released in Britain soon and have an Irish tour and college and university gigs lined up. Stewart Irving was upbeat on the band's return, "The visit to Holland was a promotional tour for the new album and although the going was hard, we were given a great reception by the Dutch audiences. We were called on to do encores at every gig and during the tour we did an interview on Dutch radio. They were very impressed with the band and this puts us in a good position for the next tour which should take place in August. The band is currently working on new material for the next album. "First Offence" is our own work and we are now rehearsing for the next tour and writing new material. The album is selling very well on the continent and it should be released in this country later this year.

Before the band leave for their next tour, which should include Norway, Germany, France, Belgium and Holland, they will be making two appearances in Corby on July 22nd with a daytime open-air concert and an evening performance at the Raven Hotel. Plans are also in the pipeline for an extensive tour of America to promote "First Offence". There seems to be no stopping the rollercoaster ride for the band who made their London debut in June at Fulham's Golden Lion pub for an audience of agents, the music press and top musicians."

Stewart Irving said, "Originally Gavin Dare had wanted us to just record singles but we wanted to do an album. We were getting into writing our own material. We should have listened to him but we were too arrogant. You had to get the record company enthused, excited. They fixed up the European tour to promote the album. We were settled in a nice apartment near Arnheim and meeting a top guy, Tio Stocken, who was Head of A & R at EMI Holland. Bob and Norman Hickens couldn't be bothered with it and went out to a nearby clubhouse and got pissed, leaving me and Jimmy to do the interview. The guy wasn't impressed. Bob and Norman then rocked up with an entourage of people leering through the windows.

Tio was asking bland questions like, "What's your favourite breakfast?" and "What's your favourite records?" and mundane stuff like that. Bob piped up with "Ballerina," "High and Dry," both off our album. Tio could see what was happening and said, "Right, I get the message" and he left. We were our own worst enemies. I went to Skipple airport later to meet up with him and Gavin Dare, wanting to apologise and attempt to build some bridges but Tio had already told Gavin, "Scene Stealer are a very nice band, he liked me but not my friends."

"The gig at the Golden Lion, which had a great PA system and stage, was attended by Dave Dee of Dozy, Beaky, Mick and Tich fame. And to be honest, we let ourselves down. Dee was A&R for A & M Records. We had a meeting with him afterwards where Bob and Norman drank all the booze that was on offer, which didn't go down well. Dave Dee left and told Gavin that he wasn't interested. Which was disappointing."

Gavin Dare (from Rebel Records) added, "Their performance at the Golden Lion was acclaimed by the music profession. It was amazing. My telephone hasn't stopped ringing since they appeared. Although the band has been kept out of London in the past, we now feel the time is right for a blitz on the city, it can only be a matter of time before their music carries them to stardom."

For all the accolades and hype surrounding the band and their debut album, Bob Grimley was far from happy and his despondency continued to nag throughout the summer, which would ultimately culminate with the demise of the band just before Christmas. In 2008 Bob recalled his disillusion.

"We spent what seemed an interminable time in the recording studio cutting that album and at the end of it, Gavin Dare and Dave Howman then told us they would go and work on the mix, probably adding some strings and a choir on it. I couldn't believe it and told them in no uncertain terms. Gavin Dare looked at me, and said, half-jokingly, "We're in control of the cheque book!"

Howman was a composer/musician/producer who had worked with T. Rex, Sweet. Mud, Gary Glitter and on the soundtrack for Monty Python's Life of Brian film.

Bob said, "We had no input whatsoever with the mix and when they called us in to hear the finished product I was appalled. I hated it. It left me totally disillusioned with the business. Apart from the addition of a choir and the string section they had squashed the sound of the guitars, putting compressors and limiters on them. We were a guitar band! We were given half a dozen copies of the album each and I felt that bad about it, I gave them all away and never listened to it again. The video, which was a comparatively new innovation at the time, was another joke. During the filming, the director stopped the production and said to me, "Do you think you could move around a bit more instead of standing stock still?" Stewart, who was a great front man, danced all-round the set, Jimmy was also good at the choreography.

It wasn't for me. I looked at this guy and replied, "I'm a guitar player, if you want a dancer, go and get Fred Astaire or somebody!" He shrugged and then moved me to the back and gave me a pair of shades to wear! I also felt the management let us down by failing to promote the album to any degree. They promised us national music press coverage, a tour of Europe and America, which never materialised. It all came to a head when the band was preparing to leave for Stranraer to catch the ferry to Ireland for a ten-day tour following a gig in Hamilton."

Bob explained, "We were depending on the money from the Irish tour to see us over Christmas. It was working out just right, and then out of the blue we received a telegram from our management telling us that they had pulled the gig. The IRA were making noises about another bombing campaign at the time and I suppose because we had a big orange van and a GB sticker on the back, they deemed it didn't particularly bode well for our health!

However, it was the final straw for me. We came back to Corby skint and peed off and I decided to quit. Stewart described it as "a premature end" for the band. I got myself a job at York Truck earning £75 a week because I didn't fancy going back to the steelworks. And would you believe it, both Stewart and Jimmy went to the steelworks and a little over a year later, they received over seven grand each severance pay when it closed down! Typical of my luck I thought!"

Bob Grimley passed away, very suddenly, aged 57, on August 13th, 2008. Living in Bedford at the time, he had been coming over to Corby for a series of interviews, and loving the nostalgic trip, recalling his life and times in the town. News of his demise came as a real shock as he appeared relatively fit and healthy. Along with brother John, Bob was regarded as one of Corby's finest musicians. His funeral, held at Kettering Crematorium was attended by many of his old contemporaries and friends from way back. One of the songs played at the Crem, chosen by his sister Lillian, was Lynyrd Skynyrd's 'sweet Home Alabama". A favourite track of Bob's and one that he played and excelled at. A fitting tribute.

Following the demise of Scene Stealer and Corby Steelworks, Stewart Irving left town to find work in South Africa. "My parents were over there, dad was working at a steel plant in a place called Whitbank and I was able to get employment there and stayed for around six weeks." Long enough for Stewart to decide it wasn't for him.

A bio on the website Discogs tells Stewart's story. "Originally hailing from Scotland, Stewart Irving was on an extended trip to South Africa and was just about to return home when he got invited to front the then popular South African band Ballyhoo. He made the position his own and quickly established himself as one of the most popular vocalists in SA. He also made an impact as a solo artist, with hits like "Superstar" and "Heart of Stone" elevating him to the musical elite in South Africa."

Stewart said, "I was still in touch with Gavin Dare and it was through him I met a guy called Kevin who was an employee of Warner Brothers. "Get yourself a band," Kevin told me. I saw a few, one of which was called Ballyhoo, a top South African outfit who were formed in Johannesburg in 1974. They had a number of albums and top selling singles to their name and they were excellent, slick, great singers too. The line-up was Derrick Dryan on vocals, Attie van Wyk keyboards, Mick Matthews guitar and vocals, Fergie Ferguson bass and vocals and Cedric Samson drums. Mick Matthews was a member of 60s hit makers Hedgehoppers Anonymous who were based at an RAF station near Corby. They had a big hit with "Its Good News Week" in 1965.

I was told Derrick was leaving so why didn't I enquire about an audition to replace him. I phoned Fergie and he said, "OK let's meet up and have a try out." He gave me a tape to learn the songs and a week later, after another session he told me to come back to his place for a meal. I didn't know if I had passed the audition or not. So I asked him.

"You wouldn't be here if you hadn't," he said.

"So I found myself back working in a band and as the gigs grew more regular I was finding it hard to keep the job at the steel plant down. In the end the gaffer, a Welsh guy called Viv Richards, not the West Indian cricketer! asked me what I was going to do. "Are you going to stay here or go off with this band?"

That was it! Off I went! For the next nine years! We had a number of hits including 'shattered Silence" which I co-wrote with keyboard player Deon du Plessis who had joined the same time as me, taking over from Ati, and also 'superstar" which I recorded solo and it reached number six on the Capitol Radio charts in 1985."

"Superstar" was included in a list compiled by music journalist John Samson entitled "1001 South African Songs You Must Hear Before You Go Deaf" in the early 2000s.

"Everybody's trying to be a superstar/But nobody knows what for." So sings the one-time singer with Ballyhoo. The ironic thing is that he does it in what we would nowadays refer to as an Idols/X Factor voice. Not only does he do the voice, but it is one of those songs competitors in the aforementioned competitions would have no problems singing or attempting to sing as the case may be.

The thing with Irving is that he does it so well with this song. He does have a great voice (although he wasn't the voice behind "Man Of The Moon" – he joined Ballyhoo just after they recorded that) and the song is a solid (bordering on power) ballad. Irving puts a lot of emotion into the performance and it paid dividends as the song made it to number 6 on the Radio 5 charts in 1985 and it was included on Ballyhoo's 1989 album "Alive".

Despite the pleading note in Irving's voice, the answer is quite simple. People want to be superstars for fame, money and (in the case of male rock artists) to pick up chicks, although they may not necessarily be in that order. Ballyhoo were Superstars in South Africa and in putting out this solo effort, Stewart Irving enjoyed his 15 minutes (or 6 weeks according to his Radio 5 chart run) of superstardom."

Stewart Irving with his wife Wendy still rocking the boat

Chrome Molly

Chrome Molly were Scene Stealer's biggest rivals at home. Graham Binley vocals, Colin "Fez" Pheasant and Tony Haselip guitars, Mick Haselip bass guitar and Alistair Brodie drums. Mick tragically lost his life in shocking circumstances during 2003. His twin brother Tony later wrote this moving obituary.

"Mick and I both started playing guitar at the age of 11. We shared an old acoustic that we learnt to play with the aid of the compulsory "Bert Weedon" book of chords. It wasn't long before we could play "Apache" and other Shadows hits and then in 1963 along came the Beatles and we were hooked. Dad bought us another acoustic and as playing bass whilst singing was far more difficult than strumming Mick got the short straw and the old acoustic became the bass.

Mick was a bass player of tremendous talent, he played in a large number of local bands starting in 1967 (aged 16 years) with gigs at Nellies Bin right up to his death in 2003 still playing with the local 12-piece soul band AeroSoul. Mick travelled throughout Europe and the UK and won many an accolade during his 12-year professional stint with Campbell's Country frequently appearing both on television and radio. Mick was a true professional and in all those years I never knew him to miss a gig, no matter what, he would not let people down, he would always say "The show must go on".

Mick the philosopher would often quote the Latin phrase "Ars Gratia Artis" (Art for the sake of art) and in his case this is certainly true. I still wind up the bass and listen to his wonderful playing, on a wide range of recordings from the varied professional Campbells Country collection to the extremely tight intricate playing on Chrome Molly's old demos. I often get asked, "What happened to Mick's old fender precision bass guitar?" It is a 1961 original and collectable. It is in the family's safe keeping and who knows, maybe one day a young Haselip will pick it up and make it sing again. I truly hope so. Mick had a happy disposition, he had lots of friends but tragically Mick was brutally murdered in 2003. He is sadly missed by all those that knew him, none more so than his family and all the musicians who worked with him over the years. RIP Mick.

Tony Haselip

Feb. 14th 2006

Chrome Molly were sharing the bill with Scene Stealer at the Raven Ballroom on July 22nd 1978, a gig memorably recalled by Colin Pheasant in 2012. "There was a rivalry between us, friendly but keen. The hall was packed to the limit, it was a great venue and promotion by Franny Lagan with Dougie King as DJ. We more often than not always began with Springsteen's "Born To Run" with Alistair Brodie pounding out a steady beat on the tom toms before we all came in. I was in a boisterous mood, full of devilment and asked Alistair to keep the tom toms going until I climbed up on to the top of the stack of speakers and cabs.

He thought I was mad! I hadn't told Mick, Tony or Graham so they didn't know what was going to happen. Alistair went along with it and I started climbing with my guitar strung across my back. What I hadn't realised, was that Scene Stealers' gear was below ours and so that by the time I was standing precariously on top, I must have been 16 feet off the ground! It took me a little longer than I expected and the rest of the boys were looking at Alistair and wondering where I was. It was to be a grand opening. I jumped off the stack, simultaneously striking down with a loud power chord! What a way to begin a gig! Despite nearly breaking both my bloody legs! And we blew Scene Stealer off the stage!"

Asked of his memory of this, Stewart Irving laughed, "I have a clear memory of that gig, It was a great night at the Raven. There was a bit of a rivalry between us and the Chrome Molly boys, they were a great band, but I can't honestly say

I remember Fez jumping 16 feet off the PA stacks! Can you imagine that!!"

Colin said, 'Music was in my family. My granddad was the leader and pianist of the Wally Stafford Band, a well-known and popular local dance band around the scene in the 1940s and 50s. One of my earliest memories is of standing alongside my granddad's piano on tiptoe to watch him tinkering the ivories, totally fascinated. My first guitar was bought from Alf Bailey's shop in Kettering. My mum and dad took me over, I was only ten. This was 1965 and I was already feeling the influence of The Beatles and such like. The sixties was a great time for youngsters, music wise, the best ever. Everybody wanted to play drums or guitar or something.

Probably my first band of any consequence was called Wildlife with Richard Oliff, Paul Willis, Rod Morris, my brother Martin and Roy Garlick, whose brother had invited me over to see them play at Kettering Central Hall. I thought they were awful! I joined them all the same and our first gig was a wedding reception at the Nags Head, Corby.

We also recorded a demo at Beck Studios which was fun. The highlight of our brief career, apart from entering a recording studio for the first time was entering a Battle of the Bands contest and winning through to the final at a pub in Leicester. A coach load of our friends went over, got half pissed and then started threatening people, "Give these boys any stick and you're in trouble!" "You'll get your head kicked in". They heckled and cheered all through.

Rod Morris, our guitarist, played with an extra-long lead which was a bit of a thing at the time. Stan Webb of Chicken

Shack probably started it all, wandering through the audience playing his guitar. This day, Rod forgot his lead and plugged in with a much shorter one. A trick he liked to perform was climbing on top of his amp and cabinet and then jumping off as he hit the first chord. Which is where I got the idea from! Rod leapt off the amp, the lead came flying out, the sound went dead and we were left looking a right bunch of dick heads! No need to say we lost!"

Richard Oliff, presenter on Forest FM Radio in Dorset posted a heartwarming memory of Rod Morris on his Blog in 2015. "From time to time, I think of someone who pops into my head whenever I see or hear something that reminds me of him. His name was Rod Morris. I say "was" because he died a long time ago, and he was my friend. Rod was a bright intelligent and quick-witted young man who had the ability to unnerve the unsuspecting with his knowledge of poetry, literature and music.

My mother liked Rod, despite his unkempt appearance. He liked to shock with his old leather bikers jackets emblazoned with images of skulls or Hells Angels chapter logos. He would wear jeans with holes in them long before jean manufacturers hit on the idea of selling such ripped clothing as the latest 'must have" fashion accessory. Back then Rod was being a rebel without a cause. He would listen to Grand Funk Railroad or Status Quo then fire up his Norton 750 motorbike to come over to my house. "Yes Mrs Oliff." "No Mrs Oliff."

"He's such a polite boy," my mum would say as Rod would reel off another poem by Browning, Keats or William Wordsworth. Then one day, Rod asked me over to his house to hear a new album that he'd bought. I duly arrived fully expecting to see our mutual friends to also be there: but no. On this occasion it was just me. Rod made his way to the large "gram" style record player that stood against the wall. As he was taking the LP out of its sleeve he turned to me. "Don't think I've gone soft or anything will you, Rich?"

"Of course not, Rod, what is it?"

The stylus hit the vinyl and the orchestra began to play. It was the album Hot August Night by Neil Diamond: a record released in 1972, several years before this living room "premiere". Two weeks ago, a listener brought this album in for my album of the week feature, and I thought of Rod.

Colin Pheasant was working in Corby Tubeworks when he met Alex Henderson, a musician new to the town. Alex said, "We got talking about music one day and I told him I'd spent three years in Glasgow taking drum lessons off a guy who lived in the Gorbals. Following that we decided to get together, and with a couple of other guys, and a few rehearsals, we played a jam session in the Nags Head as The Out Patients, having borrowed an amp off Bip Wetherell who was away for a short holiday. It turned out to be disastrous when guitarist Rod Morris blew the amp up! Bip wasn't amused.

We bought an old ambulance for £90 which we considered to be ideal for a band van. Unfortunately, it was riddled with rust and problems, failed the MOT and cost us an arm and a leg!" The ambulance did manage to make it over to Wellingborough though for a recording session at Beck Studios. We put down a couple of tracks, written and sung by Colin, "Ghoul" and "Hardman," with me on the chorus.

Not the greatest songs ever written, but as Colin has said, "I was only 20 years old!! And we were having a great time...."

Colin Pheasant added, "I was working in Cunnington's hardware shop in the High Street when Eddie Devine, the ex-Blueswailer and Carnation, came in. Eddie told me his brother Frank's band was looking for a bass player and wanted to know if I'd be interested in an audition. Sure I said, I was never short on self-confidence, give anything a go. As far as I was concerned, this band, which was the embryo of Chrome Molly and named Buck was just a bunch of some old blokes. I knew their names from the past, they were all three or four years older than me. Alistair Brodie was even older."

Chrome Molly

They were legends in my eyes but I wasn't in awe of them. I was chuffed that I thought I was talented enough to maybe join them. Turns out I got the job ahead of such established players like Jack Murphy and Kenny Payne who weren't too impressed. That did bother me, especially Jack. He had a fearsome reputation, a bit of a wild card. Years later, when I was reminiscing with singer Graham Binley in the 90s, I asked him why they chose me instead of Jack and Kenny.

"Easy," Graham explained, "You were new on the scene, younger and less experienced and we felt we could mould you into the way we wanted to go. Jack and Kenny would have been too set in their styles and less flexible, besides being argumentative!"

"A memorable gig with Buck was at the Nags Head, shortly after sax player Norrie McMullen had been to visit a dentist. His two front teeth were full of decay so he had them taken out and replaced them with a plate. Norrie started playing his sax and there was nothing but a din coming out. He kept on spluttering, starting again, taking the reed off and twisting it around, blowing again, spitting, it was terrible! Eventually, Binley asked him, "What the matter?" It was Norrie's two new teeth. Exasperated, he took them out and threw them away, "Bollocks to 'em," he said. He then proceeded to play as normal again, great style!

I was a cocky sod, always have been. I liked to walk out into the crowd with my long extension, take a drink out of somebody's pint then stroll back to the stage. It was always good for a laugh. Bit dodgy at times though! I've always lived for the day, and the future. Don't mind looking back at the old days, but I don't dwell on them. Too much living to do. It stems from my schooldays when a friend died of cancer at the tender age of ten. That was a hell of a shock.

You just don't expect to lose a school friend through an illness. Ever since then I've lived for now.

I remind myself that I've had a good life compared to my old pal. Sometimes I went too far but I can't help myself. An early rehearsal with Molly at the Corby Youth centre was typical when I overstepped the mark! I hardly knew the boys but I still couldn't help winding Alistair Brodie up. I told him he wasn't playing right! That coming from me! Alistair was a legend, been playing drums since I was still running about in short trousers. Mick and Tony Haselip both warned me. Graham was just waiting to see how things developed. I had another go at Alistair, only a wind up, and the next thing, he's jumped up from his seat and grabbed me by the throat, pinning me against the wall with my feet dangling in mi- air! Talk about being put in my place! He threatened to knock the crap out of me if I opened my mouth again! 'Told you," Binley said!"

We played an RAF base one winter's night, freezing and snow on the ground. A lively gig with the punters in the mood for a scrap or whatever. You could feel the tension in the air some nights. It wasn't long before there were MPs standing next to the stage with Alsatians on the leash and itching to oblige anyone. A number of fights did break out but the abiding memory concerned a guy we had noticed with his arm in a sling. It was while we were packing the gear away in our van. Alistair was standing in the back sorting it out as we brought it out. There was a groaning noise coming from somewhere, whining sort of sound.

"Did you hear that, Fez?" Ali asked.

We continued to pack our gear away ignoring this whimpering. It was when we finished and closed the doors we spotted this feller with his arm in the sling, stuck right underneath the van! He'd come running out of the club, chased by an MP, slipped on the snow and slid right underneath the van and couldn't move. He was wet, cold, sore. We were all pissing ourselves laughing.

A gig in March, Cambridgeshire was a dud. We were booked for this club, a big ballroom type building. After setting the kit up we took advantage of the club's snooker room. Must have been around a dozen tables. Thing was, every time we took the rack off the reds to begin, the balls spread all over the table. Every table was the same. Hopeless. A waste of time. I think it was Graham who said, 'this isn't a good omen". We went off to a pub across the road before going on.

Coming back, we were amazed, or even alarmed, that there was only about two people there! The manager was looking worried, the two big heavy bouncers were looking unfriendly. This didn't feel right. We played our set and had a break. It was then Graham said, 'that's it". He decided we weren't going on again. Well the club manager soon realised what was happening, or what was not, and sent the two bouncers to threaten us. Alistair and Graham jumped up immediately, and told them, 'Don't even think about it".

The rest of us stood behind them, cowering a bit, I have to admit. Well I was! I was no scrapper, couldn't fight my way out of a paper bag! Ali and Graham were bruisers in my eyes, when they got angry you kept out of the way! The bouncers retreated and informed the manager, who by this time was almost in tears. Because he was in such a state, head in his hands, crying, Graham did show some compassion and told him we'd go on again. There was still only about four people in! They hadn't advertised the gig. Sometimes I think these places just took it for granted that the punters would turn up."

Alistair Brodie (2009): "We used to do the Meatloaf type of stuff, "Bat Out Of Hell" and all that. Graham was a great singer. We were working all over the place, we would get home from a gig in North Wales or somewhere, just in time to go to work the next morning, crazy really, we were always knackered."

Alex Henderson was in the Phoenix watching Chrome Molly when sax player Rick Dodd came in and asked him if he knew of any local musicians, as he was looking to form a band. "I told him I had a drum kit, and he invited me to his house in Cottingham, next to the George, which proved very handy, to listen to some Johnny and Edgar Winter records. Great stuff said I. Rick then got hold of Tony 'soggy" South who was a talented guitar/keyboards teacher, plus Kevin Harnett, an ex-RAF feller who was a classically trained violinist to play bass. Next to join was John McHarg on lead guitar/vocals.

We practiced at Rick's house and the landlord of the George was going loopy. The landlord who'd previously chased Mick Ferguson and his mate Angus McKay for making too much noise revving their Lambrettas up outside the George.

Rick managed to talk him round and we actually played our first gig in the downstairs tiny room in the pub. Proving that he wasn't completely oblivious to the potential as he'd also given Mick an opportunity to play the pub piano on Saturday nights when he discovered he was keyboard player. Ricky had his dog, a bull terrier which slept inside the bass drum. Never moved! It used to crack us up, and the punters. It was a vicious thing as well. Must have been deaf! We also played at the Queen Elizabeth School as the Hertz Brothers. I thought we were pretty tasty. Tony South's playing on the Dobie Gray number, "Drift Away" was brilliant.

Another gig was at The Bluebell, Gretton. The neighbours complained and stopped the gig. We played White Trash's "Alive and Well", "Some Good Old Rock and Roll", "High Heeled Sneakers", "Shame, Shame, Shame" etc. and, of course, some of Rick's own material, which we recorded at Derek Tompkins" studio in Wellingborough. Rick did the arranging as well as playing sax, harmonica and the vocals. It was good earthy R&B stuff. "Securicor Lady" and "Break Balls" were my favourites, the others were "Investigator", "Don't Think You've Won," "Hypnotised" and "Looking For Something Sally". For whatever reason, Soggy left, which I thought was to the detriment of the band, but we could still rock it. Virgin Records came to see us at the Hunting Lodge, but obviously we weren't what they wanted at the time."

Colin Pheasant later formed the Bronson Brothers in 1988 with Steve Thomas, Dave Smith, Andy McShane, Gordon Foley, Dave Whitehouse and Dean Bronson.

The press were optimistic. "All of them have wide experience having played with a number of bands including Swing, Swamp Women and Cry Wild. Their music is varied but they've put their act together and set their sights on reaching the top. Lyrics are written mainly by Steve, Colin and Andy, and they have a host of original ideas. The

Brothers have been doing studio work and are set to record a single at Pineapple Studios in London."

CORBY band The Bronson Bros, fresh from their recent Battle Of The Bands heat victory, aim to have their first single on the streets around the end of August.

Indie label Buzzin' Records have given the thumbs up to their demo tape, but the band aim to retain as much product control as possfble on the product.

Wednesday's gig at Corby's The Office, therefore, will be their last public outing for some time as they concentrate on recording and marketing the vinyl.

The Bronson's current line-up includes, from left — Steve Thomas (bass), Colin 'Phez' Pheasant (keyboards), Dave Smith (drums), Andy McShane (vocals) and Gordon Foley (guitars) plus sax duo Dave Whitehouse and Dean Bronson.

The Bronson Brothers with former Chrome Molly axeman Colin 'Phez' Pheasant.

Part Five

I Will Survive

1979

Gloria Gaynor's karaoke classic hit might well have been adopted as an anthem by the those holding demonstrations across the UK during the final year of this decade. Schools and airports closed, ambulance drivers walked out in protest at their "paltry wages of £36 a week," hospitals refused to treat anything but emergencies, which wasn't much comfort for those on death row. When Gravediggers, anticipating an increase in their workload, dug in for a 14% pay rise, it was clear the Government's policy of a 5% limit on pay rises was snowballing out of control.

Prime Minister James Callaghan was under attack from the Tories for refusing to acknowledge the country was in a state of chaos. Returning to Britain from an overseas jaunt he responded to the question by asking, "Crisis, what crisis?" James might have got an inkling if he had walked through Leicester Square where rubbish was piled high on the street. When Bin men on garbage pay had walked out, looking for a 11% pay increase, Leicester Square was designated as a recycling centre by Westminster Council which provided a feast for the local rat population. Disappointing for the rats, the bin strike ended on February 21st.

Tanker drivers joined in, halting deliveries and forcing thousands of petrol stations to close. Callaghan's response was to engage the army under a 'secret" plan called Operation Drumstick to transport fuel to petrol stations. Thanks to the Tanker drivers, Supermarket shelves were soon running out of food due to the shortage of diesel for their delivery lorries. The knock-on effect being that crime was increasing, as the *Northamptonshire Evening Telegraph* reported, "Thieves have cleared allotments of cabbages in Wellingborough." Likely a scenario repeated around the country.

Corby's future in steelmaking was again the focus for attention following an article in a national newspaper which stated, "Closure plans would involve dismantling Corby's iron and steel works which have been suffering massive cash losses for some time."

The vultures were circling. On 24th January, a team of London consultants, following a commissioned report costing over £20,000, proclaimed, "Corby is on the brink. Action must be taken quickly before unemployment and social problems run amok. Corby has pleasant surroundings, good housing, amenities and social services. But its location away from major roads has helped make the town isolated from the rest of the county."

A town in a similar situation to Corby was Bilston in the West Midlands where it's steelworkers were being backed by the unions for an all-out strike to save their Steelworks. Which prompted the warning, "It would be industrial suicide for Corby to support the proposal."

An announcement from Brussels that "BSC workers who are laid off because of steel closure will get more than £1.5 million from the Common Market to help pay for retraining" didn't do much for confidence either. Union leaders, including John Cowling, Corby Councillor and National Executive of the Iron and Steel Trades Confederation, travelled to London for a meeting with MPs at Westminster to discuss the situation. Cowling was in defiant mood, 'there can be no doubt in anyone's mind that BSC has it in mind to shut the plant down. It is an outrage that they would think of doing this to a town like Corby which depends entirely on the work for its livelihood. It must be stopped at all costs."

On February 9th, came the news everyone was dreading, "Steel axe has fallen. BSC reveal a decision that will tear the heart out of Corby. 5500 jobs are to go. The BSC regards Corby as a wasting asset."

ISTC spokesman Bill Homewood was pugnacious in his response, "We will tell the BSC we are not even prepared to consult with them on the issue. This kind of savage action would devastate Corby."

Immediate support came from the *Evening Telegraph,* "The rest of the county must join in Corby's fight. If Corby dies, many other county regions will find job prospects have died with it."

Estate agents were quick to voice their concerns, claiming house prices in and around Corby would slump. "If everyone who is made redundant puts their house on the market, the effect will be chaotic."

Meetings and rallies were organised to galvanise support, not all met with sympathetic ears. Tory councillors were criticised for refusing to allow the action group ROSAC (Retention of Steelmaking at Corby), to use the Civic Theatre free of charge for a public meeting. Leaders of ROSAC were told they would have to pay £21 for the hire of the council owned building even though the meeting was to fight plans for more than 6,000 redundancies in the town's steel industry. Chairman Brian Wright was dumbfounded, "It amazes me that the councillors think this building belongs to the council and not to the people of Corby - especially when the town is facing a crisis."

Council Chairman Fred Harris considered ROSAC to be a political organisation and therefore didn't qualify to use the facilities for free. "We cannot override the council's policy."

Nationwide, the strikes continued. Civil servants walked out on a 24-hour strike in a bid to force the government to increase their offer of a 9% pay increase. Museums, courts, custom officers, immigration officials, traffic controllers, the Royal Mint were all affected. Dole payments were hit which saw postmen on the front line, left to face the ire and abuse of those out of work, temporarily or permanently.

Clive Smith said, "I was snarled at on more than one occasion. "Hey you! Where's my Giro!" was a regular morning welcome! One Thursday, I was delivering the mail on the Exeter estate and entered The Lantern pub not long after it opened its doors at 10.30 am. I was amazed to find the pub was packed. The locals were drinking, playing pool, darts. Smoke hung in the air. Giving me the impression the Lantern had been open all night! It probably had! As soon as they saw me the cries went up, "Got my Giro postie?" "Want a drink?" Laughter cascaded, and I couldn't help but think, "Who's the mug here?"

This was my first winter working for the Royal Mail. Severe frost and down falls of snow were sweeping the country. Norfolk, cut off for two days by deep snow, prompted a headline describing the situation as a "White Hell".

Traipsing around the Westfields Road area in Corby with a heavy postbag laden with Christmas cards, packets, presents, bills and ordinary mail in two feet of snow made me wonder why I'd left the Tubeworks six months before. For all that, "It was well-known that posties did alright at Christmas," apparently.

All the guys in the office bragged about the tips they received from their customers. As such, I looked forward to picking up a bonus or two. The snow was getting deeper by the day. My nose and hands were constantly chapped with the cold. I might as well have been in the bloody Antarctic. Five days into this "Christmas period" I still hadn't had as much as a 'thank you'. Have to admit to feeling pissed off. Then one morning in Tanfields Road, I was feeling decidedly sorry for myself as I trudged along with the snow tippling down like confetti.

Breaking my train of thought, and misery, a voice called out through the blizzard. "Postie!" Stopped me in my tracks. Turning around, I saw an elderly woman standing by her gate at the other end of the street from where I'd just come from. She was waving an envelope at me. "Christ almighty!" I thought. "Can't you put the bloody letter or whatever it is through your neighbour's door yourself?!" I trudged back, head down to shelter as much from the driving snow as I could, and looking up, saw the lady standing there, wrapped in a coat and head scarf. Looked like she was freezing."

"Yes?" I asked impatiently.

"Merry Christmas!" she said, and handed me the envelope. On the envelope was the word "Postie". Inside was a card and a five pound note! I couldn't believe it! I felt humbled, chastened. Ashamed at my thoughts. What a lovely old lady!! That was my first tip. And last. I didn't get another one on that round! But, from then on, my eyes were peeled for other old ladies standing by their gates wrapped up in their head scarfs, looking out for me. Maybe I was dreaming! It didn't happen. But nevermind, that little old lady in Tanfields restored my faith in humanity!"

***

A catastrophe occurred in the town on March 24th when the town's library was gutted by fire. 40,000 books, some of them irreplaceable, on the history and development of Corby were destroyed. Damage was estimated to be at £1million. Police suspected arson.

Corby Library destroyed by fire, 1979

A new modern building was promised to replace the George Street Library though not many held their breath. It did turn out to be modern of sorts, having been built just six or seven years earlier, the room had been lying dormant, on top of and at the back of beyond in Queen's Square. It would never have the ambience of the original library where apart from anything else, SILENCE was paramount. It was handy for a pint in the Corinthian afterwards though.

By the end of March, Jim Callaghan's Labour government was coming to the end of the road. A "vote of no confidence" by the Tories succeeded in forcing James to call a General Election. Waiting in the wings was Margaret Thatcher, who enjoyed the support and rallying call by the nation's ladies of "It's about time a woman was given their chance!"

On May 3rd, she duly became Great Britain's first ever female Prime Minister. Standing on the steps of 10 Downing Street, she pouted, "Where there is discord, may we bring harmony…. where there is despair, may we bring hope." The St Francis of Assisi quotation calculated to stamp her name in the history books. Not everyone was impressed. Corby Royal Mail union official Cliff Hughes's sardonic response was, "It should have been, where there is hope, we will bring despair!"

With the Conservative Party back in power, Kettering and Corby MP Sir Geoffrey DeFreitas decided it was time to retire. The former barrister and Squadron Leader during the Second World War had begun his parliamentary career by winning the Nottingham Central seat in 1945 and was appointed Private Secretary to Prime Minister Clement Atlee. In the 1950 general election he became MP for Lincoln and held a succession of front bench posts throughout the decade. De Frietas was appointed British High Commissioner to Ghana in 1961 and was knighted in October of that year.

Geoffrey said goodbye with what was described as "a verbal lashing" in April 1979, during his farewell speech at Northampton Guild Hall. "For successive governments refusing to allow Corby to diversify long after it was apparent that the steel industry would not need the enormous manpower for which Corby had been designed and built."

***

Cliff Hughes put his despair over Margaret Thatcher to one side and enjoyed the opportunity to catch some genuine 'rock and roll" legends appearing at Corby Festival Hall. Bill Haley and the Comets supported by The Flying Saucers and The Wild Angels.

Over eight hundred "Teds," ageing Teddy Boys, including Cliff, rolled up from as far afield as Leicester, Northampton and Wellingborough to jive the night away to "Rock Around the Clock", "See You Later Alligator", "Razzle Dazzle", "Piccadilly Rock" and all the other old favourites.

"The whole show took me back 25 years," said Cliff. Theatre manager Ross Jones was equally thrilled, "There wasn't a hint of any trouble from the fans. They were all very polite to my staff and helped to make it a really memorable evening. The atmosphere was tremendous."

The much-maligned Civic Centre was in the news when it was claimed that the building, built at a cost of £230,000 in 1965, was wrongly designed. "Only way to make it perfect would be to pull it down and start again" was the consensus. A settlement figure of £87,000 against the designers of the building was agreed, with 'the money being used to repair and maintain the building" a spokesman claimed.

The Civic Centre, encompassing the Council Offices, Festival Hall and Theatre was eventually demolished in 2009, 30 years later.

Another rock and roll legend to appear in the town was Freddie 'Fingers' Lee who was booked to appear by Entertainment Secretary Billy Mathieson at Corby's Glasgow Rangers Club.

"Fred had been a regular on the 1950's TV rock shows "6.5. Special" and "Oh Boy!" performing his own brand of Jerry Lee Lewis style piano bashing," said Bill who was clearly impressed, "Fred doesn't play piano by ear - he plays it by his nose! He's also been known to tickle the ivories with his feet!"

The 'Freddie "Fingers' Lee story began when he had moved to London from Newcastle in the early 1960s, teaching himself piano on an old upright belonging to his landlady. Reading the Melody Maker he saw an advertisement by Screaming Lord Sutch looking for a piano player and decided to go for it. 'there were millions of guitar players but not many piano players around in those days," Fred explained. He duly introduced himself to the Lord and got the job, staying with him for a number of years, which included numerous stints in Hamburg at the famous Star Club.

The Rangers night was well remembered by rock 'n roll fans John Black and Charlie Johnson. John said, "I lent a pile of my old Sun records and 78s to Chris Madden who was the DJ and I was standing by the doorway when Freddie Lee came in. A short stocky guy, he stood there posing for a minute and then turned to me and asked, "Who are the local scrubbers here then!" I was flabbergasted, told him I didn't know, I never went to the place as a rule. Then he asked me and Charlie if we could do him a favour. He told us part of his act was standing on his head when he played "Great Balls Of Fire" on the piano! Only he needed someone to hold his legs. So the time came and me and Charlie went up and grabbed a leg each. Lee started belting out the number, it was ridiculous! After a couple of minutes I got fed up and said to Charlie, "I'm going for a pint" and let his leg go. Charlie looked at me and said, "Yeah, me as well." Fingers went sprawling and the place erupted in laughter!"

Fred also made an appearance at the Stardust Centre where he is remembered for taking his glass eye out and putting it in his pint while he sang.

Guitarist John Grimley added, "I was asked if I would like to join him. We didn't know each other but somehow he got hold of my phone number and rang me up. Told me he had a gig in the Stardust the following week so I could go along and see him. Yes I went, no I didn't approach him. You can guess my reasons why."

Opening its doors for the first time in March was the Grampian Club on Patrick Road, next door to the Irish Club, with Eric McKenna as Steward and boasting a membership, "Already at 1200 with a waiting list of 2000." It was said to gain membership, one had to have come from or have an association with the Grampian region. A policy that eventually, over time, would be relaxed. With typical Corby wit, both clubs were soon given nicknames, 'the Meanians" and 'the Fenians'.

A "Halloween" gig in October gave the Meanians an opportunity to run the rule over a new band called Cherish featuring Corey Gray, Frank Mullen, Frank Malone, Mick Ogden and Ian Palmer, all wearing Corey's clothes!

Frank Mullen recalled the night and his memories of working with some of Corby's elite musicians in 2012. "Cherish was actually a smart band, wearing suits but we thought it'd be fun to dress up for the Halloween night. Oggy had one of Corey's slips on playing the drums. The Grampian crowd must have thought we were a right bunch of queers! Corey was always a good singer. She went on to do a Tina Turner tribute act which I told her she should have been doing years before. She was a natural.

The demise of the band came soon after an Australian guy called Dom started hanging around with us. I didn't like him, thought he was a scrounger, a right tosser. He decided to get up and sing with the band one night and then the rest of them wanted him in. I said no way and left. Corey jacked in as well. The guy started acquiring some gear, PA stuff and left the band with two grand of debt and headed back to Australia. "We should have listened to you Frank," they wailed.

I joined up with Mick Harper and played with him for around forteen years. What a character! Mick stole a lump of cheese off the yanks one night at an Air Base and stuck it in my guitar case without me knowing. When I went to put my guitar away I said, "What the hell's this?" Mick said, "It's ok. I'm taking that home with me."

We used to have some right fun with his false arm. He'd take it off and throw it on somebody's table! You can imagine the reaction! I'd grab his fingers and bend them right back, people used to look and think I was a right cruel bastard. He used to me crack up. Frank Malone's dog took a bite out of it one time so Mick took it off and gave it to him. Fantastic singer but he was Mad as a hatter!"

I used to try and get him to pack in smoking. Putting his fags in the pocket behind his false arm. He would always struggle to twist his other arm around to get the ciggies out. Billy Mathieson on drums was another case. He had a habit at the end of every gig of standing up and dropping his biggest cymbal right on the floor. Crash! It would go and everybody jumped with fright!

We changed the name of bands regularly. "Dynasty", "Happy Days", 'Scotch and Rye", "Junction Four". I think it was all tax dodges! Scotch and Rye was Mick and I with Barry Bryden on drums and ex Carnations bass player John Hill, who was a wee bit deaf. I said to him during one gig, "We'll play 'Do You Wanna Dance?'" next. John proceeded to play the Shadows' "Dance On" When I stopped him he broke his finger nail and started whining. It became a standing joke.

Gigs at the Welfare were always good. Peter McKay, the committeeman, was always moaning, "not you shower again, you're crap!" A regular there was a character called Raymond who would get up after Billy introduced him, "Let's have a big hand for the star of the show!" Raymond would usually sing "There's A Hole In My Bucket". Billy would then get all the women to form a queue up and ask him for his autograph. He loved it!

My last proper band was Prisoner with Harry McCormick, Mark Plant and Jim Muircroft, who was a right evil looking guy, dour looking with his droopy moustache but he was a great drummer and good fun. Jim flew at Billy Mathieson one night at the Phoenix. Don't know what had been going on or said but Jim dived right over the drums and belted Bill. Then he left. I asked Billy what that was all about but he reckoned he didn't know. I think they had been winding each other up. We used to play down London a lot and in the end it got too much for me. I told Harry I couldn't whack the travelling anymore, not when I was up for the 6-2 shift in Avon next morning. I've only played jam sessions since."

By the end of the 70s, there was a general feeling that 'live' music was on the way out. Prog Rock, Country Rock, Folk Rock whatever was on the wane, a diminishing audience that even Punk couldn't sustain. James Truman in the Melody Maker was clearly disillusioned, bemoaning, "Few acts have recognisable personalities, it's a faceless genre."

It seemed that disc jockeys were now becoming more famous than the recording artists. Even in Corby, DJ's were now as well-known as the local bands and beginning to make a name for himself was Pat McMahon who had started out working part-time as a glass collector for his dad at the St. Brendan's Club in Beanfield Avenue. Watching the DJ's in action at the club galvanised Pat's desire to progress from washing the pots to spinning the platters.

"Best Of My Love" by the Emotions, a hit in 1977 is a song that sticks in my mind from that time." says Pat. "I was 14 and it was the year I met Dave Mulheron who had the great name of Firefly for his disco. I was introduced to Dave by his brother John who was a doorman at St. Brendans. John was well known on the pub and club scene and would go on to manage and own various venues in Corby. The Strathclyde (including The Pigalle Bar and Hamilton Suite which became The Rafters Bar and The Embassy nightclub), the Corinthian, Rockingham Arms, Open Hearth and La Poste. Dave worked in all of them as DJ and I would often make the odd "guest" appearance.

On the night in question at the St Brendan's Club, Dave gave me an insight into what he was doing. I was fascinated and hooked. It was a night that changed my life forever. Dave suggested that if I was interested in becoming a Disc Jockey he was happy to show me the ropes. He had a regular gig at the Abington Road Community Centre in Corby, a teenage disco every Wednesday.

For several weeks, I met Dave there and watched him set up the decks, amp, speakers and lighting. Dave was a dab hand, even at that age, in designing and building his own lighting effects. Eventually, after much cajoling from Dave I plucked up the courage to start to cue up his records for him. I was terrified of screwing it up and embarrassing myself in front of my peers in the audience, many of whom were friends and schoolmates. A few more weeks passed, and I was able to set up the kit, pack it away. I was learning how to format a show and not only how to get the audience on their feet but keep them there. However, Dave was unable to persuade me to pick up the microphone and introduce a song.

One evening he said he was off to the loo and would be back in 5 minutes. Twenty minutes later, I was putting on records with no link from the DJ (sounds a bit like the lazy jocks today). I was managing to keep the crowd on their feet but I thought to myself I need to do something. So I cued "Best

Of My Love," a guaranteed floor filler and blurted out a nervous and hesitant introduction. That was it, that was the moment. Some might say I haven't shut up since.

When John Mulheron took over the bars in the Strathclyde Hotel, Dave became resident DJ and whenever possible I would assist, even on a Monday night when I had school next day. Because Monday was a quiet night John decided to put on a late-night disco in the Hamilton suite. This was the Strath's old function room and would become legendary after it was transformed into The Embassy. It was stunning at the time. This nightclub attracted punters not just from Corby but across the county and further besides.

For me, it was Monday nights in the Hamilton that set the tone for what was to come. Dave would DJ in the Le Pigalle bar, on the ground floor of the hotel. He would then hand over to me as he kicked off his second show of the night in the Hamilton. Tasked with finishing the night off in Le Pigalle I was in at the deep end. The place was buzzing and what a thrill it was to be part of it at such a young age. I bought my first set of disco equipment from a Kay's catalogue when I was 16 in 1978. A lovely lady who worked for my dad in St Brendan's, Linda Waterhouse, agreed to order it for me and I had to pay her ten pound a week for a couple of years.

This was the start of me heading out on my own. Sadly, Linda was tragically killed at a young age in a car accident. My first solo booking after buying my own equipment was a wedding. I thought the couple were brave booking me but the bride, Cathy Neeson, was laid back about it and said "just play anything". I have to say, the light show that day was borrowed, homemade and basic but the day was great and everyone had a wonderful time. It helped that it was an Irish American wedding and the booze was flowing (much of it brought over from USAF Alconbury, I think).

The venue, by coincidence, was the Abington Road Community Centre. I started to slowly pick up bookings for a variety of events such as weddings, engagement parties, 18th birthdays etc."

Thus began the 40-year career behind the decks for Pat McMahon. A career that would lead him to have his own Sunday morning show on Corby Radio in the 2000s which featured the very popular quiz "Aboot the Toon".

DJ Pat McMahon ready to interview Raging Speedhorn guitarist Gareth Smith

The show rapidly became the most essential listening of the week. The music Pat would have been playing when he was standing in for Dave Mulheron at the Abington Road Community Centre would have included hits by The Village People, a U.S. band of individuals attired in Red Indian, Naval and Vaudeville fancy dress costumes who kicked the year off with the chart topping "YMCA". A dirge that became a staple for discos and parties where "fun lovers" could make an arse of themselves singing and dancing along in unison. The Village People followed up "YMCA" with "In the Navy" which was just as awful, as was Gloria Gaynor's excruciating "I Will Survive", the song that would be immortalised and bore everyone to death with by millions of wannabe singers on karaoke.

Thankfully, there was still music being made to keep the "old stagers" happy and two outstanding albums this year came from the Rolling Stones with "Some Girls" and Eric Clapton's "Just One Night". Punk was dealt a fatal blow with the death of 21 year old Sex Pistol Sid Vicious from a heroin overdose. Just as Sid was awaiting trial for the murder of his girlfriend, Nancy Spungeon.

Fellow Pistol John Lydon was less than sympathetic, "It didn't come as a surprise to any of us, we could see it coming. Sid was a wanker. He bought the whole trip: sex, drugs, rock 'n roll and death."

A highlight of the summer of 1979 was The Stranglers appearing at the Festival Hall on July 23rd along with a band called The Baldheads, or Bawheeds as they were called in Corby. Stuart Allen, working in the Job Centre recalled, "The show was part of their 'Who Wants the World Tour,' though it was advertised as a 'Benefit for Steel Workers' gig. It was 35p to get in, at a time when normally tickets were around £2 or £3. They ran out of "proper" tickets on the night and I was given one that had Corby Swimming Pool on it!!

After a couple of numbers, the Stranglers stopped playing as some punks down the front were spitting at them. Corby kids thought that's what punks were supposed to do but the band said they were going to quit if it carried on. You would have thought following the Tom Robinson Band show, the so-called local punks would have cottoned on. The show eventually got moving again and the spitting stopped, though fights broke out with a mob from Northampton."

The night was also recalled on a Stranglers fan website in which the writers were left distinctly unimpressed. "A bit off the beaten track and not a place where many bands go but The Stranglers were gaining a reputation for visiting these places. The gig was a benefit in aid of the local steelworkers. It's not too far for us, a train to Kettering then bus to Corby. It's not a big venue but seems well-packed. The band come on to massive cheers and kick off as usual in fine style.

Unfortunately, there are some idiots down the front who start gobbing at the band and it seems to get worse and worse as the show goes on. JJ and Hugh are obviously not happy at this. I'm surprised JJ hasn't jumped in the crowd yet! The band go off after a shorter than usual set and, after a bit of a wait, it becomes obvious they aren't going to do an encore. This irritates some of the crowd who shout and jeer, calling the band popstars! WHAT? Mick and myself argue back that the band have come here to a place where hardly any other bands play, it's only about 75p a ticket and you repay them by gobbing constantly! As Hugh might say, bunch of morons!!! With that, we were off. A disappointing end to the night."

Those yearning for the nostalgic days of the 1960s could delight with the release of "Quadraphenia", a film based on the Mods and Rockers 1964 Bank Holiday "Battle of Brighton". Starring Denis Waterman, Ray Winstone and Leslie Ash the film was shot on location and witnessed by an alarmed Fred Jelly, one time Corby disc jockey who had debunked to the south coast some ten years earlier after a riot at one his gigs at Corby Festival Hall. Back in his home town Fred recalled the moment he was caught up in the filming and proudly claimed he was to be seen in the background of a particular scene.

"I was standing in a shop doorway in Brighton town centre and wondering why all these motorbikes and scooters were racing around. Then one of the scooters crashed into a parked car and to my surprise, not one soul ran to help or to see if the rider was badly injured. Well I couldn't help myself. I ran over immediately, saw the boy was covered in blood and shouted for someone to call an ambulance! Then even more surprising, this bloke shouted at me. "Charming," I thought. Then I noticed the film crew and realised it was a stunt! I felt a right knob."

The 60s Mods and Rockers cult was later recalled in a pop magazine by "Bugs" of Wolverhampton. Rockers stood in solemn groups on street corners and watched enviously as everybody else enjoyed themselves, their devotion to their BSA Bantams left them greasy and smelly and wondering why there were so few girl rockers. They saw themselves as Easy Riders but appeared as camp caricatures of Marlon Brando in 'the Wild Ones". Their knowledge and appreciation of music was nil but stand them in front of a mirror with a jar of Brylcreem and they'd keep themselves amused for hours. Mods were a true working-class sub culture with a passion for music, clothes and scooters.

The Mods would spend a week's wages on a mohair suit and a day's pay on an American Chess label import. They would spend hours discussing the latest Etta James or Doris Troy single while dismissing the Searchers and Swinging Blue Jeans as just light weight music for the masses. The Mods were pioneers in appreciating Ska and Bluebeat long before the more commercial Reggae labels appeared. The 60s belonged to the Mods but the absolute decadence of the all-nighter lifestyle was a well-kept secret then and remains so to this day."

Bugs would have appreciated the efforts of Bip Wetherell who organised a Mods revival dance at the Welfare Club in aid of a Kidney Machine Appeal for his friend and former drummer of The Friction, Brian Read. Chrome Molly, Energy and a Friction reunion revived those heady days of the 60s that had been committed to celluloid with Quadrophenia. "It was a great success for the fund and great fun getting Friction back together," enthused Bip.

Three of the biggest films of the year, along with Quadraphenia, was the latest James Bond offering, "Moonraker," the Vietnam epic "Apocalypse Now" along with Monty Python's "The Life of Brian" which had councillors scuttling to private viewings to judge on whether the public should be allowed to watch such blasphemous material.

The movie industry was facing a crisis of apocalyptic proportions with the sudden emergence of the video. Many predicted the end of the cinema now that it was possible to watch films in the comfort of your own home. When movie legend John Wayne bowed out after a long fight with cancer, the industry was in deep mourning. A golden era had passed. "Big Duke's" death was like the final curtain.

Video did appear to be the future. Stores were springing up everywhere. Getting in on the act was former St Cecilia guitarist John Proctor and his friend John Knox, opening a shop in Rockingham Road, Corby. Very successful the Johns became too and soon competition was coming up all around town. Notably Ann's Video Shop in Occupation Road. Doubtless it was the same story elsewhere in the country.

Energised

Energy, Iain Wetherell, Mike "Bozzy" Bosnic, Mark Stewart and Stephen "Flapper" Fulton had built up a huge following since their formation in 1976. In 2007 Iain and "Bozzy" relived their Energy days during an interview at Iain Wetherell's Premier Studios.

Mike Bosnic had told his dad in 1976, "When I grow up, I want to play in a rock band." The response from his pa was typically caustic, "You can't do both son!"

Iain said, "Energy was full-time for nine years. Though Bozzy calls it his retirement years! When the band split up, we all had to go back to work!"

Bozzy took up the story, "We first started playing when we rehearsed in the Nags Head where Iain's brother Bip was proprietor. Then after a few weeks Bip threw us in at the deep end and told us we were playing the Sunday jam session! It was the first time we'd played in front of an audience which was daunting but a great experience. Bip was great, lending us gear when we needed and giving us the opportunity to learn our craft.

Our first gig proper came at Corby Samuel Lloyds School on October 2nd, 1976 thanks to teacher Frank Holmes, a one-time skiffle man himself, who encouraged pupils with musical aspirations. The dance was packed out. All our school friends were there, of course. Iain sang the first song, Bryan Ferry's "Let's Stick Together" before Flapper made a grand entrance, running in from the back of the school hall with a duffle coat tied round his neck like a cape as Iain played the theme from "Batman"!

Iain said, "Initially we sorted our gigs ourselves, or with the help of Bip, and then eventually decided to sign up with the Concorde Ham Acts Agency. It didn't take us long to realise that they were booking us in air bases for less money than what we were getting for doing it ourselves! So Bozzy took control of affairs. Calling himself Pyramid Promotions, he used to phone venues where live music was played and ask if they'd be interested in booking us. He would send them a copy of a collage we'd made of Energy, a record for their jukebox and ask them how much they paid, which was usually around the £100 mark. Boz would give them some bull, tell them we normally played for double that amount but as a favour we'd do the show for £150, and after a bit of bartering we'd get the gig! We became probably the most organised self-controlled band on the circuit. We had a data base of people who followed the band. We'd phone what we called the ringleaders and tell them we were playing at such and such a place and they'd put the word around and the gigs were often packed out."

Energy

The record in question was an EP titled "Energised". The songs "No Go", "Don't Show Your Face", "Lovely Lady", "Spoilt Choice" were recorded at Derek Tompkins Studio in Wellingborough. The tracks were produced in a collaboration by the band.

Bozzy said, "I used to tell people we've sold over two million copies of our first record. And if you don't believe me, come and look in my garage! "Conquer the World", "Make It", "Lawbreaker", "Nowhere To Hide", "Fight For

Your Freedom" was our second release. All are now collector's items, you can find them on eBay!"

The band were featured in *Musicians Only,* a weekly music newspaper published between 1979 and 1980. "It can be argued that a lot of bands in the early stages of their career fall by the wayside, not through a lack of ideas or musical direction, but because they have not got the business end organised properly. That's why it was refreshing to meet the four people who make up the Corby based rock band Energy, and to witness for myself not only their unbounded enthusiasm onstage, but also their professional approach to the marketing of their name. Energy was formed out of the remains of two school bands, The Hardly Worthit Band and Lipstick. Mike Bosnic was asked why the band had parted company with their manager (their first and last) a year or so back to go it alone. His reply demonstrated the band's ambition and self-belief.

"Although his opinion was valued, we valued his opinion in many ways on many things, we thought we could accomplish more on our own. It's as simple as that."

Certainly if you study the bands track record since they started handling their own affairs, you can see they made the right decisions. Mike handles the booking arrangements and publicity while Iain sorts out the accounts and insurance. Agents are used as much as possible, the reason being purely financial. Equipment such as the PA, lighting system and the transport are bought out of the kitty.

"Basically, it's the money that's left after expenses. Sometimes one of us might dig into it for our individual instruments, but it is always paid back, always," stressed Mike.

A new van is the next thing on the shopping list, as the two they have now don't warrant a decent set of spares between them. Turning to the subject of touring, Mike told me apart from a three-day stint in Middlesbrough a while back, the band have never been on a full tour. That's not to say that they have been sitting around waiting for the phone to ring. Energy, clapped out vans and all, have averaged two gigs per week for the last sixteen months or so, taking in places like Cinderford in Gloucestershire, Ashford in Kent and Leicester where they were runners up in a national competition sponsored by Premier.

They have also been support to big names like Love Affair and Chairman of the Board. "We wouldn't have done half of this under our old manager" said Steve Fulton.

"No, he organised a tour of Denmark for us, but nothing came of it, it all fell through," added Mike, who showed me a copy of the itinerary for 1980. Energy will be gigging consistently, but as before, it's not an organised tour. And although it will take them right through to mid-summer, there are no London dates mentioned. I put it to Mike that it might be a good idea to try and slot some London venues in between the local haunts.

"We would love to play London," Mike replied, "but what would be the cost of a mini tour down there?" True, in financial terms, (time off work etc) it would be a bit of a struggle. But what about the long-term effect? "Yes, you're right I suppose if we made the effort and the gigs came together it would probably lead to something."

One drawback I did note was the playing of non-original material mixed in with their own compositions. This is a shame, for their own songs had far more going for them, in terms of depth and style than the bulk of the pop/rock which made up the two sets that I saw them play. That's not a criticism of their playing ability because they played numbers like "Message In A Bottle," "Black Betty" and "Since You've Been Gone" with just as much finesse as the original artists. It would be hard to pick out any particular star in the band, although I must say that at times front man Steve Fulton stole the show with his antics, dashing here and there, offstage and onstage, as though possessed.

At the end of the second and highly impressive set, I joined the lads backstage, where they presented me with a copy of their EP "Energised" self-financed, on the BIPS Record label. The number which impresses me most was an out and out rocker called "No Go" which reminded me of early Nazareth. Mike said, "We have had a thousand copies pressed and we've sold about half. They're available through the local branch of John Menzies and mail order through me." Their immediate plans? 'to keep on gigging" said Mike, "We would move to London as a band if we thought we could make a living at it. But at the moment, it's just one gig and one stage at a time."

Energy have ability but what they need to do is to get right away from Corby and its surrounds. If they made that all important move and wrote and performed more of their own material, their chances of making the big-time would be greatly enhanced. Energy are the best band I have seen this side of a lucrative record deal. Now it's a question of finding an enthusiastic producer to channel their ideas into something commercially viable."

As Autumn encroached, Energy announced that they were taking the next step to going fully professional. Leicester Trader's *The Insider* was optimistic of their chances. "Like most other things, the music industry bares large, seeping wounds, inflicted without mercy by the recession's cast iron teeth. Hardly a week goes by, without news filtering through the record and entertainment jungle, that somebody or other has been released from what looked like and indeed was, a mouth-watering, zillion dollar contract.

Bands, like trends and fashions, come and go. Some disappear as if in their sleep, while others are condemned to a series of ups and downs, followed by slow, painful erosion which can and has broken the spirit of each individual concerned. It is with this in mind, why I have the utmost respect for the voice of voices who say goodbye to 9-5, cross "no man's land" and plunge headlong into the uncertainty of the professional musicians world. Four such voices belong to Energy, a rocky-type, all-round entertaining quartet from Corby.

"This will be a real test for all of us, in every respect," said vocalist Stephen Fulton in a recent conversation we had when the band played The Windmill. Steve is a front man par excellence and the same can be said for the guitar, drums bass combination of Iain Wetherell, Mike Bosnic and Mark Stewart. In the last three and a half years since the bands inception, Energy have averaged twelve to fifteen gigs per month, playing everything from seedy backroom bars with wall-to-wall sawdust, top plush nightclubs where even the Gents and Ladies powder room don expensive shag pile.

Playing regularly up to four, five gigs a week around the country, Mike told me that Energy will go "pro" sometime this autumn, possibly in early October. All four members giving up careers "to pursue the golden trail in the music business." Iain a trainee accountant, Mike a trainee computer programmer, Steve Fulton a fitter and Mark Stewart a trainee engineer. As they handle all their own affairs, all are aware, that once the bridges are burnt, the future will be full of animal traps, parasites and hollow promises. But all are equally aware, that at the end of it all there could be success. Will they stay the course? I think so.

Bip Wetherell explained, "It's going to be a bit of a struggle and I suppose cars may have to be sold but we mean to make a real go of this. We are planning to record another EP soon and it should be pressing about 2000 copies. And, of course, we will be after a record deal. Giving up our full-time jobs means we will have more time to chase these things. Of course, now, it's just a case of bookings for exposure - we need money to live!"

Self-sufficiency was the band's aim, which extended to taking care of the group van. Before a tour of Scotland Bozzy decided it needed a service, "So outside Iain's house in Studfall Avenue, I changed the plugs, HT leads, rotor arm, oil, points, everything. Then when I finished, I couldn't get the thing going! Checked everything again, got the set of feelers out to recheck the gap in between the points, distributor cap was clean, etc. Still nothing. I said to Iain, 'tell you what, we're on a hill here, let's give it a push and see if we can jump start it.

Well, the van rolled down the hill, failed to kick in, and we were standing there bemused and scratching our heads when a taxi pulled up. The driver, Robert Knight, got out and asked us what the matter was. We told him the story, he said he'd give it a go, turned the ignition key, just a grunt as usual, then he discovered there was no fuel in the tank. That was my last attempt at being a motor mechanic!

Mark Stewart would later complain, "I'm only in the band because a drum machine can't push the van!" Iain used to do most of the driving. He was the only one who'd passed his driving test. Coming down long lonely highways like the A1, often in thick fog, or so it seemed, I'd be sitting next to Iain steering the van while he kept his foot on the accelerator, trying to keep his eyes open and stop from falling asleep! When we reached Stamford, I'd give him a shake, "Right, come on, it is a bit trickier from here on in!"

Another trick the band came up with was to join both the AA and RAC motoring organisations. Iain, "We thought it was a good idea. We could use one to tow us to a gig if necessary, and the other one to tow us back home afterwards. I said we were organised!"

A headline making night to remember for Energy, for more than one reason came the night the band competed in a RCA sponsored "Battle of the Bands" contest in Birmingham. Three coach loads of supporters travelled from Corby, and only two made it back! One of the coaches had to be abandoned on the way home when it went on fire on the M6! Onboard was a shaken Cathy Bates who said, "Somebody shouted there was a fire and a man banged on the window of the bus and told everyone to get out."

"52 escape coach fire," screamed the *Birmingham Evening News*. "Passengers had to scramble to safety when a coach burst into flames. They escaped the smoke-filled coach through emergency doors and windows after a night out in

Birmingham. Passengers were transferred to two other coaches and police were called. The three coach loads of people, who were delayed for three quarters of an hour had been to Birmingham to support their band Energy in a contest."

On the March

The fight to save Corby Works continued despite BSC Chairman Sir Charles Villiers" view that BSC was determined to press ahead with the closure and 'the town had better come to terms with the fact."

Disregarding his remarks, thirty steelworkers, including council leader George Crawley and leading ROSAC members Mick Skelton, John Cowling and Jimmy Wright, marched out of Corby on Saturday June 23rd to embark on a 100 mile "Jarrow Style" crusade to present a petition and bring world attention to the steel crisis at the House of Commons.

George Crawley far from the madding crowd with actress Vanessa Redgrave

On arrival, they were greeted by the sight of thousands from Corby and actress/political activist Vanessa Redgrave, a star of 1960's cult movies "Blow Up" and Richard Attenborough's satirical "Oh What A Lovely War". Redgrave supported a range of human rights causes, including opposition to the Vietnam War, nuclear disarmament, independence for Ireland, aid for Bosnian Muslims and other victims of war. Her opposition to Soviet oppression led her to join the anti-Stalinist Workers' Revolutionary Party on whose ticket she twice ran for Parliament.

To coincide with the march on the House of Commons, a song, "Corby's Army" was written by Johnny Mack to the tune of "Ally's Army". (Ally McLeod, Scotland manager in the previous year's World Cup in Argentina), and recorded at the Stardust Club by musicians Frank Mullen, Billy Mathieson and Mick Harper.

"They're going to close the steelworks and put us on the dole,

Put us on the scrapheap and so destroy our souls,

But we might just surprise them all and give them such a fright,

For we're not going to let them do it, we'll put up a fight.

We're on the march with Corby's army, we're out to get a fairer deal,

With our target square in sight, we will carry on the fight,

For we're going to save our jobs at British Steel."

Support also came from the man labelled a 'Scottish political firebrand" Jimmy Reid, leader of the Upper Clyde Shipbuilders Anti Redundancy campaign in 1971. Reid told the people of Corby to "fight for their jobs or watch the town become a refugee camp" during a speech at the Civic Hall.

Daubed on the side of the giant gas holder in Lloyds Road, a slogan S.O.S. SAVE CORBY caused controversy when the BSC ordered it to be removed. John Cowling was outraged, "It is stupid and petty for the BSC to get rid of that sign. I'll climb the gas holder myself and replace the slogan if I have to."

A press release soon after, indicating that a new lease of life could be given to the tubeworks, "if steel strip is supplied from a modern large-scale iron and steelworks" invoked another similar reaction from Cowling, "Only Corby strip will be used in Corby Tubeworks and nothing else!"

As emotions continued to ebb and flow, steelworkers, expecting to be given confirmation in July that Corby would close were surprised when negotiations took a new turn with a possible reprieve for Corby on the cards.

"A stay of execution is granted to Corby's 6000 steelworkers," a report claimed, "but BSC still want to close the town's iron and steelworks. Unions will have the chance to formulate a case for keeping the iron and steel sections of the giant complex running, though they face a three-fold problem.

Firstly, how to save the Corporation £42 million it would have recouped in a year by closing Corby.

Secondly, how to suggest where new steel capacity on stream this year on Teeside, to be sold.

Thirdly, their cash would come from for new investment in parts of Corby's complex.

BSC remain convinced the most economic strategy available was to end iron and steelmaking at Corby because of the high costs involved. This would leave the field clear to bring in cheap steel from the new Teeside Works to Corby's tube mills. BSC lost £309 million nationally in 1978."

The response from Rosac Chairman George McCart was belligerent, "There is no way we will allow closure, whatever happens."

Emphasising their determination, steelworkers posted another message SAVE OUR STEEL on the side of the Strathclyde Hotel in George Street. Made from scrap metal produced by the tubeworks, it was designed and constructed by engineers in their spare time.

George McCart said, "Now everyone coming in and out of Corby will know about our fight and we are determined not to give away 6000 jobs."

Another mass meeting at the Festival Hall on July 20th attracted thousands of Corby people cheering and carrying banners, the biggest demonstration the town had ever seen. Gathered outside the Civic Centre, where a series of emotional speeches inside were relayed outside, Secretary of ISTC Mick Skelton was overwhelmed by the response, 'this shows the country is united in its determination to keep the works open. Response has been overwhelming."

AUEW member Ken Dawson spoke for all. "Let's not forget we are fighting for our children's future either."

Emotions finally boiled over during September when violence erupted during a massive demonstration by 10,000 Corby people as yet more talks on the future of steelmaking, held at Graham House in Cottingham Road, got underway. Workers laid siege to the building, and scuffles broke out when they attempted to bypass a police cauldron to gain entry.

Bob Lochore, of Corby's Post Office Union, the UCW, marching along with the steelworkers in a show of solidarity, had a painful memory of the day. Carrying the huge UCW banner with his pal Cliff Hughes at the forefront of the Royal Mail contingent, the surge towards the gates of Graham House caught Bob off guard, and the pole of the banner crashed back onto his head.

"It was so funny," recalled Cliff, "Bob thought a copper had hit him with a truncheon!"

Peter Floody, Corby Council Chairman, was pragmatic when asked to comment on the events, 'this kind of emotion had to break out sometime. But no damage was done. It was an impressive show of strength and I have to praise the police for their handling of the situation."

***

Distractions come in many ways, with or without their problems. There was chaos at the Welfare Club in Occupation Road before the start of a "Forward Chemicals £10,000 Snooker Tournament" semi-final between top stars

John Spencer and Doug Mountjoy. Seating in a makeshift gallery collapsed and sent spectators sprawling, resulting with one woman breaking her leg. The tournament got under way after the disruption with spectators standing on chairs and tables.

Jeff Stewart, a Fitter in the EWSR Engineering Shop, recalled the night. "It was a shambles. A crazy night. I went along with my workmate, Bill Kerfoot. We arrived at the Club and went into the hall where everything was set up for the evening and being so early we managed to bag two seats right next to where the players were to sit. Being inquisitive, I had a good look around the back of the two stands that were built either side of the snooker table, and to say they didn't look very safe would be the proverbial understatement. The only things keeping the planks together were pieces of very dodgy looking rope! Bill said to me straight away "I'm not sitting on there, that's a disaster waiting to happen!"

Anyway, we'd put our jerseys down to reserve our seats and off we went to the bar to get a pint. When we returned the room was packed with the two stands filling up quickly. As everyone settled down, the players came out and there was the biggest crashing noise you have ever heard with the one full stand totally disintegrating right in front of us! Shouting, moaning, swearing, dust and debris were everywhere. Absolute utter chaos and all I remember is passing planks of wood along a chain of people as they tried to get everyone accounted for under the fallen stand.

It took some time to restore some order and the only casualty unbelievably, was the woman who broke her leg and some wag said it was the biggest break of the night but how nobody was seriously injured or worse was remarkable! The players eventually came back out to play in what was then like a football crowd as everyone was standing, including all the others who had been sat on the other stand. They didn't trust the structure one bit after what they'd seen and they were soon off there sharpish. John Spencer even checked the legs of the snooker table before they started playing!"

***

The last throw of the dice in the fight for Corby's future came when coach loads of steelworkers travelled to Brighton for the Labour Party conference in October. Mick Skelton in a passionate appeal, urged the Labour party to support action "against the destruction of communities brought about by the policies of the BSC" and had the conference cheering with a fighting speech as he pilloried the men who run BSC. "These bankers and so-called intellectuals are getting paid a fortune for being butchers." Mick then turned the focus onto the Conservative Party for pressurising BSC to make cuts. "The Tories are not going to stop at Corby. They are on the road to destroying the industrial base of this country."

Skelton was backed up by Iron and Steel unions boss Bill Sirs, "If Britain allows the steelmaking industry to collapse we would lose the seed corn of industry. If we allow the Tories to close these industries - they will never come back."

Two weeks later, on Friday November 1st 1979, "5,000 townspeople led by Corby's Purple Flute Band took part in an emotive march from the Tubeworks flyover to the Town Centre - the second mass protest in three months. Waiting for them was an estimated 10,000 men, women and children, supported by union colleagues and political groups from all over the country. Thousands of police were drafted in from four bordering counties, and a helicopter kept watch from above for disturbances."

Finally, the announcement everyone dreaded and which tore the heart out of Corby was made by BSC Chief Executive Bob Scholey, confirming closure the following year. A decade of rumour and speculation was at an end. At a stroke, half a century of work, hope and development had been wiped out. The town was stunned.

"It now seems certain the town has about three months to live. Or, more precisely, three months before it starts to die. Just down the road the talk will be of very different things - the prospect of living in a ghost town, a town that some think will soon be bankrupt and ungovernable. A town, where, according to one policeman, they will be cutting them down from the rafters within a couple of years." The fact is there is not much left of Corby when you take away the steel works. From the start, it has been a one-industry, one-employer, one-class town. About 52,000 people now live there and about 11,000 of those - two thirds of the male workforce - work for BSC. The prospect now is instant redundancy. It seems likely that the rundown of the steel works will begin in January with a possible final shutdown as early as March or April.

When that comes about, 6,000 people will be laid off (the tube works are not yet threatened) and redundancy in the town could reach 30 per cent. People in Corby can only begin to wonder what that means.

"What's being proposed is beyond comprehension," says Peter McGowan, "people will just have to face in the seventies what they have already faced once in the forties and fifties. To see the works close without any due regard for what's going to happen for the town is inhuman. Nobody is pretending that the town is prepared for what is almost certain to happen. Belated attempts to diversify industry in the town have been only marginally successful. The average life of factories set up since 1967 has been two years."

Asked for his thoughts, Bill Sirs was solemn, "It is absolutely shocking. A national steel strike is now not out of the question." In the evening, a lone piper played "Amazing Grace" at the start of a special vigil of prayer at the town's Church of Epiphany. Over the coming weeks as workers fought to come to terms with the prospect of unemployment, Secretary of State Keith Joseph announced that government aid would be given to find jobs for the stricken town, declaring Corby an assisted development area. It was estimated that the redundancies pay off for 5500 could be £38 million. Turning the screw, Maggie Thatcher refused to meet a delegation from Corby steelworkers and reaffirmed that the government would not intervene to save the doomed works.

Meantime, as if they hadn't suffered enough, Corby people were outraged by remarks from Kettering county councillor Bill Asprey who called Corby's workforce 'third rate, lazy and inefficient." Bill had heard of 'men taking sleeping bags to work, clocking in for nightshift and then going off to a club, reading books and playing games of darts and dominoes."

He later retracted his comments admitting that some of the stories were hearsay. Asprey was clearly a controversial character, shortly after these stinging comments he had a go at local members of the Tory party who he called "a bunch of old women." His angry comments followed his failure to be re-elected as treasurer of the St Michael's ward in Kettering, a post he'd held for the previous nine years.

On December 15th, the fight to save Corby was officially over when 2000 steelworkers voted for shutdown to begin and told union leaders to start negotiating for the best redundancy pay available. George McCart was disappointed, 'this only shows that sometimes money is more important than people. These men may get redundancy pay but we do not know whether they will all get jobs in the future."

The threat of a national strike became reality when the BSC offered a "derisory 2% pay increase" to its workers when they were asking for between 20% to 25%. 8000 steelworkers at Corby BSC forced closure for the first time in its history in support of 100 men who lost £5000 wages following union instructions to defy BSC management's decision to start the rundown of the plant, which was due to begin on January 1st.

Part Six

Keep the Candle Burning

1980s

Celebrations for Corby's 30th anniversary as a New Town were muted with the loss of the steelworks. Corby Development Corporation handing power over to the Commission for the New Towns and vowing to build new industrial estates and over 200 factory units over the next 12 years did little to lift the spirits.

The New Towns were planned under the powers of the New Towns Act 1946 to relocate populations in bombed-out housing following the Second World War. Stevenage, Crawley, Hemel Hempstead, Harlow, Newton Aycliffe, Peterlee, Welwyn Garden City, Hatfield, Basildon, Bracknell and Corby were selected.

It was clear that the traditional industries of steel, coal and shipbuilding were coming to the end of the line. The car industry, shoe and textile industries were going the same way. "Before long, the U.K. will become the biggest warehouse in the world" a despondent steelworker opined.

Following the collapse of talks over pay and productivity the first national steel strike for more than fifty years was inevitable. On January 2nd, the steelworkers walked out.

"We are being looked upon as the worst producing steel nation in Europe" stated Bill Sirs, 'the steel industry improved productivity by 8% last year and 7% the year before and members are angered at having their pay rises linked to fresh productivity deals."

Support for the strike from the doomed Corby steelworkers was tepid. Many couldn't understand the logic in going on strike for a pay rise when they knew they were going to be out of a job come the end of March. Despite the reluctance, flying pickets were organised to stop the movement of steel in the area at transport depots, railway stations and at the east coast ports of Boston and Kings Lynn. As the strike gathered momentum, action group ROSAC wound down its operation at a meeting held in Corby Labour Club. It was a solemn George McCart who came out with the memorable declaration, "Whether we like it or not, we have lost the battle. Unfounded allegations have been made against us and it is imperative we find the alligators amongst us."

Meanwhile, in *The Times*, British Leyland boss Sir Michael Edwards was having a go at Corby motorists for buying foreign cars. "Jobs are lost every day in Britain when a foreign car is bought. Thousands of BSC jobs are axed at Corby, yet half the cars driven in the town are foreign."

The rant received a mixed response. Datsun owner and Country & Western star Ray Brett was unrepentant. "Foreign cars are more reliable and economical. I disagree with Edwards" comments. It's nothing to do with steelworkers at BSC."

Geoff Peart of Clarke Road had a different view, "I agree with Edwards, if people did buy British our industries wouldn't be in the mess they are in now."

On the tenth day of the strike, 200 steelworkers left Corby by coach and in cars "to throw a network of barricades around vital supplies," with a warning from Corby Works director Harry Ford that "the strike could hit redundancy payments in Corby."

The statement was issued following rumours which had made workers worried about joining the strike. ISTC's John Cowling countered, "The statement is absolute rubbish. It is a disgrace that such a statement was made. All men of Corby Works will get their severance pay. It's an attempt by Ford to break the strike but it has been totally unsuccessful."

The reality of the situation kicked in, if it hadn't already, when the Glebe Coke Ovens closed on February 27th. 1500 redundancy notices went out. Come the end of March, steelworkers were offered another increase of 1% to take it to 15.5% which was enough for Bill Sirs to urge the men to go back to work.

Glebe Coke Ovens

Mick Skelton was indignant, "I'm amazed at the offer of just another 1%. I personally haven't been out on strike all this time for another 1%."

Help for striking steelworkers came from all quarters. The manager of Station Road Garage offered a 10% discount on fuel to all steelworkers. Various community centres around the town holding collections and arranging events to help struggling families included a weekly Frozen Food Sale, 24 Beefburgers for £1 and 5lb of streaky bacon for £2 at Corby Boating Lake. More bizarre was a scheme launched at the Focus Cinema by manager Martin Parry who revealed plans to screen x rated sex films at 10 o'clock in the mornings.

"Shows are aimed at Corby's unemployed," Martin explained. 'This is a new venture. We thought people might get fed up sitting at home with nothing to do. The first films are "Truck Stop Women" and "When Girls Undress". It'll be a £1 for the entertainment."

Well-intended or not, Martin's initiative soon attracted the wrath of Corby housewives. "Men of Corby don't need morning sex films. I can't believe they want this exotic entertainment." Also, "Alex can get wired into the garden if he's got nothin' else to do!" were just two of the more indignant quotes.

Corby stores were also suffering from the effects of the strike. "Some will have to close if the strike goes on for much longer," Corby Chamber of Commerce warned. 'things are really bad" said Jimmy Reid, manager of Franklins Furniture Store on Rockingham Road said, "I used to sell about six suites a week but now it's down to one."

Morale was on the wane but given a boost when Scottish mineworker's leader Mick McGahey pledged support of his members to steelworkers during a "Back the Steelmen" speech at Tresham College. McGahey, a life-long Communist Party member, urged steelworkers to "Support Labour and the trade union movement and stand together to fight for the future of your town. This is not a steel crisis. It is a crisis for every worker in British industry."

Defending their right to picket, Denis McBlain of the Plug Mill spoke out, "Strikers are always cast as the villains, trouble makers, accused of idleness. BSC are no exception to the accusations. People shouldn't get the idea we enjoy striking. Sure, we have a laugh on the picket line. We are all in the same boat and it draws you closer. The camaraderie is one of the best things to come out of being in a situation like this. But we want to go back to work as soon as possible."

Willie McCowatt of the EWSR told of how he spent 18 hours on the picket line in Sheffield and all he received was a paltry £2.50p. "That was the last time. I remember Mick Skelton telling us to stand in the middle of the road to force lorries to stop. So we did as Mick said and then this big articulated lorry comes along, and made it clear he had no intention of stopping. We had to dive out of the way! Bollocks to this, I thought."

Dennis Taylor, Fitter in the EWSR, said, "During the strike, both myself and my dad were out on picket duty. At that time I had a van and I used to travel to picket sites taking a van full of pickets with me. While doing picket duty I would stop at food manufacturing companies we would come across and ask to see a manager, explaining who I was and asking them if they would contribute products or offer it at a lower price.

If we were successful the food went towards the food parcels which were given to strikers and their families. I don't recall any of the companies who were approached refusing to help with donations of food.

I remember I superglued the locks on the admin building at the Works and nobody was able to gain access for hours, causing disruption to those workers who ignored the picket. The worst hit were those families who had all the adults in the household out on strike. I would always double the food parcels I delivered to those households. The steelworks closure affected tens of thousands of people and I believe there are people today who never recovered from it. Their fellow workers were their families, so socialising both in and out of work were the same people. Never again will this country see the rise and fall of integrated iron and steelworks all within the span of 50 years."

Pickets were sickened by an announcement in the Government's Budget that strikers' families were to have their social security entitlement slashed by £12 a week and BSC chiefs were to get rises of £340 a week. There was massive resentment against Prime Minister Margaret Thatcher's "terror tactics". Complaints that the original offer of 2% wage rise was a deliberate strike provocation. "Why then should they victimise young families by cutting down on social security payments?"

Dennis Taylor said, "It just shifts power into the hands of the bosses who can force strikes when they feel like it and make us suffer."

DJ and Save Our Steel Campaigner Dennis Taylor

As the strike entered its eighth week, rumours began to circle that support was crumbling as some men were thinking about going back to work. John Cowling's response, along with Peter Floody on the ISTC National executive, was to demand £2 million from steel union's funds to pay the steelworkers on strike.

After fourteen weeks, the steel strike was at an end. For Corby's steelworkers, it was all over. Tom McConnachie, future Mayor of Corby, regretted the strike, "It was all a waste of time, the plant was going to close anyway. There were complaints afterwards that people had lost money on their pensions."

Train driver Edwin Andrews said, "We had no money coming in for three months and we were all concerned about what we were going to do after the closure. I was broken hearted when it did close as I loved working there."

Blast furnaceman Jimmy Kane added, "People knew that regardless of what happened with the strike, they were going to be made redundant."

Kelvin Glendenning, leader of Corby Council, recalled, "It was very depressing because not only did the steelworks close but so did much of the surrounding subsidiary industries."

Many felt this was only the beginning. The signs were there, the whole of Corby Works would die in the 1980s. Patrick Foynes of the Rolling Mills lost £1700 through the strike, "It's alright for the tube workers, they've got a job to go back to. But I'm finished and that is that."

BSC claimed they were saving £13 million a week in wages while the strike was on - yet were still losing £18 million a week. The ISTC estimated the strike cost BSC £500 million whereas the dispute would have been avoided for less than £50 million.

A kick in the teeth for long term workers came with the news of a loophole in redundancy payments. Men with 40 years service taking home £3000 instead of £15,000 they were expecting. BSC claimed that men and women who reached retirement age by March 31st 1982 were excluded from lucrative severance pay packets. This only came to light when men from the Coke Ovens and Minerals collected their "golden handshakes".

Loco driver Jack Langley couldn't believe it, "We've been led to believe we'd collect a lot more than the £2226 I received."

Unions demanded action for the BSC to pay up. Corby MP Bill Homewood called for an adjournment debate in the House of Commons as support for the 600 workers grew. Any hope was dashed by Charles deVilliers the Chairman of BSC, "It would cost the company many thousands of pounds."

A temporary reprieve for the Corby Works came on April 2nd when workers agreed to go back to work to help BSC out of a crisis though 'trouble was expected" with steelworkers refusing to work with lorry drivers who had crossed the picket lines during the long strike. On April 21st, the last iron was tapped from No. 4 blast furnace and the next day, the last steel was produced at the BOS plant.

The reality of factory work, if jobs were available, would come as a culture shock for men who had worked in heavy industry for most of their lives.

Postman Andy Dickson was one who took advantage of a recruitment drive by Vauxhall Cars, "I was in the Coke Ovens, my job was on the Exhauster. I went straight to Vauxhalls in Luton. They had set up a recruiting office by the Main Gate in the Works. There was a bus with about fifty blokes travelling every day at first. They charged us £10 to go on the bus. Gradually many dropped out and we started hiring a minibus. Then it was down to a few cars before everybody jacked it in. I was there for three years. I then got a job making Barbecue pots for six months, moved on to another company called Pakraft and then the Post Office."

Fellow postman Craig Douglas explained, "It was a devastating blow. I was a steel erector with E.N. Wrights working in the Coke Ovens. I had four young kids and was out of work for six months before I got a job at Snakpack packing crisps."

Jim Wykes worked in the Coke Ovens and was later landlord of The Beeswing in Kettering. In between times he too gained employment at Corby Post Office. Jim recalled his memories of life in the Ovens, "Originally I worked in the ERW where the hours were pretty good, two shifts, every weekend off, but when I got married I needed to earn some extra cash and I was told that the steel side was the place to work, all the overtime I wanted. I got a transfer and what a difference in the working conditions!

The first job they gave you was basically shovelling up crap, coke that spilled out of the wagons, hoppers they were called. It was a thankless and tiresome task. The crazy thing as well, there was no protection for your eyes, mouth, whatever. You had to tie a scarf round your face! Talk about health and safety! The second day I was in the Coke Ovens the gaffer asked me if I wanted to stop on and he gave me the job of releasing a railway truck, one at a time from a line of about twenty, by taking the brake off so it would roll down to a section of track which was called a tipper. The tipper would lift the wagon up and empty the contents into the oven.

I was a bit nervous about this, never seen or done it before but the gaffer told me it was a piece of cake, 'don't worry about it" and I released the brake, the wagon began to roll and before I knew it, the whole lot of them started rolling. Whoever had parked these wagons had only put the brake on the front one! The wagons gathered speed, went racing on and ended up about half a mile away, near the West Gate! They had to get a diesel engine to bring them back! I was one of the more fortunate ones, getting a job with Royal Mail before deciding to go out on my own as a painter and decorator. That lasted a couple of years until I moved into the pub trade."

On receiving their redundancy payments, many cast aside their blues and reacted by going on a spending spree. "We never expected this," a delighted Garth Webster, Manager of Travelounge, admitted, "business is booming, travel agents are finding it hard to keep up."

On April 28th the National Front, whose rally call was "British Jobs For British Workers. Ban Foreign Imports," selected Corby for its annual St George's Day rally. NF organiser Martin Webster admitting, "There's a chance of recruiting more members in Corby."

The prospect provoked an outcry. Bill Homewood called for the Chief Constable to ban the march. "It's a recipe for disorder and violence.

Chairman of Wellingborough's Unity Against Racism Campaign, Dr Brian Silk, was appalled by the prospect, "Corby should be spared this insult."

Council chairman Peter Floody and the police urged people to stay at home. Police leave was cancelled throughout the Anglia area. Traders advised to shut up shop for the afternoon. On the day, eight coach loads of national front supporters from as far afield as London, Bristol and Manchester converged on the town, all directed to St James's Road where police searched the buses and frisked the occupants.

The Rally held a thirty-minute meeting on land adjacent to the Post Office in Lloyds Road before marching behind the National Front Drum Corps and headed for the Town Centre down Oakley Road. Crowds jeered and shouted anti- nazi slogans. The first real sign of trouble occurred when police fought to hold back angry counter demonstrators in Elizabeth Street. Police used riot shields as demonstrators threw eggs, bricks and beer cans. Martin Webster was punched in the eye and a constable was hit by an egg.

"Cracking shot," postman Ian Easton laughed. Police made fifty arrests.

Sporting a black eye, Martin Webster claimed the day had been a success. "We chose Corby because it's being murdered by foreign imports. It is a symbol of the country's problems."

John Cowling at the forefront during the NF march

On a brighter note, there's always something that comes along that provides some light relief. One such occasion occurred at Corby Stardust Centre during a "Wrestling Night" when local wrestler and steelworker Tony Rowney was fighting Rushden's Ken Joyce and kneed him in the balls. Tony was disqualified, and left the ring to a chorus of boos, pursued by angry wrestling fans, including the obligatory "granny" who belted him over the head with her walking stick. She was bundled away by stewards and then complained she had lost the rubber from the end of her stick.

Stardust manager Arthur Pitcher was bemused by the incident, "We usually get some crowd trouble, but this is a first! In a few weeks we have Japanese wrestler Yasi Fuji here - and the last time he was here he poked a spectator in the eye. We will have to have another look at our public liability insurance policy before that event."

The myth that was "WonderWorld" lifted spirits temporarily, perhaps that was its only intention as hundreds of firms capitalised on the free Enterprize Zone so heralded by the Council as the major success story of Corby. Companies poured into the town, basking in the glow of the 'saviours" and recruiting former steelworkers to their ranks. The reality was that they were coming to Corby on the cheap, moving into virtually rent-free premises, offering piss poor wages and the opportunity to work as many hours as you could want, at a bare rate.

Initially, the redundant steelworkers were content to enjoy themselves, spending their cash on new furniture, televisions, cars, a holiday. "Living for today" was the mantra. Underlying this though was the fear that gaining employment and especially that with good pay and prospects was going to be at a minimum. Some were lucky to walk straight into another job with the Post Office.

Clive Smith explained, "If this was received with some reservations from the posties, eating up the overtime of which we all relied on to get a half decent take home pay, the fears were soon allayed when the news, genuine this time, came through that a major company was coming to town which would create employment for hundreds if not thousands. And by association, for the Royal Mail as well. R.S. Components, an Industrial and Electrical supplier of components and tools with over 130,000 products depended on the Royal Mail to collect and deliver their goods, thousands of items on a guaranteed next-day delivery contract, Datapost, as well as ordinary packets, parcels and, of course, mail. Wondering where the next slice of 'docket' was going to come from at the Corby Sorting Office soon evaporated when R.S. was up and running. Overtime was coming out of our ears! This was on top of the extra jobs created to handle the overwhelming deluge of work. R.S. stepped into the breach and saved the town from complete disaster."

Steelworkers were willing to work anywhere basically, as long as they were employed and not thrown on the scrapheap. The fact that the majority of them had their wages boosted by 'severance pay' for a year or two was a huge bonus for the employers.

Employees of contractors E. N. Wright, H. B. Pearce's, Shanks and McEwans all benefited from the severance pay. Unfortunately, those working for PED were less lucky, deemed to be "only temporary" in the "Works" they missed out on the payments. Such was the feeling of being "brushed off" the men from PED carried their fight all the way to the House of Commons. It was to no avail and left a bitter taste.

If you believed everything you read in the newspapers, WonderWorld was going to be the saviour of the town if not indeed, the whole of Northamptonshire. The announcement of a theme park to rival that of Disneyworld was being proposed on the soon to be derelict British Steel site, providing an estimated 8,000 jobs.

The WonderWorld promise was, "For everyone, everything wonderful in a world of its own." The propaganda machine went into overdrive with an exhibition at the local council building displaying models, articles in the Evening Telegraph and glossy pamphlets.

"WonderWorld, an idea proposed by Group Five Holdings Limited, promises a theme park that goes beyond the root purpose of entertainment to add thoughts upon existence and education. It is to be a kind of edutainment resort that will at once impress and blend in with the local countryside. The heart of WonderWorld will exist within a massive, enclosed environment where the widest variety of attractions can be housed, themed in history, folklore, fairy tales and the future. It will be a massive project spread over a decade or more of development, starting in early 1983 with land clearance, construction, services, utilities, staff and more besides. The whole project will use only leading specialists in all required fields guaranteeing the highest possible standards. It will involve schools, old people, families, local companies - the whole community."

Quotes from the Leader of Corby District Council, Kelvin Glendenning, and the Right Honourable Sir John Eden MP, proclaimed the opportunities for employment, building the community and offering unsurpassed facilities. TV personalities including botanist David Bellamy and golfer Jack Nicklaus had their names associated with different aspects of the project.

Attractions would include a ride through an enormous Pythonesque body, starting in a pool of lime green soup and travelling aboard an enormous pork sausage. Yes, you couldn't make this up. Could be that this was where the idea for I'm A Celebrity Get Me Out of Here was thought of!

Hands-on entertainment in the world of film-making and craft displays. An invitation to the Butterfly Ball, which was a great themed party event filled with costumed fairy tale participants. The Jack Nicklaus master class golf simulator which was to take advantage of the cutting-edge motion technology of the time with a full 18-hole golf course that spanned the full length of the WonderWorld location. A World War II flight simulator allowing visitors to take the pilot seat of a fighter amidst the Battle of Britain. Space age facilities, such as a massive, domed Communications Centre. The Lost Village of Rhyme, which was a gathering of fairy tale and nursery rhyme sourced buildings, including a teapot house, a liquorice-roofed corner shop and bookshelf-shaped library. A massive open air concert arena styled to look like one of the Martian tripods from Jeff Wayne's "War of the World" all blended into the surrounding countryside. The description created a vision of glass and metal fused with the countryside. It was an incredible project that excited the whole community, well some people anyway, and promised not only a feast for the eyes but a hands-on world of participatory entertainment as well.

It did sound "out of this world" but scepticism towards this sort of enterprise has never been in short supply, particularly in Corby, and right from the beginning doubts and laughter was the reception this project received. As the venture dragged on, it was with amusement when a huge billboard erected on the site depicting the sign WonderWorld, which was supposed to be a signal to passers-by on the nearby Weldon Road that all was going as planned, someone had scrawled out the "World" and substituted it with When? indicating that most people regarded the whole charade as a load of balls and fantasy.

New Horizons

As is often said, everyone remembers where they were when they heard Elvis Presley had died in '77, JFK in '63. Maybe Martin Luther King in '68. In December 1980 you could add John Lennon to the list after he was assassinated outside his apartment in New York City. His death reverberated around the world. A dagger through the heart as it felt like another part of our youth was taken away.

Clive Smith said, "I visited the Dakota Building, scene of John's demise, in 2018, as much out of curiosity as well as paying homage. It was a strange feeling standing there thinking back to when I heard the news. I was driving a Royal Mail lorry at the time, and I couldn't resist approaching the two doormen idly chatting away. "This is where John was shot?" I asked, thinking immediately that this was a gormless thing to say! They looked at me, both with that look on their faces, obviously thinking "another dickhead…"

Lennon was joined by AC/DC singer Bon Scott and Led Zeppelin drummer John Bonham for the big gig in the sky this year. Earlier, in January, John's old Beatles buddy Paul McCartney was in the news when he was arrested at Tokyo International Airport for possession of marijuana. What John thought of that is anyone's guess. Looked like Paul's career was going to pot. He was imprisoned for nine days before being deported.

As if this wasn't enough for us baby boomers to digest, the ship that housed the fabled pirate station Radio Caroline, the

MV Mi Amigo, sank off the coast of England after a "battering in gale force seas."

It all had the feeling of the end of an era and to kick it further into touch, a genre emerged labelled "New Wave" with Spandau Ballet, Duran Duran, Human League, Depeche Mode, Adam and the Ants in the vanguard.

For those less than enamoured with what was also labelled the "New Romantics," the "wave" would ebb in the 90s with the arrival of the Manchester, or "Madchester" scene. The "Britpop" of Oasis, Blur, Pulp, the "boy" and "girl bands," Take That and Spice Girls. Along with the Stock, Waterman and Aitken's 'music Factory" dirge of Kylie, Rick Astley and X-Factor wannabes, it was a veritable bowl of tripe for the baby boomers brought up on Elvis, Beatles, Dylan and the Rolling Stones.

"Everyone to their own generation." Indeed.

During the 90s and 2000s, groups were still being formed in Corby. New "boys on the block" included bands with the grand monikers of Sack the Drummer, Sick On the bus, Theodore Green's Orange Machine, Little Green Men, The Inline, Prisoner, and Raging Speedhorn, who unbelievably achieved worldwide fame with a number of 'thrash Metal" albums, playing Wembley Arena, Ozzy Osbourne's Milton Keynes OzFest, the National Indoor Arena at Birmingham, the Texas Rock Festival at Austin, the Donington and Reading festivals, touring Europe, America, Japan.

Not bad for the boys who started out as Sect and The Box playing Franny Lagan's Nags Head gigs in the mid-90s. Frank Regan, Gareth Smith, Darren Smith, Gordon Morison and brothers Tony and John Loughlan, like Energy before them, had an unbelievable ten-year career.

Speedhorn's first official gig happened to be at the Rockingham Arms, which was memorable for a transit van being torched outside in the car park. A distraction it may have been but the Horn showed their mettle and played on. As the years passed, like most bands, they would have a few changes in personnel along the way, which is par for the course, and their final gig came on November 30th 2008 at the Club Squad, Yamaguchi, Tokyo.

Frank Regan and Gordon Morison reformed the band with some new guys a few years later and continue to perform across the continent and play festivals to the present day. Gareth Smith emigrated to Sweden in 2002 where he remains with his wife Jenny and daughter Polly. After a brief go at semi-retirement he joined Stockholm band The Victims, a trio who had been touring the world for close on ten years like Speedhorn, and who were looking to expand their sound with a second guitarist. Gareth's first gig with them was a month-long tour of the United States.

The Victims ironically fell victim to the Covid pandemic in 2020, bringing an abrupt end to their career just as they were due to play gigs in Paris and Berlin. Gareth and drummer Andy Henrickson resurfaced in 2022 to form a band with a bunch of friends called A\\Void, playing a more jazz style which has been going down really well.

Returning to the guys who have been intrinsically involved in the sequel of books that have covered the local scene from the 50s to the 80s, the most prominent of them include Bip Wetherell who reformed 60s chart toppers The Tornados with original drummer Clem Cattini, a world-famous session drummer besides being a former Pirate with Johnny Kidd, and Tornado, in 1988. The Tornados played on for another 20 years, partaking in many "60s Golden Oldies" tours and shows around the continent, working on cruise ships, on one memorable occasion they met Buzz Aldrin, the second man on the moon, which was a massive thrill for helicopter pilot Bip.

"I told him we had something in common," Bip recalled with laughter.

Chrome Molly drummer Alistar Brodie was working for Engineering contractors PED at the time of the Corby steel closure and was feeling disillusioned, wondering which way his career was going to turn. Living in the West Country, Bristol way, he relived those troubling times when home in Corby in 2010. "With the Steelworks closing down and the uncertain future that thousands of people feared, there was a pall of doom lingering over the town that left a scar like a shadow on a lung. I applied for and got a job as a Welding Lecturer at Tresham College during which time I did a teacher's training course. After a couple of years an opportunity arose for a job with the Aramco Oil Company in Saudi so I decided to go for it and it was a move I would never regret. Though I had an eye opener as soon I arrived there. I had to go to the main administration building in Dhahran to get my travel documents and was told by a Saudi National to leave my suitcase at the bus stop which was quite some distance from where I had to go."

"Don't worry about it, nobody steals anything here," I was informed, 'the penalty if found guilty of theft is designed to discourage the thief from doing it again, it's off with the right hand, quite literally!"

Saudi, of course, is also a dry state, violating the laws can have consequences unimagined, as some have found to their cost. A Scottish acquaintance of mine ended up in jail for drinking the amber nectar and I visited him with my workmates. The conditions were awful, no meals, no comforts. The cells were just little square rooms with a mattress on the floor and a bucket in the corner for toilet and no air conditioning. Normally in such circumstances, the inmate's company provides what meals and necessities they can, if they don't, they have to scrounge from other inmates."

Alistair lived in Saudi Arabia for a number of years, though it wasn't all fun and laughter down the line, he suffered a serious injury when he jarred his back during a marathon run and had screws in his spine to keep it together. He also found himself caught up in the 1991 Gulf War, "Dodging scud missiles to deliver a truck load of Pepsi cola and packs of cold ice to the U.S. troops."

The United States deployed thousands of soldiers to the Gulf and in particular, Saudi Arabia which was under as real a threat of invasion as its neighbour Kuwait. Alistair and his pals had joined up with the British Volunteers Force 'to aid in any way we could," leading to the escapade which gave them an insight into what life was like on the front line.

"We were aiding the crack U.S. 82nd Regiment in their efforts to thwart the threat of the Iraqi dictator Saddam Hussein. It was scary," Alistair said with understatement. "A couple of scuds dropped nearby to our compound and there was a genuine fear of invasion all the time. Though I did manage to salvage some shrapnel and turn them into mementoes which now adorn my walls.

"The heat was awful and there was little refreshment for the troops. We left at dusk one night and drove for several hours into the desert. It was pitch-black and all we could see was the stars. When we arrived with the 'mobile oasis' at what we thought was the designated rendezvous, we alighted from the truck to stretch our legs and immediately froze with fear when a voice broke the eerie silence. "Who are you?"

I was trembling. "We're from the British Volunteers Force and we've got a truck load of Pepsi Cola and ice."

The reply was equally as menacing. "You better not be messing with me, man."

Suddenly, we were surrounded by all these soldiers with Kelvar helmets and desert fatigues. They took off their helmets and filled them with ice and helped themselves to the Pepsi. It didn't take long for them to empty the trucks. What was scary was that we hadn't seen a thing, yet they had been all around us.

Back at base, the cordiality continued as the 82nds used the BV camp's facilities and Alistair and his buddies repaired tank machine guns and supplied plastic ties to be used as handcuffs in anticipation of taking Iraqi prisoners, should they invade. Telecommunication links were also set up for the soldiers to phone home from the base, though it was under strict control. The soldiers weren't allowed to say where they were, where they had been or where they were going.

Alistair said, "It was basically to enable them to contact their folks at home to let them know they were alright. They had to change into civvies, which we provided and they were only allowed in at six at a time, and only on a certain night."

In return for their hospitality, Alistair and his chums were taken on a trip to witness a 'live fire," a practice range where the troops simulated an attack on an Iraqi base. Live "ammo" was used and they witnessed a demonstration on how to repel an Iraqi tank by piercing the armour plating with a TOW missile, which vaporised the vehicle, sending the temperature soaring to thousands of degrees in a second, literally melting everything attached to it.

For their efforts, the boys were awarded a White Falcons medallion which Alistair proudly carried around with him. The coins are issued to the troops and have to be presented when confronted, particularly in the field. A lack of response to "Where's your coin?" could be seen as detrimental to your health.

Before the sojourn in the Middle East was interrupted by Saddam, Alistair had been settling down to his new life very well, helped considerably by the discovery of an "almost complete drum kit" in the company's Mess Hall. "It was a Ludwig set as well, superb. I got hold of some sticks and formed a trio with a Scottish guitarist and a Welsh accordionist. It was terrific fun. One night we even got hold of a girl singer and smuggled her into the camp because women weren't allowed out. The place went mad. The workers who were mainly Filipinos and Thais who hadn't seen a hint of a woman's leg in years!

Back home, many of Alistair's musician pals were still on the road. Jack Stewart, Tommy Smith and Bob McAuslen in The Tartan Combo played throughout the East Midlands and the USAF bases.

Carousel, featuring Campbell Baxter, John Hanvey and Laura Handyside played at the Wembley International Festival of Country Music, appearing alongside country legends, Tammy Wynette, Crystal Gayle and Emmylou Harris. They won through to the finals of the "Britain Country and Western Best New Acts" festival at Wembley where Campbell later complained strongly after the event, "I noticed they were counting the votes while we were still playing! Talk about a stitch up, I told the organisers exactly what I thought."

Campbell Baxter was born in 1941 at 16 Ollis Close, Corby. Went to London and returned when he was 15 to begin an apprenticeship as a mechanic at Blanchflowers in Kettering earning £1.92d a week. Having been around since the early 60s in various bands he formed Campbell's Country in 1971 with Kettering musicians Dave Anderson on lead guitar, Dave Bryant on drums and Nicky Evans on bass guitar.

"We were semi-pro, we all had jobs, I was manager of the stores at Stockwood Motors at the time. Dave Anderson came up with the name for the band, a play on the film and book by Hammond Innes, Campbell's Kingdom. We went full-time in 1973 as a backing group to Patsy Montana, the first woman to sell a million records with "I Want To Be A Cowboy's Sweetheart" released in 1935. An album was recorded along with Patsy's daughter Judy Rose in 1976 called "Mum And Me Visit Campbell's Country", the liner notes written by Gene Autry. The record was released on Luke Records."

Campbell's Country

Campbell's Country split shortly afterwards and reformed again with Dave Anderson on lead and steel guitar, Mick Bembridge piano, Chris Page drums and John Fellows bass in 1983, and became "one of most sought-after professional Country and Western acts in Britain" with Festivals at Peterborough, Harlow, the Isle of Wight and Pontins in Somerset. Dave Anderson was well pleased, "We are in the very happy and enviable position of having to turn down work. Since we reformed we haven't looked back. We had to turn full-time as it was impossible keep our full-time jobs. But we're not complaining, its hectic but we're enjoying every minute of it."

The band recorded and released a single "Cotton Eye Joe" at Derek Tompkins studio in 1987.

Another Corby stalwart, banjo player Joe McIlvenney, was still going strong as we headed into the 90s, playing with Bluegrass/Folk trio The Old Grey Dogs, which also featured Barry Ford mandolin and Bob McLean guitar. They had been around for a number of years on the folk circuit.

Joe McIlvenney

Joe explained, "I started out in the folk clubs back in the very early 70s playing mostly Donovan and Dylan stuff on guitar. the banjo entered my life at this point - I heard one being played and the guy was actually selling it for eleven pounds. I bought it. I was sold! And it was goodbye to the guitar. I then bought my first Bill Monroe record and set about listening intently to Earl Scrugg's magic being spun. In those days books were spar sew and needed ordering from the local music shop. the two available were Earls book and the Pete Seeger book. I bought both.

Learning from Earl's book was inspiring and I recall at the end of each exercise he wrote "x1000" that was the amount of time I played each lick to get it best I could. Things were going as well as possible for me. I had only my records to compare myself with… I knew no other player close to me and there was no social media back then! I saved really hard and bought a Shergold banjo. It was wonderful. I also remember my father taking me to London and buying me a lovely Antonia EB250 copy, pure bliss.

My apprenticeship consisted of at least two hours every night in my bedroom. I strove really hard to become a good clean picker, using Cripple Creek and other such tunes as my guide. I would go to the local folk nights and play them with my good folk guitar friends helping me out. I wanted so bad to be good on this instrument, my soul was touched by its magical sound.

One night while visiting a folk club in a neighbouring town, I met Bill Forster, a real eureka moment. Bill played superbly and we became good friends. He told me of a festival that was just into its second year in the Peak District. Off we went, there was twenty of us at the most and for the first time I could compare my work with others. The people I met there are still my friends today."

A bio of Bill Forster tells us, "Bill is an Englishman living in the wilds of Clare on the west coast of Ireland. Exposed to Bluegrass music at an early age he developed his natural talent for playing with a passion. In addition to playing with his local band, the Harrison family band, he visited the States early in his career to immerse himself in the music. For over twenty years, Bill Forster has been "the" talent of the five-string banjo in the U.K. He can play flat out Scruggs style, melodic like Bill Keith, or in the more pyrotechnic modern style. Bill added his considerable Banjo prowess and musical influences to the Acme band sound in 1983. He is one of the most versatile of Banjo players covering a broad spectrum of styles in his playing which incorporates some fine classical pieces. He's much in demand in the UK in teaching and promoting Bluegrass."

At the time of the steelworks closure, Mick Ferguson was working in the Glebe Coke Ovens. He joined forces Derek Cowie to form Kez, a band put together for a gig in the Isle of Wight. Others recruited were bass player Jack Murphy, also on the redundancy list, from E.N. Wright's, Reggy Knowles on keyboards, drummer John Donovan and guitarist Chris Beesley.

They received this glowing report in the *Isle of Wight News*. "If it hadn't been for the Star Wars movie theme, I would have missed just about the best middle of the road group I have seen on the island. Having endured another marathon Sylvia Thorley Showcase at Cliff Tops, I prepared to slip away after well over three hours of rather contrasting fare. The exciting opening bars of my favourite space theme stopped me in my tracks and Kez did the rest.

Amazingly, the band has only been playing together for just three weeks. They drove down from Corby especially for the showcase and literally stole the evening with some beautifully tight and electrifying sounds that brought an instant buzz of excitement from those who had stayed the course. Unfortunately, some bookers and local musicians had already left. They don't know the treat they have missed. Kez play chart material, waltzes, quicksteps and also present a delightfully mixed bag that included "Feelings," "Music," "Love of My Life," "Cavatina" and, of course, "Star Wars".

In Mick Ferguson, they possess a singer of immense talent and class. Seldom have I ever seen such emotion from a group singer as he produced from Maurice Albert's gorgeous song "Feelings". The tears were streaming down his face. Pop singing at its best. At present, Kez are only a semi-pro outfit but in March, three of them, who are steelworkers, are being made redundant and then they hope to go full-time into the business.

The lads told me they'd love a summer season on the island, the only problem as far as I can see is where they would play. They seem ideal for establishments like Keats Inn but there aren't too many of them dotted around. Any of the big holiday camps would also be very suitable. Most of the band has been fully professional in the past, in different outfits, and some have worked on the continent. I certainly hope they summer on the island. If they do, I am certain they will also attract a huge local following."

Kez at Camber Sands

Mick said, "On the back of this, we secured a summer season at Pontins Holiday Camp on the south coast, which in the wake of the steel closure was welcome news. Playing six nights a week and four dinner times we were paid £460 a week, roughly £115 each, out of which we had to pay £22 for a chalet. We each had our own in a two-tier block. Changes were inevitable and Reggy and Chris left, Bob Grimley replaced Derek Cowie who acquired a job in Australia and then two weeks into the season, Big Jack threw in the towel!

Temporarily in the lurch, I put an advertisement in Melody Maker for a bass player and a guy from Bristol applied. As he didn't have the means of getting to Pontins I made the 450-mile round trip myself to pick him up. I should have saved my time, the bloke was awful! That bad I wished a big hole would open up on stage so we could disappear! I took him back and told him, "Don't call us." When I returned, I was told a feller from Chester was on his way down to audition. Owen Ricketts was his name. And he was brilliant!

We had a great time socialising with the punters. Bob locked himself out of his chalet one night and made a terrible racket trying to get in. Woke everyone up, this was about half three in the morning. His chalet was on the left down this corridor and after trying to barge his way in, he decided to lean back against the door behind him and push his door with his foot. Well, all hell was then let loose as the door he was leaning on crashed open and Bob went sprawling into this chambermaid's bedroom! The girl was terrified! I became friendly with a couple who lived in Essex and they invited me over for a break whenever I had the time. Which I accepted.

Funny thing was whenever I went over there, the husband was always away! He didn't seem to mind though. At the end of the summer season we called it a day, finished on the spot. Owen went back to Chester and was never seen or heard of since. The rest of us went home to Corby to pick up from where we had left off. Redundant. I was given a couple of options on our return to Corby, one was to rejoin the Roy Bishop band and the other was an offer from a Peterborough showband. It was then my old mate Derek Cowie contacted me again with a proposal - to help him form a band to be called New Horizon. It was a band that would last for over 15 years."

Derek Cowie added, "I had spent three months working on a pipeline in Kalgoorlie near Perth in Australia. When I came home I wanted to get playing again and formed New Horizon with Mick, drummer John Donovan and bass player Jim Smith. It was one of the hardest working bands I ever played in, three, four, five nights a week."

Jim Smith said, "New Horizon was a band that worked throughout the 1980s with a core of musicians led by Mick who utilised any 'muso" that was available and over the years his line ups read like a Who's Who of the best of the local talent. Ricky Dodd had a spell with the band, somewhat inauspicious, he never lasted a gig! Always fell asleep in the lounge. Jimmy Gourlay who had started life as one of the Jack Knives vocal ensemble in the early 60s and often referred to the band as The Variations, an apt name if ever there was one. Alan Booth, Bip Wetherell, Roy Walker, Tony Paul, Joe McElvenney, Tim Richards, Bob and John Grimley all had a spell with the band."

Mick said, "One of the problems we had was the perennial lack of reliable transport, which I solved when I was working as an Insurance Salesman, my first 'proper' job after the steel closure. Walking down Chelveston Drive, I spotted this old British Telecom van parked up and decided to find out who's van it was. Taking the bull by the horns, I knocked a door and asked the guy if it was his van and if he was interested in selling it. To my surprise, he told me that he hadn't been intending to but as it had been vandalised, somebody had poured a bag of sugar into the engine, he said, "Give me £25 and you can have it." We did about four gigs to pay for it!

Jim Smith was a genius at fixing things up and he took it home, stripped the engine down, changed the carburettor, took the petrol tank off - and made a new one at work! He was a welder at Oxford Welders, Rothwell at the time. The new tank had two holes in the top, one for a big tube to go through the roof to let the fumes out. It was hooked up to the carburettor. And believe it or not, it worked a treat! Needless to say, the fuel gauge didn't work so Jim devised a method by dipping a piece of wood into the tank.

It worked a dream! Jim's expertise was called for again the night we were booked to play at Hitchin Football Club. About a mile from the club, the van's exhaust blew and made a hell of a racket. When we pulled up in the car park the punters were looking out the windows to see what all the noise was, it was that bad. Jim immediately went into the bar and ordered four pints of lager for the band - and asked for a tray to carry them on. "No probs," said the barman. It was the last time he saw the tray. Jim folded it in two and wrapped it round the exhaust, tied on with wire. It lasted for months!"

"We were regulars at Corby Grampian Club, mainly because we would play anything the punters wanted, rock and roll, country, waltzes. One night, I was looking at the 'Forthcoming Attractions' board where each individual section had their programme. I smiled to myself when I saw the name New Horizon spread right across the whole gamut. The bowls section, darts, dominoes, travel club."

New Horizon

Derek Cowie said, "A good laugh was the night Ray Haggart showed up. Ray had been out of Corby for years, living and working as a salesman in Stratford on Avon. His friend from the Crows Nest days, committeeman Charlie Smith announced that there was a very special guest appearing, 'Emile Ford from the USA!'

Ray came walking through the doors at the back of the hall, smiling and shaking everybody's hand as they cheered and clapped. We thought it was hilarious. He had almost everyone fooled. Ray was a great singer, full of panache."

Everybody fooled, except Grampian Saturday night regular George Bradshaw who used to be a neighbour of Ray's in Stevie Way! George stated, "I was in the toilet after Ray had finished his stint and my mate Tommy Dorrian came in and said, "he's some singer that Emile Ford!"

"Yeah, he's terrific," I replied, laughing my head off. Ray was always a right smooth feller, poser, a great bloke and singer.

Derek said, "Me and Mick also teamed up with drummer Pete Buckby for a sixteen-day trip to Jabeli, Dubai to play three gigs, one of which was on a Russian ship, with 600 nurses on board! Pete had stepped in at short notice for New Horizon when John Donovan left - and helped us land the New Years Eve booking in Dubai - and Mick to shed the shackles of his wife."

Mick added, "She hindered my career, every time I went out, which was regular, she did nothing but moan. She hated the music business. I was in bed when Pete phoned, it was 1.30 in the morning. The phone was above my head and initially I was speaking through the wrong end! "Speak up," I said.

When I realised it was Pete, I turned the phone round, and Pete came straight to the point. 'Listen," he said, "I want an answer right away. No ifs or buts or wherefores, it's yes or no. How do you fancy a 16-day trip to Dubai to play three gigs over New Year?" At first, I thought it was a wind up, gathered my senses, weighed it up and said yes. I didn't have a clue where Dubai was. Might have been next to Mablethorpe for all I knew!

Pete had received a call from his old Canned Rock buddy Don Maxwell. A contact in Dubai had tried to book Canned Rock for a gig, discovered they had finished and then asked Don if he could put a band together. The guy in Dubai was awaiting an answer.

So it was that Pete, Don Maxwell, Derek Cowie and I headed off for the sunny climes of the Middle East from a cold and miserable Gatwick Airport on December 28th."

How did Mick's long-suffering wife receive the news?

"She was lying next to me in bed when I was having this conversation with Pete and she told me that if I went through the door and off to Dubai, I needn't come back. So I went!"

His good lady had the last laugh though. On returning home, she'd cleared the house out and gone!

Derek Cowie said, "Flying to Dubai, we were sitting at the back of the plane having a bit of a sing song when some people ahead of us started grumbling. They'd probably been reading too many stories in the papers about Led Zeppelin and rock stars getting bladdered on flights. Mick got up and went to have a word with them. When he returned he told us he'd been talking to the owner of the aircraft! I said, "What would the owner of the plane be doing sitting at the back with everybody else!" Mick reckoned he'd ask the feller if he could go into the cockpit when we were coming into land so he could video it. "No problem," the guy said. Sure enough, just before we started descending, Mick goes up the front and videos the landing! We couldn't believe it."

Mick claimed, "A guy complained to the stewardess about the noise we were making and I went to apologise to him. I said, "Look, can I get you a drink?" A vodka and coke he said. I told the stewardess to make it a double. When he finished that I got him another one. By the time we had finished having a chat and he'd knocked back about four or five vodkas, he thought I was great bloke! He'd forgotten that the drinks on the aircraft were all free!

Regarding the video, I'd asked the stewardess if it was possible to visit the cockpit and she arranged it. The pilot was an American, nice guy. I told him that we both had something in common and when asked what that might be, I told him that I fly as well. Gliders. He showed me all the controls, lights, everything. One hell of a dashboard! He told me to get my video, sit next to the window but when we began the descent, everybody had to be quiet, no talking. I put the video on my shoulder, then one of my headphones over the mic to capture all the requests and orders from flight control. It was amazing. You could see the lights on the runway from about six miles. Tremendous experience which since the Twin Towers disaster on 9/11 would be impossible to do now."

Mick said, "We kicked the trip off playing on New Years Eve for all ex-pats in Jebu Ali, next night at the International Seaman's centre and then three nights later played in the poorer quarters for people who worked in the port. Filipinos, Indians, the ethnic community. It was a real eye opener. We were the only white people there. The people were great though and made us feel really welcome.

The Dubai trip was such a success we did it for the next three years. The flights were paid for, as was a chalet/villa for each of us. The equipment was all there for us. We took our own guitars and Pete took his sticks and cymbals. All we had to pay for was food and drink. And we were paid over a grand for the pleasure! One day we were sitting in a restaurant discussing the idea of hiring a car to do some sight-seeing when a feller overheard us and came over. He told us not to bother and if we were serious, he'd sort one out for us and have it at our door at 7.30 the next morning. True to his word, he dropped off a brand-new Range Rover! We were taken aback, "bit heavy on the petrol" was my first thought. Chipping in about a fiver each for petrol, we were amazed when it filled the tank up! It was only about 33p a gallon!

We played on a Russian hospital ship which was weird. Only one person on board could speak English. He was also a bass player with the ship's band. We used their gear and played for around three quarters of an hour, went really well. Then the Russian band did their spot and the bass player paid tribute to us by dedicating an Elton John song to us. It was 'Nikita'. Sung in English by Russians who didn't have a clue what they were singing! That was strange.

Though not half as much as that of a barmaid I had my eye on! I told Derek that before the end of the night, I'd be off with her. I bought her drinks, chatted her up and then she opened her mouth. It was full of gold teeth! Christ! We called her Klondike Kate after that. That first trip was when we encountered our compatriots from Corby, Energy. Their drummer, Chris Page, asked me to do him a favour by taking £450 home to give to his partner, Jane. It was easier and cheaper than telexing it which would have cost him around £30. Good job he trusted me!"

Energy 1980

Energy's decision to "give up the day job" just as the unemployment figures were set to rocket had been a brave one, but who could blame them for taking the chance? For the four lads, some far reaching horizons and exciting times were ahead of them, and their share of embarrassing moments, as guitarist Iain Wetherell admitted.

He said, "We played a venue in Peterborough when during the AC/DC number 'Whole Lotta Rosie', Bozzy jumped up in the air too much in the same place and eventually the boards on the stage gave way. He went straight through it! Corby Civic was another cringe maker. Flapper (Steve Fulton) did his usual routine of jumping off the stage and running around the hall, singing and whipping up the fever. He ran back to the stage and couldn't get back up! The Civic stage was a bit higher than most of the others. He had to sheepishly walk to the side and got back on via the stairs. Everybody took the piss out of him as you'd expect in Corby! We used to have an intro, 'Thunderbirds 54321' till one day we decided to change it to an air siren. Unfortunately, the first time we used it was at an air base, and it caused a panic as they thought it was an air raid! A red alert! They weren't amused."

"In 1984 we secured a deal with Nigel Gray, who had seen us play at the Ad Lib Club, London. Nigel was the producer of the first three Police albums and 'Message In A Bottle' and 'Roxanne". We'd sent him a demo tape, he liked it and offered us the use of his 24-track recording studio for free. We demoed all our songs in the same studios The Police had used which had a big impact on me as I was even then, interested in the recording and producing side of the business. A showcase was arranged for us at the famous Marquee Club in Wardour Street, home of the British blues in the 60's. Three coach loads of our fans travelled down to support us. Unfortunately, none of the invited Record Companies bothered to turn up. This soured our relationship with Nigel. We were disappointed and disillusioned but later on we realised it was typical, it wasn't particularly Nigel's fault, it's just the MUSIC BUSINESS!!"

Despite what some may have felt was a setback, Energy continued to tour the UK, Europe and the Middle East where a trip to Dubai, lasting six months, netted the band £11,000 which gave them the opportunity to take a stab at America.

Energy

Iain said, "We thought Dubai was a dry state and a typical Middle eastern country, women in veils etc. On the plane journey there, we decided to make the most of it and got rat arsed drinking bottles of wine. This was going to be our last drink for nine weeks! Then we discovered everybody was pissed! The women were all wearing miniskirts, right up their arses! It was unbelievable. We played at a five-star hotel, where there was a Rolls Royce in the foyer which was a raffle prize! Which was something of an eye opener. I mean, you don't see that sort of thing in England. We played for an hour a night, and the way we performed it was hard to work in that heat! Bip came out for a visit, told us that with all the spare time on our hands, we should be concentrating and doing some writing instead of just holidaying. He basically gave us a kick up the backsides."

Boz added, "I was suffering with my ears in Dubai and went on board a Royal Navy ship to have them syringed. They pulled out a solid piece of wax the size of a peanut. And I suddenly realised I could hear the fan in the ceiling whizzing around. Back on stage, the volume of the band amazed me. It was deafening!"

In New York, Energy discovered, quite coincidently, a "Showcase for Talent" at the Marriott Hotel in Times Square, within walking distance of Broadway, Fifth Avenue, Central Park, Carnegie Hall and the Empire State Building.

Iain said, "We took part in a cavernous auditorium, it was scary, the first two rows were occupied by these music people who we had to impress. It was the scariest gig I ever did. It was so sterile and the atmosphere was zilch. Gigs are all about atmosphere and this wasn't going to be achieved in this situation. Despite not giving our best, we met up with a guy who was very keen to become our manager and he arranged a few gigs for us in New York and the West Coast to play at the famous Whisky A Go Go in Los Angeles amongst other venues. That was terrific but by this time Mark Stewart was becoming restless, and admitted he'd had enough of the travelling. On our return he decided to quit. Chris Page took over on the drums."

Page had played with a number of local bands including Buzzard, Mystik and Vision to name but three.

Buzzard featuring Jimmy Cave

Chris said, "I got into the drums thanks to my brother Barry who was a friend of Johnny Robson, drummer with local band Legal Matter. Johnny used to set his drums up in our house, and when they went out I used to get on the kit and have a bash around. I was only three or something! My first set of drums was when I was aged 15, a mix of snare, bass and Toms. I sold my chopper bike to get these and Ned McGuigan, former Blueswailer, Magic Roundabout and Sasperella drummer, gave me a cymbal.

My influences back then were Johnny Heron and Jim Muircroft, both great local drummers. Also, Pete Buckby and Billy Mathieson. I was a Led Zeppelin and Deep Purple fan and John Bonham and Ian Paice were my idols. Jam sessions at the Nags in Corby were my first gigs, playing with the Grimleys and Johnny Heron and company. It was Bip who gave me the opportunity to sit in with these guys. He saw me in the room, knew I was only 16 and shouted, "What you doin' here?!" I said "You should know, you served me a pint in here" It was all in jest and that's how I came to play my first ever gig!

My first gigs out of Corby came with Mystik, a band comprising Harry Thomas on bass, John Dolby and Derek Cowie on guitars. We worked up in the north east a lot, Middlesbrough and places, the main memory I have though is being designated to share a room with Harry, me being the youngest as it turned out. Derek and John knew what they were doing! Harry had a terrible habit of crunching his teeth when he was sleeping. Sounded like squealing, I wondered what the hell it was! I hardly slept a wink.

Another gig was when I sat in with The Headboys, Stuart Wetherell's band. We had a few gigs in France which was memorable for us stopping one time at a filling station, and Stuart got out to pay for the fuel and have a leak. The rest of us decided it was a good time to clean the van. It was full of rubbish, papers, plastic cups, cans. We emptied it all in a bin. Stuart came back and was astonished to see the car so clean. "What's happened?" he asked. We told him we'd cleaned up, and he went over to the bin, returned with it, and emptied the contents back in the van. "Nothing gets cleaned up until we get back home!" he said.

With Buzzard, I was playing with Jimmy Cave whose son Leon now plays with Status Quo. When Quo played in Bournemouth, near where I've lived since 2006, Weymouth, Leon gave me hospitality tickets for the show."

Having got over the disappointment with the Nigel Gray affair, Energy were back in the studio during 1986, recording a self-penned single 'Radio Radio'. Described later as an "unashamedly poppy song which Energy would rather disown now!"

"It was a stab at being commercial," said Iain. "It's a good pop song but not really our style."

'Radio Radio' did get airplay on Radio One, albeit, in the form of a jingle! But the single did get a lot of airplay on UAE Radio Dubai FM92.

Chris said, "It was phenomenal, when we were out there last time we went to buy a Hi Fi and our song was actually on the radio when we put it on. What I also remember is being in a bar with Flapper when we were playing in Abi Dabai and we started talking in a Kettering accent, we'd had a drink! We'd got rat arsed in there the day before, drinking Jagermeister. They called it a Bamber. 'Starter for ten!'

Anyway, it started with me asking Flapper, "Where you goin' sarternoon m'duck? and such things." The barman was listening and asked us where we came from. We told him Corby. "Ah!" he said, "I'm from Higham Ferrers! Didn't expect that. All the way over in the Middle East and you come across a guy that's half hour away from Corby! Small world." Think he realised we were taking the piss though!"

Chris Page

Early in 1988, Energy were interviewed by Adam Coulter for a feature in the *Weekend* magazine, "Could 1988 be the year when Energy will really make it big? They've now got their dream set on wider horizons."

Steve Fulton (Flapper) said, "In the two years since Chris has been in the band, everything has been good. Confidence has been at an all-time high."

So what happened in the other nine years? Eleven years is, after all, a long-time without a major breakthrough.

Steve said, "The first five years you can just cancel out because we all had full-time jobs. You can also cancel out the first two years after turning professional. A few things weren't right in the old band. Mark was not enjoying it."

"So what is Energy's style?" asked Adam Coulter.

Chris Page said, "Queen's a big influence, and then you've got individual influences, John Bonham of Zeppelin."

Iain added, "I think Zeppelin definitely, and Brian May, Hendrix, Clapton, Jimmy Page. I think there are Police influences as well."

Bozzy suggested, "AC/DC."

Adam Coulter said, "Steve now believes they made a mistake of writing songs for commercial reasons. We now feel we're going to write songs which either appeal to us or that we want to do."

One such song is 'Dream the Dream', a ballad which the band are particularly proud of and feel may lead to major commercial success. The aim is to go to the United States and play several venues there with emphasis on the single. If it goes down well Stateside the band will turn their energies towards the British market and hope for success. It's a ploy used first by The Police with their single 'Roxanne'.

Unfortunately, the striving for success and recognition, at home and abroad, eventually turned to disillusionment, "Dream to Dream" proved to be, for like so many before, and afterwards, just that.

Iain said, "We all decided to call it a day."

Boz continued, "The dread of having to get a 'real' job raised its ugly head and it's when I started my own wheelie bin cleaning business."

Iain was devastated as the band was all he had known for over a decade but his talent for recording was noticed by his brother Bip who was in the process of setting up Premier Studios. Bip recruited him for the job "behind the desk" where his years of experience and perfectionist attitude quickly saw him inundated with recording projects and Premier Studios rapidly gained a reputation to qualify its name.

Energy would reunite, "for a one-off gig" in 2002, playing at the Corby Pole Fair, on the back of a lorry in the middle of the roundabout between the Cardigan Arms and what was the Old White Horse. Thousands turned out on the hot summers day to recall some great memories when following the band in their heyday. In a unique kind of way, Energy can claim a piece of history as being the only band to have appeared at two Corby Pole Fairs, having played on the Nags Head roof during the 1982 event.

Chris Page joined Campbell's Country with whom he'd play for the next dozen years or so before heading south to reunite with his cousin, former Little Green Men drummer Ricky Stevenson who had settled in Weymouth, Dorset.

"I went to visit Ricky, thought Weymouth was a real nice place, and I never came back!" Chis recalled. "There was plenty of work down there, music wise, and I sat in with a number of bands. One included session guitarist Chris Spedding of "motorbikin'" fame and Andy Fraser the former Free bass player. When that ran its course I was approached to replace Ginger Baker's son Kofi in a tribute band called Sons of Cream. Jack Bruce's son Malcolm was on bass and Eric Clapton's nephew Will Johns was on guitar. Will was the son of Andy Johns, famous record producer who worked on the Stones' "Exile In Main Street", The Free's "Heartbreaker" and countless other albums. We went out as Fresh Cream, named after Cream's debut album in 1966.

Cream were a 1960's British Rock Super group power trio with guitarist and singer Eric Clapton, bassist and singer Jack Bruce and drummer Ginger Baker. With 15 million albums sold worldwide, their music included songs based on traditional blues such as "Crossroads" and "Spoonful".

A bio released to publicise the band commented, "Get ready to rock out with tribute band Fresh Cream. They bring the sound of 1960s icons Cream back to life. And they do it with all the aplomb, gusto and brilliance that you'd expect. They will be playing hits such as "Sunshine of Your Love", "White Room", "Spoonful" and many others. This respectful tribute to the world's greatest power trio enables Malcolm Bruce & Will Johns to take a break from their own respective careers as original artists to perform this incredible music from their fathers' era.

The highly-acclaimed Chris Page joins them on drums. "We definitely are making this our own. It would be pointless to me to simply ape the material. They cannot be matched within what they did," said Peter Bruce. 'so we simply play and interpret and hope to capture the spirit of the music, and I think we do something rather special with it in our own way."

Will Johns's other uncles also include George Harrison and Mick Fleetwood, of Fleetwood Mac.

Chris Page has been a professional drummer for all of his adult life. He is accomplished in all styles and has played all over Europe, Japan, the Middle East and the States. He has played for numerous Blues artists such as Big Bill Morganfields, Eddie Kirkland, Ben Waters, Phil Guy and The Colin John Band to name but a few.

Ashes To Ashes

The road to recovery had to start somewhere with unemployment in the UK hitting a 44 year high of somewhere near 1.9 million. Corby steelworkers joining the national strike in support of their fellow comrades at Bilston in the West Midlands must surely have been asking themselves, "What was the point?"

The demise of Corby's steelworks was all but complete just months before the Blast Furnaces at Bilston Steelworks were demolished.

The demolition of Corby Works, spread over 680 acres, left the feeling of desolation, as described later in the *Financial Times*. "In the early 1980s, Corby became the grim face of Britain's unemployment crisis after the decline of the steel industry that had long sustained it cost thousands their jobs."

Councillor Peter McGowan reflected, "The skyline was dominated by the black smell of soot, smoke, the lights, the smell. There was the feeling of devastation throughout the town. People couldn't talk about anything else, people couldn't think about anything else."

Support came from far and wide, including an album 'Steeltown' by Scottish band Big Country who'd had hits with "Chance", "Look Away" and "In A Big Country". Singer/guitarist for the Dunfermline-based band, Stuart Adamson, had no connection with Corby as far as I can gather, but felt for his patriots in exile and dedicated this album to all those who had emigrated from north of the border in the early days and who were now having to contemplate returning home.

"Steeltown, recorded at ABBA's Polar Studios in Stockholm, was written about the town of Corby, telling of how many Scots went to work at the Stewarts & Lloyds steelworks when it opened in 1935 at the height of the Great Depression, but later found themselves unemployed when the steelworks declined in the early 1980s." (*Wikipedia*)

More support came from The Clash who released their third album 'London's Calling' in December 1979, the same month when the fate of Corby was sealed. On the face of it, 'London's Calling' had nothing to do with Corby or its steelworks but the town's fate was brought to the attention following a "clash" between The Clash and Radio One disc jockey Annie Nightingale in a national music paper.

'London's Calling', written by guitarist Joe Strummer, was a track highlighting the threat of environmental catastrophe amid the economic malaise at the end of the 1970s. The chorus references the sensationalist tabloid headlines of the day, which carried news of possible harvest failures, flooding, oil running out and the "nuclear error" of Three Mile Island, when a partial meltdown occurred at a Pennsylvanian nuclear power station in March 1979.

Joe Strummer explained to Melody Maker, "I read about ten news reports in one day calling down all variety of plagues on us. There was a lot of Cold War nonsense going on, and we knew that London was susceptible to flooding. My girlfriend told me to write something about that. Hence, the line "London is drowning and I live by the river."

The track reached No. 11 in the UK charts, a significant achievement because The Clash refused to appear on BBC's Top Of The Pops, which was a necessity to break into the Top Ten for all but the most successful and well-known artists. Strummer knew this and, despite a favourable critical reaction, doubted it would make the Top Ten.

Annie Nightingale was so confident that it would she wagered a Cadillac with Joe. She said, "I was astounded by how good it was. I said to Joe Strummer, that's a Top 10 record. He said, "No, it isn't. I bet you a Cadillac it won't go Top 10." I took the bet and the track went to Number 11. Not unreasonably, I thought 'Right, next week it'll break into the Top Ten."

However, the following week it dropped to 15th and then to 20th the following week, I had lost the wager! I was horrified! Now I'm thinking, "How on earth am I going to get them a bloody Cadillac!" Thankfully, a kindly listener phoned in to my show and said he would spare my blushes! It turned out he had an old Cadillac and he even went to the trouble of delivering it to the Radio One studio in London.

After it arrived, the band called me to say although they were grateful and impressed that I (or more accurately this generous chap) had honoured the bet, none of them knew how to drive! The American gas-guzzler was raffled by Strummer to a lucky fan but, according to author Marcus Gray, this Caddy didn't guzzle any gas at all, it wouldn't even start. Perhaps the listener had an impish sense of humour… the song contains the line "Engines stop running."

According to the official Clash Facebook page, the proceeds went to the industrial town of Corby, 140 kilometers north of London." Well, how many remember that! Corby descended into nothing much more than a ghost town in the 1980s. Shops closed, stores were boarded up, teenagers leaving school had little prospects and little for them to do as venues and youth clubs closed their doors. Regeneration was a fine word to bandy about, but it would take over two decades to achieve.

Gareth Smith, guitarist with Raging Speedhorn and Swedish band The Victims, reflected on his early days growing up in Corby during the 80s and 90s. Born in 1978 he left Corby after meeting his future wife Jenny in Stockholm at a Speedhorn gig in 2002. "Obviously, I don't remember the Steel Works. It lay there on the edge of town, at least the shell of it did. Little left but ghosts and memories. Corby, which had at one time been one of England's most productive towns, was a desert of unemployment.

Even the train station was closed, as if to hammer home that the way out was closed. The town centre was littered with darkened stores that had gone bankrupt. The only thing still doing business was the pubs. None of this made any impression on me when I was little, of course. The only things that existed for me were my street, the field behind the house where I played football every day with my best friend Neil and some other kids from the estate, and the woods where we played the same games that my dad and his gang had done twenty-five years earlier."

Achieving A-Levels didn't inflame any aspirations when there was the feeling that they weren't worth very much. Working for agencies who offered short term work slicing cabbages, counting chicken legs, shovelling coleslaw, packing books didn't herald the way ahead. Or maybe it did.

Gareth's way out couldn't have been foreseen. Too far-fetched you could say. Forming a band with his friends, playing their own interpretations of "heavy metal" in his dad's garage, they would never have believed, had they been told, they would tour the world and play at such prestigious events and venues as Wembley Arena, the Reading Festival, the OzFest, the Whisky in Los Angeles, punk venue CBGB's in New York, record albums at Richard Branson's Manor Studios in Oxfordshire.

Music was Gareth's, and his bandmates, escape.

***

£3 million was designated by the Government to help prepare sites for new industry in Corby, sandwich factories included, with a promise of "immediate consideration" to grant the town assisted area status. Which was received with great scepticism. The policy, tried elsewhere, hadn't proved to be very effective. The total cost of Government subsidies needed was estimated to be £330 million - two-thirds of the annual Government regional aid programme.

Councillors complained that repeated appeals over the previous 10 to 15 years for Government aid to sort out their housing problem had been ignored, producing a "ghost town" atmosphere already in parts of Corby. So what were the chances of aid to create new industry?

As one councillor said, "Drive down Stephenson Way and you see the evidence. Out of about 280 houses, 54 are boarded up with bits of wood and corrugated tin. On the more modern Exeter estate whole blocks of flats and complete rows of houses have suffered similarly."

The social argument was a powerful one with a high crime and vandalism rate, and an infant mortality rate and an unemployment rate nearly twice of that anywhere else in the country.

Dennis Spiers, head of the town's social services department, revealed there had been an increase in domestic problems, financial stress, juvenile crime and mental illness. Corby people felt increasingly that their town had been continually neglected while neighbouring towns had been encouraged to flourish.

Ray Jobling, a Corby-born Cambridge sociologist, wrote at the time, "The other towns have better transport links, more money for housing and for industry, which has always been more diversified. The danger is that all the next generation towns will take away people with transferable skills. The people with a genuine contribution to make to Corby will be the very ones who will leave."

Steve Purcell, an instrument mechanic recalled in his book *Corby Iron and Steel Works,* "Around 10,000 people lost their jobs and another 10,000 jobs were lost in allied businesses. The day I walked back in after the strike was the same day that I got my redundancy papers. It was April 1st. It had to be a joke but it wasn't. The effect on the town was immediate. Everybody was down, quite despondent and depressed. They couldn't see what on earth they were ever going to do again. What use is it that you used to be a pusher driver on a Coke Oven? It was a one-horse town, for the men there was not a lot other than the iron and steelworks and the quarries."

The demolition of the works took four years to complete. The coke ovens, blast furnaces and chimneys were constructed to withstand incredibly high temperatures and as such, were tricky to demolish. The "Corby Candle" was the most recognisable of all. A large chimney that burned off gases produced by the steelmaking process that could be seen from miles away. "Keep the Candle Burning" was the hopeful anthem. Until it was extinguished.

Demolition of Blast Furnaces begin

Des Liquorish worked in the blast furnaces. His wife Jacqui reflected, "It was a sad time when the demolition was taking place. It had become such a huge part of the landscape in Corby. You could see the Corby Candle burning from every direction. When the demolition of the blast furnace happened neither me nor Des could watch. Thankfully, Des was lucky enough to get a job when the steelworks closed, working as a bin man. The BSC were making the wages up to whatever salary the workers were previously on with the severance pay so it wasn't too bad."

"Thatcher's government made Corby an Enterprise zone to attract new jobs to the town and the Labour controlled council worked with other bodies to bring European Community grants to the area. Businesses moving into the zone were exempt from business rates, could reclaim some of their capital spending and benefited from other incentives such as fast-tracked applications to receive tax relief on specified imported goods. There was also a near complete relaxation of planning controls in the zone, meaning most types of commercial development - warehouses, factories, office blocks and retail units - could be built without specific planning permission, although the usual building regulations and health and safety requirements applied."

Working for the Royal Mail during this time was Ian Easton who was well-known throughout the town for his window cleaning business which he started when he joined the Post Office in 1979. Ian saw the expansion of the enterprise zones and the despair former steelworkers felt. "It was amazing how quickly these new units and warehouses appeared to spring up on the industrial estates. New companies seemed to arrive and take up station every other week. A lifeline on the face of it. However, it soon became apparent that a large percentage of these new workplaces were only here for the short-term. Six months free rent and they were gone. The turnover was unbelievable.

They were taking advantage of redundant steelworkers accepting any job that was going, safe in the knowledge that they weren't that bothered about a decent wage, their wages would be hiked up with BSC's severance pay. Those who were unfortunate to have only a minimum sum were forced to work long hours on a minimum wage, the company knowing they were grateful just to be employed at this time."

To understand the depth of feeling at the loss of the steelworks, one has to remember that people born and bred in Corby and the surrounding areas were brought up knowing that all school leavers were guaranteed a job and a career if so desired.

I was one of the influx of school leavers in 1965, starting as an office boy in the Steelworks Engineering Office. All my friends were employed in various offices too. A nice way to break one in for life after school even if the jobs were often tedious, boring, making a dozen cups of coffee three times a day, running errands. You soon began to look for ways to bide your time away and a phone call here and there would get you out of the way and off for a hike to all sorts of departments and dangerous areas.

Roaming about and making your way around the Blast Furnaces, Coke Ovens, Rolling Mills, Bessemer, over a myriad of railway lines with engines shunting ladles of hot metal, wagons of scrap, iron ore, ingots, became the norm. You were almost blasé about it. Like sewer rats crawling everywhere, you were oblivious to the lack of health and safety.

When you hit the age of sixteen, as I did in February '66, you were conscripted onto shift work and a real job. Working with men twice or three times your age, learning to be respectful, when to open your mouth and when not to. Learning to be aware of the dangers that were omnipresent. Learning how to operate machinery. Learning to cope with the heat, dust and smoke. If you were ambitious, an apprenticeship in the Works was there for the taking. Electrical, mechanical, engineering, carpentry, whatever.

As two of my friends, Jeff Stewart and Ged Devlin, recalled in 2020. Jeff emigrated to South Africa in 1983. "It's amazing how certain dates stick in your mind forever from a very early age. I started my first full-time job with British Steel (BSC) or Billy Smarts Circus as some called it! as an apprentice on Aug 17th 1970. I've put that date on so many different documents over the years and it just shows, you can never plan your life out thinking that it will all fall into place. Would I have thought about living in South Africa when I walked into the training centre at BSC all those years ago?

Never in a million years but I definitely wouldn't have changed it as it's been a fantastic experience.

I often wonder where all the other guys ended up after finishing their own apprenticeships and I know some moved to different parts of the UK and some to various parts of the world while some were happy to continue working in Corby and are probably enjoying retirement today but to think it all began as long as 50 years ago is quite scary! I can still see the workshops like it was yesterday and the canteen, when we used to get sent upstairs to programmed instruction too. It was short and sweet in the training centre before we were thrown out to the big bad world and that was when you found out what Corby works was like because some of the characters we worked with were unbelievable and the stories and comedy situations are endless and it's all those experiences that made Corby the town it was! Even here in South Africa I've met loads of people from Corby and many others who've worked there at some stage and they all tell you about the Jocks!"

Ged said, "I never thought that I would emigrate to Canada and then to Australia, all on the back of the trade that BSC gave us. I've met various people who say to me, "Corby, where is this place?" Everywhere I go, I meet people from Corby, I have met many people who I didn't know in the town but met later."

A number of stories were embellished over the years about steelworkers spending most of their time sleeping, reading books and even going for a pint during a shift. This fuelled the consensus that "it was no wonder the Works died." Overall, a misguided view that this was the practise for all, but the stories are endless.

"Taffy" Thomas, a schoolteacher at Corby Boys School from 1958 until the 1980s worked regularly in the steelworks during school holidays. He recalled his memories in 2014. "I used to finish school on the Friday and be down the Works Saturday morning. There were some right characters there. In one plant the foreman and his charge hand clocked in and then disappeared to Towcester Races for the day before coming back to clock out! I worked in the tube works, 18 hours a day, the charge hand would come round and ask, "anybody want to stay on in case somebody doesn't turn in?" "Yeah no probs" I'd say. I worked everywhere, doing anything. Slinging in the tube works, brickie's labourer, driving a van all-round the works which incorporated being a "bookie's runner".

Somebody stopped me once, "You Big John?"

"No," I said.

Then this other guy stopped me and asked the same question.

"Who's this Big John?" I asked.

"He's a bookie's runner."

"I'll do it" I said. I ended up driving all over picking up bets for people and putting them on. I also worked for Pearce's, painting a big gas holder along with my mate, "Big" Greg, "Bronco" Layne, a schoolteacher with me at the Boys School. Greg climbed into the bosun's chair and when he got to the top of the gas holder he discovered he suffered with vertigo. He wouldn't let go of the hand rail! Couldn't move. Big feller like that, a giant and he was panic stricken! We managed to coax him down eventually."

WonderWorld, 'the answer to Corby's prayers,' was given backing by the East Midlands planning committee despite condemnation from its chairman Lewis Sturge who claimed 'the scheme is a misfit and too big for England, an importation from America.'

The affect this would have on the existing countryside and villages was discussed with plans to meet the Department of Transport to press on with by-pass schemes for various towns and villages, particularly that of Bulwick, where councillor Roger Glitheroe warned that too much emphasis could be placed on the creation of local jobs by the construction work. Many people working on construction jobs in Corby came from outside the area."

He also warned that many people might be driven away from their villages by the influx. "Although the area would gain from the additional rates paid by the theme park there would also be heavy outgoings on providing extra facilities like policing.

Kettering General Hospital could also feel the strain if the park went ahead. It would inevitably lead to more accidents."

Chairman of the Kettering Health Authority Paul Seddon said that they had already been in touch with planners of the complex to discuss the possibility of the company providing its own casualty unit on the Wonderworld site to deal with minor injuries.

As the years would pass, Wonderworld became so much of a joke nobody would take any serious notice of further announcements. Many were convinced from the beginning it was all just a land occupation scheme. Developers holding on to land to sell on a few years down the line for a profit.

Forgetting WonderWorld, the devastation felt with the steelworks closure was eased a trifle with the arrival of large companies like RS Components, Oxford University Press and Commodore Computers to provide greatly needed employment for thousands of former steelworkers.

Startin' Over

"Startin' Over" was John Lennon stating it was time for a reset. Released two months before his tragic death, Startin' Over from the album "Double Fantasy" was John's way of announcing he was back, starting afresh after a five-year sabbatical, in which he'd apparently been spending his time making bread.

Startin' Over was also a phrase some may have used to describe the beginning of a new era in Corby after all that had been going on over the last couple of years.

For a while, though, during 1980 we were able to forget the tribulations and join in with the celebrations for the Queen Mother's 80th birthday. It was an opportunity to dust down the bunting, organise communal street parties, rejoice with a Vol-au-vant and a sherry. Wave the Jack. During her annual Christmas broadcast Queen Elizabeth paid tribute to her mother's 'selfless devotion to duty," expressed her gratitude to the minions who waved away their woes, momentarily to be able to forget their anxieties, and above all, to celebrate the landmark of her Mother's Big Eight 0. If you were that way inclined.

Highlights from the Queen's speech included, "I was glad the celebrations of my mother's 80th birthday gave so much pleasure. The loyalty and affection which so many people showed, reflected a feeling, expressed in many different ways, that she is a person who has given selfless service to the people of this country and of the Commonwealth."

"As I go about the country and abroad I meet many people who are making a real contribution to their community. I come across examples of unselfish service in all walks of life and in many unexpected places. We face grave problems in the life of our country, but our predecessors, and many alive today, have faced far greater difficulties, both in peace and war, and have overcome them by courage and calm determination. They never lost hope and they never lacked confidence in themselves or in their children."

Those thrown on the scrapheap will surely have appreciated the few grains of solace in her heartfelt words.

The Queen Mother had been in the town as recently as 1973, when she attended the ceremony for the opening of the appropriately named Queens Square. A trip which also included the opening of the Jerry Lewis Cinema where she found herself vying for attention alongside a bunch of Carry On film stars.

Carrying on regardless, the Queen Mother was celebrating her 80th birthday in style, touring the country and waving to all who lined the streets, though not everyone was enamoured with the outpouring of devotion. Corby Councillor and Post Office union official Bob Lochore at Corby Royal Mail Sorting Office wasn't by any stretch a devotee. Bob's uniform jacket was liberally decorated with lapel badges, CND, Make Love Not War, I Love Ringo, Get Out Of Vietnam, Drop Acid Not Bombs. On the actual day of Her Majesty's birthday, Bob displayed his latest badge, featuring the Queen Mothers face. Adorned with the words, "80 years a scrounger!"

Bob sadly died after a long illness in 1989 and was remembered by his close friend Cliff Hughes. "Bob was a real character. He told me one time, when he was a bus conductor, he and his driver used to park up in the Cottingham Road depot when finishing the late shift and dash across the road to the White Hart to get a pint before closing time. The driver was a Scottish feller, Bob Cherry, who lived on the Exeter estate. Making it to the bar, breathless, Bob Cherry said to the barmaid, "Two pints of bitter hen!"

To which the barmaid replied, "Too late, I've got my towels up."

Quick as you like Cherry replied in his thick Glaswegian accent, "I didnae ask about the state of yer health hen, just gie us two pints!"

The Jerry Lewis cinema was renamed the Focus in 1980. Situated at the rear of Queens Square the cinema never really established itself and in September '83 was given a makeover by some entrepreneurs from Nuneaton and re-named the Forum. Eight years later, in September 1991 it was closed down after its entertainment licence was refused by the council due to lack of maintenance. A year later, it was open again with one screen and the other half of the building as a lazer centre. A games thing for kids apparently. Eventually the complex gave up the ghost and became an over 25's nightspot known as 'talkies".

Inevitably, the cinema/lazer centre/nightclub closed its doors for the final time in 1996 and was demolished when the shopping centre was rebuilt in the summer of 2005. Corby's Film lovers would have to wait another ten years before they could enjoy a bucket of popcorn and annoy everyone by eating a packet of crisps whilst watching a movie in the Savoy, opened in 2015.

Puttin' on the style in 1980, along with Elizabeth Angela Marguerite Bowes-Lyon, (the Queen Mother), was Lonnie Donegan at Corby Stardust Centre in February. The Skiffle king who introduced the blues and rock and roll to Britain in the 1950s with "Rock Island Line" and "John Henry" proved his popularity was a strong as ever as he entertained the bingo wallers with his repertoire of classics, "My Old Man's A Dustman," "Does Your Chewing Gum Lose its Flavour?," and "Puttin' on the Style".

The success of the Stardust inspired Bip Wetherell to broaden his horizons from running pubs to joining the nightclub circuit, as he explains in his autobiography, *My Life As A 'Z' List Celebrity*. "Elaine and I bought our first nightclub in 1980. The Freewheelers in Kettering, which we changed to Mr. Bip's Nightclub. It was a real pit. I didn't have enough money to buy the lease and do it up so I went to the local Nat West Bank for a £30K loan. Showed the manager my business plan and the accounts from the Nags Head. Just to make sure he had me tied up with Belts and Braces he took a first charge on our detached house in Middleton. He shook my hand as he authorised the loan and as I walked down the road to my car I did an impulsive Andy Capp "click of the heals" to celebrate. What a complete ejit, I didn't even think about how I was going to pay it back!

So began four years of running two businesses. I soon found out they were Chalk and Cheese and I found it really difficult to get the Kettering club busy. I discovered Kettering customers were careful with their money and I was reduced to trawling the pubs of the town centre before closing time to give out free admission tickets. This was madness as the door money was our principal source of income. The theory was if you could cover your off-bar costs i.e. Door Security, Disc Jockeys, Advertising etc with the door money, the bar profits would show a healthy bottom line. But this didn't happen in Kettering. Although, I eventually got it busy, it didn't ever make any real money. I spent time travelling between clubs, sometimes twice a night, just to make sure everything was going as it should and to show a presence to any management or staff that the money they took should go in the tills and not their pockets.

The first time I had been in the "Freewheelers" was back in the late sixties. I'd just started D.J.ing and had heard that "Emperor Rosko" was to appear at the Freewheelers. Well "Rosko" was one of my heroes. An incredible, not to be forgotten voice and he always played a great selection of music, mostly soul, a lot of which I'd never heard before. I paid to get in at the downstairs reception, climbed two flights of stairs, and entered the downstairs area of the club which housed the stage, main bar, and dance floor. You couldn't move. The place was packed. The atmosphere was incredible.

The track that was playing as I entered was "Couldn't Get It Right" by the Climax Blues Band. There were bass bins either side of the stage (I'd never seen bass bins before) and the strong bass line on the track not only shook the dance floor but hit you right in your stomach. I stood there saying to myself, "I've got to own a nightclub one day," not knowing that Elaine and I would buy it twenty years later in 1980.

Meantime, the success of the Nags Head was incredible. Although it was licensed for 300, we would be full with another 300 in the car park waiting for the "one out" "one in" rule. I remember one New Years I went to work at 6pm to get things ready for what was our busiest night of the year. As I drove past the "Chippy" in the High Street, I thought to myself "they must be busy" as the queue for the shop went 50 yards past it. I then realised that the queue was for the nightclub at the back of the pub.

```
*********************
* Mister  * TONIGHT *
** TONIGHT * TONIGHT **
* CORBY'S TOP DISCO EVERY FRIDAY *
              WITH
           DJ GILLIE
      Every Saturday our over 20s' night with
      LIVE GROUPS PLUS DISCO
  This Week's Group: THE TAPES
         Saturday February 13th: ENERGY
      Saturday February 20th, back by public demand
       * CISSY STONE BAND *
      STARTING NEXT THURSDAY FEBRUARY 11th and
              * EVERY THURSDAY *
       DJ STUART will be presenting his
        * FUN DISCO NIGHT *
        This Thursday February 11th: HAT PARTY
      Next Thursday February 18th: ST TRINIANS NIGHT
              * FREE ADMISSION *
         For all girls all night 8 pm — 1 am
           Don't forget it has to be MR BIPS
           THE TOP NAME IN NIGHTCLUBS
            We accept smart 'n' casual dress
      Bip's        High Street,
                    CORBY 3174
*********************
```

Bip's

I went in and straightaway phoned a couple of doormen to come in early. It was a fine moonlight night so, trusting it wouldn't rain, we moved all the movable furniture outside and left it at the rear of the pub. When we opened I just let everyone who was queuing in. It was ridiculous. Talk about hanging from the rafters. There are photos of that night with me and my brother, Stuart, D.J.ing stripped to the waist and covered in sweat. What a night! We desperately needed bigger premises.

During our tenure at the Nags Head, there was the 1982 Pole Fair. Every 20 years, Corby would celebrate the original granting of the Royal Charter to Corby by Queen Elizabeth 1st in 1568. The pubs were allowed to open all day that day. It was complete bedlam. I stole a march on the opposition pubs by opening at 6am. The rest of them didn't open until 9am I had done 300 breakfasts and took £1000 before the other pubs had even opened.

Because the Pole Fair was an outdoor event, I booked four bands to play on the pubs flat roof in our "Roof Top Special". It was packed. At night, I got the same four bands to play in the back room until midnight. Another resounding success. The only downside was Elaine came down with food poisoning and I spent the whole day counting tills and banking the money in the pub safe. We took 8 grand and got a massive reward from the brewery - a meal for two at their prestige pub in Peterborough! It was about this time I really started to think we needed bigger premises."

Corby Pole Fair is well-documented elsewhere but for those who don't have any idea about the tradition, the Pole Fair was granted to the village of Corbei, as it was spelt originally, in 1585. How the Fair came about, it is believed, is Queen Elizabeth, daughter of Henry VIII fell into a bog while hunting in Rockingham Forest and was rescued by villagers from Corbei. By way of a thank you, Liz granted the village a Royal Charter which contained six valuable rights. Landowners were exempted from:

1. "Pignage" - A tax that was paid to allow local people to feed their pigs on fallen acorns in Rockingham Forest.

2. "Murage" - A tax to maintain and build walls at Rockingham Castle.

3. "Passage" - Corbei men could pass through toll gates throughout England without having to pay.

4. Contributing to the expenses of the Member of Parliament for the area.

5. Jury service.

6. Giving every man the right to refuse to serve in the local militia.

Bip said, "After 8 years in the Nags, we were looking to move on. The local Welfare Club had gone bust and with the help of our accountant and several other investors we were able to sell our Kettering club for £50K to put our share in. So for a total of £250K we had a club with six rooms that would eventually be licensed for 1250 customers a night. It was a brilliant decision to buy a "Freehold" business. One-by-one, we were able to 'do up" the bars and entertainment rooms. It was amazing how replacing the fluorescent tube lighting with spotlights could alter the atmosphere of a room, carpet instead of linoleum and even soft toilet paper in the trolleys instead of the harsh "Izal" brand.

It was a struggle to finally get the much coveted 2am drinks licence but once that was in place the club really took off. So much so that we were able to buy all the investors out, some of them quadrupling their initial investment. Finally, we owned a great business in a valuable property showing great returns and employing over 50 staff including doormen, DJs, Live Bands, Bar staff, glass collectors etc. We even had a full-time carpet cleaner who would come in on a Monday to clean all the carpets which were sticky from the busy weekend trade.

The downside of operating nightclubs where the customers were drinking until 2 a.m. was you had to have good security. It soon became apparent that using local doormen wasn't going to work as there had been a few incidents where doormen had had their windows put in at home as a reaction to being barred. So I bought a mini-bus and shipped fifteen doormen in from Birmingham for the big nightclub and I kept the local doormen for the over 30's nightclub where we had less trouble.

My accountant said to me once, "Why do you spend so much on security when you have very little trouble?"

The obvious reply was, "That's why we don't have a great deal of violence to deal with."

On average, we would have fights maybe once a month. The policy for the doormen was that they were stationed at strategic points of the room with the Head Doorman being in charge of admissions with two doormen either side of the D.J. booth which had the best view of the room. There we could, hopefully, spot any bother that was brewing.

In my years of running nightclubs, I have been involved many a time breaking up fights. The procedure was the doormen nearest to the incident would immediately pull one of the trouble makers away whilst the next person who arrived would calm and control the other party. The policy was if you went in with fists flying you would increase the fighting by fifty percent whereas if you took one of the fighters away you reduced the trouble by fifty percent. Many a time I took blows from customers that were still wanting to fight so they would start on you. You couldn't react you just concentrated on removing the person from the nightclub.

Although we searched about one in six customers for weapons and illegal booze, the ladies would have their handbags searched, there was a few incidences where I have taken a knife off a guy and, luckily, I only had to take a gun off a customer once. I confiscated the weapon and took it round the local police station where they informed it was only a starting pistol. My reply to this was, "I wish my arse had known that at the time."

Bip's competition, Martines Night Club, George Street

My main competitor in Corby was the town centre pub "Martines". The main problem was if the next generation of customers preferred going up the town for their late-night entertainment there was nothing I could do to get the customers back. In the nightclub business you were either red hot or as cold as ice, there was no in between. So I decided to buy out the competition. I went to my bank to ask for a loan so I could buy the club from Northern Leisure. The only trouble was I needed a £1mn.!

In 1988 I was in a local band, playing Tornados and 60s stuff. I suggested to guitarist Dave Dean the idea of trying to get Clem Cattini, an original member, to join us to make it authentic. I managed to find a contact for Clem and it was a short while after I flew down to Torquay in my helicopter with Dave, to meet Clem who was playing in a show with his current band. When we arrived Clem said, "I've never been up in a helicopter".

So I took him for a whirl and then we came down, the band's singer Lynne said, "I've never been in a helicopter either." So I took Lynne up for a quick whirl round the resort. Later, before heading off home back to Corby, I told Dave I would have to put in a flight plan and pay a £25 landing fee before we could leave. When I went to pay it, I was told, "That'll be £100".

"I thought it was only £25!" I replied.

"You've landed four times sir, that's £100."

So, it cost me £100 for the pleasure of meeting that lot in Torquay!"

Clem said, "Bip took on the challenge of booking gigs and organising 60s tours and it was great fun meeting up with many old friends from the day still out there performing. Some weren't so great though if I have to be honest. Ricky Valance was one, a 'star" we played with a good few times during the 1980s. Joe Moretti who played guitar on 'tell Laura I Love Her" was with us at the time and after playing the hit, Ricky Valance went up to Joe and screamed at him that the solo wasn't right! I mean! Joe was a fantastic player! I told Ricky Valance to remember that the musicians always have the last laugh. I told the guys in the band that next time we back him we'll play an upper third. Course, he came on and was screaming trying to reach the notes because we were playing so high! Made him look a right idiot."

Bip said, "Ricky Valance wasn't the brightest. I asked him if he was the guy who got killed in the air crash with Buddy Holly. He said, "No, that wasn't me." He couldn't see I was taking the piss. We played one gig when he came into the dressing room before the show and told us "I'm not going on first, I'm the star of the show boyo! I don't open the show. I've got a number one record". He did have, in the Christian charts! He'd turned all religious and found God or something. Anyway, we said, "Great!" We could go on, do our bit and get off home! Another gig was when we were playing the Hammersmith Odeon on the Golden Oldies Show and he fell off the stage after taking a bow at the end of the performance. He fell head first into the orchestra pit (which appears to have been a habit) and the compere, comedian Mike Lee Taylor, quipped, "That's the best I've ever seen him go down!""

Clem said, "The best one was when we were on a radio show the day that John Lennon died. When Elvis had died the radio played his records all day long and they did the same with John, played the Beatles and Lennon's records all day. I said to the DJ, 'Thank goodness Ricky Valance is still alive!' Later on, he came up to me and thanked me for the mention!"

When Bip and Elaine moved on from the Nags in 1984, they were succeeded by Dougie King, one of the most flamboyant DJ's in Corby. A truly colourful character, Dougie sadly passed away in 2004 and was paid tribute by his friend and fellow DJ, Ian Bateman.

"I first met Dougie when I worked as a resident DJ in the Embassy Club in the old Strathclyde Hotel in Corby. He came along as a guest DJ from Hereward Radio, this was in 1981. As I was there every week, I asked Dougie what music he would like to play. He said, "Whatever is appropriate for the floor." I had quite a few 12" pre-release records in my singles box, from WEA records, they used to send me freebies every week. Dougie's eyes lit up when I pulled out Prince 1999, he loved that and kicked off his stint behind the decks, introducing himself as the undisputed vanguard of bad taste. We had a cracking good night, the atmosphere was brilliant. We kept in contact after that and became very good friends."

Dougie had returned to Corby after working on Radio Clyde and Forth and worked for Hereward Radio in Peterborough. He was also working in local pubs and clubs, Shafts, The Rock, The Raven, Rugby Club. He always classed himself as one of life's lucky ones. It soon became apparent that he was never ambitious to be rich, he just wanted to entertain and be comfortable. He loved technology and had a good understanding of how things worked. I am sure anyone who used to go to the Raven to see the Dougie King Show on a Friday night had their ears enveloped in the loudest sound coupled with thunderous bass that made the hall shake. He was the first in the area to use four Citronic speakers, which were bi-amped.

Off stage, he went through many highs and lows, many of which I was part of. When he was about to move from his home in Woodlands Avenue, he asked me if I would look after his record collection for a few weeks. I had plenty of loft space, so I thought. It took five journeys in my estate car to collect the majority of the boxes, they included mostly 7" and 12" singles and albums I would estimate to have a value of, to a collector, to be around about £25,000.

I am convinced that during this period, Woodlands Avenue was probably one of his lowest times. He had the ability to build himself up to a height, then come crashing down to earth with problems under his own admission he created. I had many a late-night call when Dougie told me he'd had enough of life. I decided to meet him and have a Sunday drink down at the Talisman. Dougie poured his heart out to me, but he was still very angry with life. A customer accidentally knocked into him, and Dougie started to set about him. I said to him, "If you carry on like this you will get yourself hurt." He said, "I am scared of no man". I gave him a slap with the back of my hand. He looked stunned. I just about crapped my pants but thought sod it, I'll stand my ground. Suddenly, he's done a sergeant major walk to the gents, come back to his pint at the bar and said, "if that was supposed to teach me a lesson, it didn't."

Since then, whether it was in person or on the phone, or even a text message, we always offered each other a fight. My last text message to Dougie included, "You want a fight?" The reply was, "A fight sounds very appealing."

The Nags breathed life again when Dougie took over as landlord. He booked many bands including the late Steve Marriott from the Small Faces who appeared there on more than one occasion with his band Packet of Three. After one gig we went into the bar and had a late drink where it became clear that Steve Marriott and Dougie were of the same personality. Steve was another who did not want to be rich, just wanted to entertain and have a drink.

People came from miles around to the alternative music night with Dougie's unique style, he used to call it several names, the harder edge or spiky night. Dougie never really believed in the paranormal but some strange things went on in the Nags. One night after every everyone had gone he was cashing up when all of a sudden the price tags flew off the optics one by one. I joked with him and said he must have been outside and sniffed the white lines in the middle of the road. Strange as it seems though... landlords have said the place was haunted.

Rick Dodd was asked to try and get a Jazz Night going at the Nag's Head when Dougie was the landlord. Dougie advertised it over the air continuously on Hereward, leaving the rest of the organising to Rick. He asked his friend Ronnie Scott if he could play but had to turn him down because he wanted too much money. Rick then turned to another old friend from the Bulls Head, Barnes days, Dick Morrissey. The evening turned into a damp squid with Rick feeling really downhearted, "Ronnie wanted about 300 bucks and we couldn't make it but Dick was just as good. I got a terrific rhythm section from Leicester to back him and we were all excited about the night. Unfortunately, it didn't work out and only about 40 people turned up, it was a disgusting response."

I went over to Hereward Radio with Dougie several times to help out on his breakfast show, and I learned to never play a trick on Dougie and expect to get away with it. One or two pranksters at Hereward tried to catch him out and put him off while on air. This normally happened when he was reading a serious news broadcast. One day Dougie entered the studio while his colleague was on air reading out a lengthy news item. Dougie timed it until the last few sentences before setting fire to the news script and all that could be heard from the radio was the presenters words becoming increasingly faster and faster.

Many radio stations have a play list of songs to play, and the presenter is left to fill in as he chooses between songs during his show. Dougie had an invisible aardvark in the studio that he struck up a rapport with. There were phone calls asking where he kept it after the broadcast and did it live in the station studio. He helped raise money for charity over many years and was always keen to help when he could. Nellie Connaughty from Nellie's Bin was very keen to raise money for her local charities and one of her stops was the Nags at the weekend. Nellie always looked for a chat with Dougie before going around with her collection tin."

Clive Smith added, "Dougie King was a big Bob Dylan fan and I bumped into him, not literally, at the NEC Birmingham in 1981. Whilst the music scene was all New Wave, Romantic, Electronic, Dylan never one to follow a trend, was in the midst of a Christianity kick. His most recent three albums were all embracing the Lord, 'shot of Love," 'slow Train Coming" and 'saved". Not to everyone's taste but the show as you would expect, was a sell-out.

I was huge fan of Bob myself and it was the first time I'd seen him, so whether the songs weren't entirely what I expected or not, it was still a thrill. And I realised that most Dylan fans at his concerts didn't go to hear the quality of the set, more to be able to say they've seen him. Human nature I suppose.

I witnessed this again a few years later at the Echo Arena, Liverpool, which was another sell out, and proved my point. Dylan's voice was always an acquired taste and never in the same league as Sinatra say, but he confounded all his followers by going down the road of the "Great American Songbook", performing "Fly Me To the Moon", "It Had To Be You", "Stella By Starlight," which just didn't sit right. It was bloody awful! He received rousing applause from the fans all the same, even if they were expecting to hear more of his renowned repertoire than the stuff from the "Great Bob Dylan Songbook." Felt phoney somehow. What Big Dougie would have made of it I can only imagine."

I wrote a blog on the show in 2017, reproduced here:

"Echo Arena, Liverpool May 8th.

Bob Dylan, walked on stage, played his set, walked off, nearly two laters later, and never uttered a word. Now, Dylanologists will know that since the 1960s this is par for the course. Bob never went into the show-biz baloney of 'Hello Wembley, everybody havin' a good time?' etc.

Part of the mystique surrounding Dylan is his embracement of non-conformity. It's been a long time since Greenwich Village, Newport, Isle of Wight in which Bob has morphed and crossed musical borders many times.

It could be that many in the packed audience may have been disappointed. The show started well with "Don't Think Twice, It's Alright" from "Freewheelin'", the crowd responding with all the enthusiasm of old. "We love you Bob!" a voice rang out which was almost an intentional reminisce of the cry of "Judas" at the Manchester Free Trade Hall in "66. It brought loud cheers and laughter. Bob remained unmoved. Tonight's set was a ramble through some of his 2000s albums which many, if they would admit, had never heard of.

"Duquesne Whistle," "Scarlet Town," "Early Roman Kings" from 2012's "Tempest" were well-received. Interspersed was the rapturously received "Highway 61" and "Desolation Row", bemusing arrangements of "Tangled Up In Blue" from 1974's "Blood On The Tracks" and the anthem for Civil Rights, "Blowin' In The Wind". It was obvious that the crowd were restless, many came expecting to see the Dylan of old, guitar and harmonica strung around his neck, speaking pearls of wisdom, songs of protest… frequent trips to the bar was witnessed all night, irritating it was as rows of people were constantly asked to let some ignoramus pass by, carrying a tray full of pints.

Dylan is now in his 80's, been 60+ years on the road, stockpiled a massive catalogue of songs. He sits down for most of the night behind his piano, the electric five-piece band driving him along, until he steps out from behind the shadows, takes a stance like Gene Vincent of old, right leg straight and stiff behind him...and sings a selection from a recent album release called 'triplicate" - his take on the Great American Songbook. And to be honest, it was crap. No Bob, you're not Sinatra or Bennett, leave it out. Nobody wants to hear it. They want to hear the stuff that you're known for, not only the 60s and 70s albums but from "Infidels", "Modern Times", "No Mercy" "Slow Train Coming". Wouldn't be Dylan though if he conformed, or did the expected. I mean, can you imagine Dylan entering the stage and yelling out Tina Turner style "Hi everybody!!," I said, HYYYY Everybody!!!"

As if to remind everybody that he was still the Dylan of old and not drifting off into middle-age or indeed old age cabaret, he came back for the encore and brought everybody to their feet with "Ballad Of A Thin Man," arguably the highlight of the night. Whatever you think of Dylan, he still has a presence of the icon we all know, one of the greatest 20th century poets and artists. Who knows if he will return. If he leaves it another five years or so, Zimmerman might just be walking on stage with a Zimmer frame! Don't think I would like to see that.

During the mid-1980s, a new music genre called Grindcore was characterised by heavily distorted, high-speed tempo, songs often lasting no more than two minutes, and vocals which consisted of growls and high-pitched screams emerged. Grindcore drew inspiration from some of the most abrasive music genres – including death metal, industrial music, noise and more extreme varieties of hardcore punk.

Foremost of the bands entertaining the legions of enthusiasts was Napalm Death, who emerged from the crust punk scene. Napalm inspired other British grindcore groups, among them, Extreme Noise Terror, Carcass and Sore Throat. Brilliant name or what? Other bands to follow with equally wonderful names included Collapsed Lung and Rotting Christ. Cannibal Corpse is another good one.

Riots erupted around the country in 1981. Liverpool, Bristol and London bore the brunt, fuelled by the unemployment crisis in the wake of the miners" disputes and steel closures. Two television programmes this year highlighted the issues with both despair and humour.

"Auf Wiedersehen, Pet" was centred around seven redundant British construction workers who left the U.K. to seek employment on a building site in Germany, which echoed what was happening all around the country where once stood industries such as the steelworks. A number of Corby steelworkers followed the trail and went to work in Holland. Likely seen as a temporary appointment, it was the cause of much angst, some families were torn apart by the arrangements.

"Boys from the Blackstuff" written by Liverpudlian Alan Bleasdale was described by the British Film Institute as, "A warm, humorous but ultimately tragic look at the way economics affect ordinary people… TV's most complete dramatic response to the Thatcher era and as a lament to the end of a male, working class British culture."

Bitter Memories for Pat and Yvonne

DJ Pat McMahon and his wife Yvonne decided there also had to be a better way of making a living than engaging in occasional agency work to supplement his disco earnings. Encouraged by his dad, Joe, steward at the St. Brendan's Club in Corby, Pat looked at the options advertised in the trade paper Morning Advertiser, which is where they saw a vacancy for a trainee and assistant manager at The Burrell Arms, Haywards Heath, Sussex.

The licencees were a middle-aged couple running a thriving business situated right next to the railway station. The pub was packed out all the time, picking up the custom from commuters disembarking from the station. It appeared to be a great opportunity to learn the trade. Pat and Yvonne's application was accepted and they bagged up their belongings and headed south to start their adventure.

Pat and Yvonne McMahon kicking off the karaoke

However, for all their optimism, things wouldn't turn out as they expected. It was clear from the beginning that the landlord and his wife were looking for a couple of dogsbodies, and Pat and Yvonne fitted the bill. They were very soon being taken advantage of, the proprietors taking a back seat, "hiding away" upstairs and not offering any substantial help or guidance. Pat's Celtic blood would soon see his patience wear thin and an altercation with a customer who was drunk and volatile was the tipping point.

Receiving no backing from the landlord, Pat had to sort the problem out himself, chucking the guy out. As the weeks passed, Pat and Yvonne were to grow more exasperated by the day. Things finally coming to a head when the landlady, an "oafish and ignorant woman," ordered Yvonne to clear a bin bag of rubbish out at the end of the night, forgoing to tell her there was a broken glass in the bag. Yvonne picked it up, the bag split open, and the glass gashed Yvonne's leg. Pat immediately told the landlord to phone an ambulance. "Not at this time of night" was his reply.

Raging, Pat phoned a taxi and when it turned up, the driver refused to take them to hospital because they might get blood all over his cab! Pat wrapped Yvonne's leg up best he could, the driver relented and took them to Burgess Hill Hospital where Yvonne's leg was cleaned up and eight stitches were inserted. They arrived back at the pub around 4am. Next morning, Pat was up early and the landlord asked him where his wife was. "She's in bed," Pat told him. "What! She should be down here working!"

Pat told him that thanks to his pig-ignorant partner, Yvonne was lying down resting with eight stitches in her leg. A row kicked off which ended with Pat telling the landlord where he could stick his pub. "We're finished!"

"Well you won't get your wages," he threatened.

"Stick your wages up your arse!" Pat told him. Adding that if he didn't receive them in the post by the following week, he'd be getting a visit from friends of his in Corby. And if he didn't believe him, to check it out.

"You don't mess around with Corby folk," was Pat's final shot. They returned home to Corby where they still had a council house in Kingsthorpe Avenue. Their wages did duly arrive, and Pat and Yvonne's dream of running a pub was over. The episode left a bitter taste. Pat went back to concentrating on building up his disco business. Yvonne gained work at Hunters Crisps. They never looked back.

The Battle of the South Atlantic

The Falklands War came at a time when the Thatcher government was under increasing pressure and cynics viewed the war as a convenient distraction. Nobody as far as I know, gave any thought to the remote islands in the South Antarctic but apparently Argentina had long laid claim that the islands they called the Malvinas had belonged to them. Was this ever mentioned during our schooldays? No, so when right out of the blue, the Argentines invaded the South Georgia islands as a precursor the invasion of the Falklands, most people in the U.K. were asking "Where's that?"

Clive Smith remembers walking into the Rockingham Arms for a pint, and someone said, "Argentina has invaded South Georgia." My initial reaction was "Really? Where's that then". And I always claimed I was decent at geography at school! It did sound serious though, for some reason. As events unfolded, it was serious! And an old pal in Corby's Royal Mail Sorting Office, Alex Shaw, was soon to be heading that way with the Task Force to help reclaim the Falklands.

Alex was a former Lodge Park Schoolboy who joined the Royal Marines on leaving, left to get married to his girlfriend Ann and ended up as a postman in Corby. He had a great sense of humour that was infectious. Coming back from holiday I once asked him where he'd been. He replied, "Ma - balla - thorpe."

"Where?" I asked, thinking it was on the Costa Brava or somewhere.

"Mablethorpe," he said laughing, "Ma - balla - thorpe sounds better though!"

I cracked up laughing too. Sounded so funny.

Alex eventually grew bored with the Post Office and rejoined the Army. Walking the streets and posting letters wasn't fulfilling for him and it came as no surprise when he informed us all he was going to join up again. This was a matter of months before the Falklands War kicked off.

We were all aware what was unfolding as the weeks rolled by, leading up to the Task Force departing Portsmouth. News bulletins every night giving the latest developments did seem unreal. Nobody of our generation expected our country to be going to war! And somewhere near the Antarctic!

As the Task Force sailed south on the three-week journey, everyone expected that Argentina would back down. It soon became clear they had no intention of doing so. Argentina was in turmoil under the dictatorship of General Galtieri and this war was a distraction for them as well.

We were all concerned for Alex. He kept in touch with a series of postcards which were upbeat, full of optimism and dare I say it, bravado. Alex's postcards were pinned on the notice board at work and there was a sense of foreboding as each one arrived.

Alex Shaw served alongside the 3rd Battalion of The Parachute Regiment (3 Para) during the battles. On the night of 11th June 1982 they were assigned to capture Mount Longdon overlooking Port Stanley, the capital of the

Falkland Islands. Along with attacks on the neighbouring Mount Harriet and another peak called the Two Sisters, victory would give the British control over all the high ground around Port Stanley and leave the Argentinian forces in a much-weakened position.

The fighting was vicious. By the end of the night, the British had lost 23 soldiers killed and another 50 wounded. Argentinian losses were 31 killed, 120 wounded and over 50 captured. Vitally, Mount Longdon was now in British hands and the remaining Argentinian troops retreated back to positions around Stanley. Despite suffering heavy losses and being forced from the mountains the Argentinians didn't surrender and instead started to shell the British troops who dug in on the mountains.

It was the day after the heavy fighting on Mount Longdon, Alex was flown on to the mountain by helicopter to give support to the mortar platoon and machine gun platoon. Some of their weapons had become inoperable during the heavy fighting on the mountain and the fear of an Argentinian attack meant they needed to be fixed quickly. Having left the helicopter, Alex moved to the exposed frontline positions to fix the broken weapons. Shortly after he arrived, the position came under fire from Argentine artillery. Alex was hit and fatally wounded, despite gallant efforts from the unit's soldiers and medics to save him. He died from his injuries on June 13th 1982.

When news came through that Alex had perished, on the eve of the Argentine surrender, the news was devastating and received with utter shock. It was a terrible time and all of us at Corby Post Office felt for his wife Ann and his parents. How do you deal with that? Unfortunately, thousands have had to deal with such news but it makes you feel just grateful, if selfish, that most of us haven't had to deal with it, or sacrifice ourselves.

As a postscript to this, and to my ignorance, I was talking to a tourist guide conducting a survey in a hotel in Buenos Aires in 2017. Asking the usual banal questions about my visit, I stopped him in his tracks when I asked him his views on the 1982 conflict "in the Falklands". His eyes went cold, as did his manner. 'the Malvinas!!" he said. To say I was taken aback was an understatement. He then went on to remind me and educate me on the history of the islands and to inform me that the schools in Argentina still taught the pupils about the war and that the Malvinas belonged to them! Argentina would never give them up! Christ! I was sorry I spoke. I did mention my friend Alex but it didn't make any impression. "We lost…, whatever it was," he replied. I was glad when my taxi turned up.

George Reilly and the Rocket Man

George Reilly became only the second local boy to play in an F.A. Cup Final when he turned out for Watford against Everton in 1984. George was following on the heels of Len Chalmers who played for Leicester City against the "double winning" Spurs team in 1961.

George scored the only goal in the F.A. Cup semi-final against Plymouth Argyle at Villa Park and on May 19th he stepped out at Wembley as Watford faced up to the might of Everton in the Cup Final. Unfortunately like Len's day, George's was to end in defeat with the same scoreline, 2-0.

Despite the disappointment, George still has a great memory of the event, "We had a big party after the final at Elton John's manager John Reid's house in Rickmansworth. It went on all night even though we'd lost. There were tents and marquees put up all over the grounds. Kiki Dee was there and she got up with Elton to sing Don't Go Breaking My Heart. Then next day we went on the open-top bus parade. Everyone came out, you couldn't have got any more people if we'd won it."

George was a young centre forward for Corby Town in the mid-1970s. His prowess in leading the line soon brought the attention of league scouts to the Occupation Road ground and he was duly signed by Northampton Town in the summer of 1976.

With the Cobblers, it wasn't long before he was attracting more attention, scoring goals for fun in Division Three of the Football League. Cambridge United came in for him and paid a record fee of £140,000. From Cambridge he moved to Watford, signed by future England manager Graham Taylor and his chairman "Rocket Man" Elton John.

George recalled his career at Vicarage Road, and more during an interview in 2016. "Elton was always around, dressed in his crocodile-skin suit, real crocodile skin, and a white hunter's hat. It was unreal and he got a fair bit of stick. But he could do what he wanted, he was the chairman! Graham Taylor's style with two wingers, John Barnes and Nigel Callaghan suited me down to the ground. I was an out-and-out centre-forward. Before games, Taylor would say, "In the first 10 minutes, I want Barnesy to fire the ball into their goalie and I want George to clatter him to let him know he's there."

"We played hard and partied hard. I shared a flat with my strike partner, Mo Johnston. I was his minder on and off the pitch. He got into a few situations where I had to bail him out. Charlie Nicholas at Arsenal was also a pal. I used to look after both of them on nights out. They used to go out in their leather trousers. I'm from Corby, thinking *what is this?* But they loved the limelight.

John Barnes was just a kid back then. He was terrific, it was only a matter of time before he went to the top. He and Paul Gascoigne were the best I played with. Mo was my best strike partner, along with Alan Biley at Cambridge. Mo could sense where I was going to head the ball and was on to the knock-ons like a flash.

I once got sent off against West Brom after the final whistle had gone. Ali Robertson went to throw a punch and I poked him in the eye to stop him. We were both charged with bringing the game into disrepute. When I signed for West Brom later, I walked into the changing rooms and found a pair of boxing gloves on my peg! Another red card was against Nottingham Forest, for a late tackle. Brian Clough told the ref to send me off and he did!

When I signed for Newcastle, Jack Charlton said he'd heard I had a reputation but he didn't care as long as I did the business at three o'clock. When Jack left and his assistant Willie McFaul took over, I knew my days were numbered. The year before I'd thrown him into a swimming pool with his suit on. We were in Fiji on tour and Willie wanted to fight me. So I threw him in with his clothes on. That is why I left Newcastle."

Asked if he had any regrets about his rollercoaster career and life, he was clear. "No way! Every summer after the season finished, I'd take myself off to Marbella for 12 weeks and have a great time. So I didn't waste my money!"

A year after the Watford Cup Final, George's former club Corby Town was on the move. The Steelmen had played at the Occupation Road ground since their formation in 1948. But times were changing. The ground was dilapidated. The terraces were a mess. Tumbleweed flourished. Since the heady days of the 1950s and 60s, the club's fortunes had been on decline. Attendances dropping in the late 70s to just double figures. It looked as if the demise of the club was only a matter of time.

However, a new board was elected in 1980, and there was a revival of interest and the team, consisting of local youngsters with a couple of older experienced heads, turned the corner and soon had football fans returning to the football ground "amongst the chimneys" as future chairman Bip Wetherell would later refer to it. To progress further, it was deemed necessary to move and the club moved up to the Rockingham Triangle where they would share the facilities with Corby Athletic Club. Not ideal and not everybody's idea of a football ground, the running track proved to be a numbing barrier for creating atmosphere. But that's where the club were. And where they would stay for the next twenty years.

Live Aid

Bob Geldorf of the Boomtown Rats was watching the six o'clock news in 1984 with his wife Paula Yates and newborn baby when a film was shown about a famine in West Africa. It affected him so much he felt he had to try and do something. Paula was working on the TV Channel Four show The Tube at the time when Bob's imagination went into top gear. He phoned her to find out who was on the show that night and asked her to tell the guests about an idea he had. Midge Ure and Jools Holland were thus enrolled and the idea snowballed. Their contemporaries in the rock world, Spandau Ballet, Duran Duran, The Police, Boy George, George Michael also joined in to help raise money and awareness for the crisis, and to record "Do They Know It's Christmas?" at Sarm Studios in London.

"Do they Know It's Christmas?" became the biggest selling single of all time. The lyrics and melody was later explained by Bob Geldorf during an interview with TV presenter Alan Yentob.

Bob revealed that the lyrics had come fairly easy but admitted he was struggling for a melody and Midge Ure was left to deal with it. When Midge felt he had it, he phoned Bob and hummed it over the line.

Bob's response? "I told him it sounds like Z Cars!"

Midge's reply was equally brutal, "It's better than any stuff you come up with!"

Bob admitted it was true!

Inspired by the success of the fund-raising record at Christmas 1984, Bob was encouraged to go one step further and organise a mammoth event on Saturday 13 July 1985 simultaneously at Wembley Stadium and at Philadelphia's JFK Stadium. The Americans had recorded their own song "Feed the World" to raise awareness of the African famine in the States and were keen not to be left out.

Tickets for the Wembley show were priced at £5 - with a £20 charity donation added on. The weekend extravaganza, broadcast on television and radio was celebrated around the country with barbecues and gatherings of friends. Various fundraising events kicked in and over £125 million was raised for the famine relief.

Celebration may be the wrong word to describe Live Aid, being the seriousness of the situation in Africa but nonetheless, most would agree it was the most enjoyable weekend. All the same you can't forget some of the video clips of emaciated children and the soundtrack of The Cars" "Drive". Chilling.

Clive Smith added, "There won't be many who remember, but it was the Coldstream Guards who opened the show with the "Royal Salute", a brief version of "God Save the Queen". No, I didn't realise either! I enjoyed the afternoon with my wife Sue and friends Don and Yvonne Gracey at Corby Rugby Club where there was a barbecue and hog roast."

Ceremony over it was down to the real business and who better to start it all off than Status Quo with "Rockin' All Over the World". The magnitude of the event must have been nerve racking, even for the top stars used to such gigs. Quo Guitarist Francis Rossi told of Bob Geldorf telling him before they went on, "It doesn't matter what you sound like, just so long as you're there"

I told him, 'Thanks for the honesty, Sir Bob."

Watching at home with his mum Irene and dad Jimmy was a young Leon Cave. Jimmy was a well-known singer and guitarist who had moved to Corby with his family from his native North East in the 1960s. He met Irene Mitchell and they were married in 1970, moving to Cheshire in the early 1980s. They could never have dreamt that 30 years after the Live Aid gig, their son Leon would be the drummer with Status Quo. How bizarre is that? Amazing.

Leon was interviewed in 2014 by journalist Glenn Milligan following a gig at the Donington Download Festival. It is reproduced here, in an abridged version.

"GM: What was your first ever drum kit?

Leon: A Premier Royale, bought from the local drum shop and it was far too big for me. I couldn't reach the pedals. It was a five-piece kit - one cymbal, hi-hat and that's what I learnt on, all the way until I was about 18. Then I got a Yamaha kit after that. There was a drum kit before the Premier kit that was a child's drum kit. A bass drum, a tom and a snare drum and I used to bang around on that. It was like a toy but had real skins and it was something that was bought for my brother Dylan initially but he never used to play it and I started banging around on it from aged 3 or 4.

GM: What songs got you going that you used to like playing to?

Leon: My dad is a musician. He was a guitarist and lead vocalist with a number of bands back in the 60s and 70s and in the early 80s he was gigging like 5 nights a week. My dad and mum used to take me and my brother to all the gigs. They wouldn't palm us off on the grandparents or with their friends, we'd go to the gigs and I heard I used to be in a cot by the side of the stage. I basically grew up around music.

My dad also has this immense vinyl collection and apparently from the age of about three or four I used to sit there with my headphones on playing loads of different records and that was everything from Black Sabbath and Deep Purple through to Queen and the full Beatles back catalogue. I completely loved it and I was used to being around musicians all the time so music was the natural way to go.

I remember, I think it was 1983, my dad had a record which was some kind of Metal collection and I remember Iron Maiden being on there, and Saxon, Manowar an American heavy metal band from New York. All those kind of bands. But it was Maiden from day one. I would count them as the band that got me into music really or got me into wanting to be a musician. It was the 'live After Death" album in particular and then the "Killers" album, which I had on cassette and bought it Spain, I remember that I used to play along with those. I became a massive fan and then in 1988 I went to a gig... I asked my dad to take me and he was like, "Yeah, no problem, let's go," and just him and me went and that was the day I was like, "Right, I just wanna play drums now." They bought me a drum kit and I was banging around and getting quite good. I started having lessons and it just developed from there really.

I loved Black Sabbath and Deep Purple albums too. "Black Sabbath" & "Paranoid". I had "Deep Purple In Rock," there was a song called "Rat Salad" and I used to try and emulate the solo. It was the right-left foot drum fill. It wasn't until later I got into The Beatles and started moving away from the metal stuff and getting into the pop and rock genres. My dad's into The Eagles so I was listening to them as well. I used to play along to everything really. I liked everything. I wasn't like, "I'm only Metal" or I'm only whatever, I played along with anything. Then when I started getting lessons later on in my early teens I got into every other style – Funk and Soul and Motown, Latin, Jazz.

I went through my Death Metal stage and started to get into the double-bass drums at about 14. I've been through everything and still my record collection is really eclectic. I just love music. If it's good then I like it. I was with a band called 'soul Drain" when I was 14 and we were influenced by the bands that were around at the time – it was Cynic, Atheist and Death so it was technical but there weren't any drum triggers then. I was trying to learn and get my left foot to catch up with my right foot. Then I got into the American progressive metal band Dream Theater. It was more precise and more about odd time signatures. Listen to Dream Theater and it brings you back again to bands like Rush, Yes and Gentle Giant and all those bands.

GM: What led you into the big league and meeting Francis?

Leon: There's a bit of a story about that. I was at a wedding and it must have been about 7 years ago, a summer wedding for one of my good friends. I live in London but I'm from the Manchester area originally. So I was up there at the wedding and it was about 11 o'clock at night and I was really drunk, you know, I'd done the wine, all the champagne – all that kinda stuff and I got a call from my mate who I went to Uni" with and he was like, "Leon, there's a gig coming up on Monday and we need a drummer urgently but rehearsals are tomorrow (Sunday) do you want to do it?," and I was like, "Ohhh," a bit drunk and that, "Oh I dunno," so I said, "alright then, I'll do it."

So I went home straight away and my mate sent me the tracks, put them on a cd, stuck it in the car, drove all the way down to London and learnt all the songs in the car as I was driving down, went to the rehearsal and then did the gig on the Monday in Glasgow – it was about 5,000 people and it was for a band called Macara. We toured the week during in which I found out that Francis was managing the band. I was like "Oh okay, that's interesting, that's quite cool." Then after that tour they'd recorded nine tracks on the album and they wanted me to do the last three tracks and it ended up being at Francis's studio. So I went and recorded there and he used to pop his head in and he'd watch me play and go, "Well done, that's really good," and I said, "Oh thanks, that's cool."

Then we supported Status Quo. We did Holkham Hall and some of those stately home gigs. He would always come in and say, "Well-played young man, that was really good."

Then he did his solo album "One Step At A Time" and I got a call randomly one day and it was from Greg Jackman who was the Producer. He said, "Francis is doing a solo album and he'd really like you to play on it," and I was like, "Oh right, amazing," so I went and recorded the album and obviously he was there a lot of the time and I got to know him quite well and then it came to the tour, he asked me to do the tour and we just clicked – we got on really well. I seemed quite quiet and quite trustworthy to him and I think he likes that about me. I wasn't acting like a fan or anything like that. When Matt Letley left, that's when I got the call. That's the way it worked really, over knowing him 6 or 7 years.

GM: What's he like to work with?

Leon: He's the nicest bloke I've ever met. Really professional – highly professional, but everything is always very humorous. You rarely have a serious conversation. It's all done with a bit of humour and fun and that's the best way because it's always a nice atmosphere. He's a loyal person. He's so famous so I'm sure he's had dodgy people trying to be his friend over the years. There's not a bad bone in his body – a top bloke.

GM: What would you say goes through your mind before, during and after a show?

Leon: Before a show from the morning, your adrenaline is really high and you're in gig mode for the day. Everything's timed so you have a time for your lunch, a time for your dinner, a time to get changed and then you go on stage. I suppose when you are on a series of maybe three or four gigs before a day off, your adrenaline is always really high and you are thinking about the day ahead. We don't drink before we play – no one ever drinks before a show.

Just before we are about to go on stage, is when I am at my most nervous and then as soon as I step behind the kit all my nerves just drop and then we do the gig and during the gig all you are thinking about is the playing and buzzing off the other band members and buzzing off the audience. When you've finished, you get onto the tour bus and your adrenaline goes boom and you reflect on the gig and talk about if it was a good one or a bad one or whatever.

What I do find when I come back home after a time away is I'm completely knackered. I don't think it's a physical thing, I think it's because your adrenaline is so high for three or four days then you get home and it drops. You end up sleeping for fifteen hours. That can be after you've done three gigs or can be after you've done a five-week tour. Your adrenaline drops because you've always got that intensity of thinking about the next gig. So that's kinda how it works as far as the feeling of it but you always feel that little bit of nerves just before you go on.

GM: What are you most proud of so far?

Leon: I think "Download" is my proudest moment without a doubt. There was so much expectation and when you have so much expectation there's a chance that it might be crap but it was what I expected it to be and even better. People going mental. It was circle pits and so many people coming over the barrier and all that and we played really well – we played spot on. Everything just went right so that's gotta be a career highlight for me.

Polly Short was living in London at the time of Live Aid and worked behind the scenes at Wembley. Brought up in Lodge Green Road, Polly left Corby and lived in London around the time of the so-called 'Summer of Love'."

Polly Short, London 1966

Now living in Buckinghamshire, Polly recalled in 2022 how it came to be she ended up serving refreshments at the Wembley gig.

"A group of us who lived in Barnet had a friend in London who owned a pub and he said he needed some extra hands on the soft drink stands in the stadium so we were all keen to go, of course, and it meant we got in free! Plus we all received a free Programme (£5). It is in excellent condition. If you know anyone who might want to buy it let me know!

We hired a bus to take us all from Barnet and we arrived at the stadium at 7.30 a.m. We had a brief about our duties and told we had to do two hourly shifts selling soft drinks and then we had a half hour break throughout the day. Our stand was right in the centre of the stadium.

During that break, we were allowed, as members of staff for the day, to use the VIP Bar and that is where I met several of the performers who kindly signed my Programme. George

Michael and Andrew Ridgley of Wham! Tracy Ullman, Sade, Spandau Ballet (3 members), Francis Rossi and Rick Parfitt of Status Quo, Pete Townshend of the Who and actress Hayley Mills. Sadly I missed out on a lot of the others! The Who's Roger Daltrey refused to sign my Programme saying he didn't have time - I wasn't impressed.

I remember posing with Spandau Ballet for a photograph for some teenage popstar magazine but they cut me out of the photo! Cheek. The atmosphere in Wembley was absolutely amazing. It was a very hot day and I actually got sunburned! I rated it as one of the best days of my life!

Disappointingly, I didn't meet Freddie Mercury of Queen in the VIP bar. I loved Queen and still do. Seeing them sing "We are the Champions" was so wonderful. I didn't want it all to end. I have been to many concerts over the years but this beats all of them - big time! Queen had come off an enormous world tour in support of their album "The Works". They reminded everyone at Wembley what a great live act they were and how many huge hits they had.

I honestly cannot remember what time it all wrapped up but it is one experience I will never forget. We all met up a few days later at our local pub in Barnet and talked non-stop of our experience. Happy days indeed. I should say that when chatting to the stars that did give me their autographs they were all charming and friendly. They dedicated most of the autographs to my kids Kevin and Kate and Francis Rossi put Pauline down as my name as I didn't change it to Polly until I had left Corby."

Roger Daltrey's mood was probably explained by the technical difficulties that marred The Who's set. John

Entwistle's bass wouldn't work at the start, causing an awkward delay of over a minute before they could start playing and then the TV feed cut out just as Roger sang "Why don't you all fade away..." The broadcast returned as the last verse of "Pinball Wizard" was played. Kenney Jones, ex Small Faces and Faces was on drums and it was The Who's first performance since disbanding after their 1982 "farewell" tour.

Paul McCartney suffered a technical hitch - his microphone didn't work properly for the first verse of the Beatles classic "Let It Be". There were also strong rumours the surviving Beatles would get back together, but George Harrison sourly noted, "Paul didn't want me to sing on Let It Be ten years ago, why should he want me to sing on it now?"

Despite the egos, technical challenges and dropping the F-bomb on live TV, Bob Geldof pulled it off and the Wembley leg ended with a rousing chorus of 'Do They Know Its Christmas?'

Meanwhile, over in Philadelphia, the highlights, or otherwise, were reported as...

"Black Sabbath crawled onstage at the unholy hour of 10am for a set of classics, clad in pure Spinal Tap threads."

"Madonna rolled out the hits Holiday and Into The Groove."

"Led Zeppelin reformed, enlisting Phil Collins to replace their late drummer John Bonham. Robert Plant was hoarse, Jimmy Page was out of tune and the band were under-rehearsed."

"Mick Jagger dragged Tina Turner on stage for an embarrassing version of the Stones standard It's Only Rock And Roll."

And we won't mention the excruciating cameo of Bob Dylan and Keith Richards...

Still, it was in aid of a good cause, and everyone was out of their heads on alcohol or whatever, so nobody cared much about how great or bad some of the performers were.

A series of disasters would dominate the news in the latter half of the 1980s. The Bradford Fire, where 56 people lost their lives during a football match between Bradford City and Lincoln. The shocking footage of the inferno witnessed live on television.

The Heysel Disaster when 39 football supporters lost their lives at the European Cup Final between Liverpool and Juventus.

The capsizing of the cross-channel ferry, MS Herald of Free Enterprise at Zeebrugge, Belgium in 1987 with 193 victims.

The Hungerford massacre where 16 innocent people were shot dead in the streets of the Berkshire town.

The Kings Cross Underground fire also in 1987, which killed 31 people. This was the year when the Archbishop of Canterbury's envoy Terry Waite was kidnapped in Lebanon and would remain hostage until 1991.

Golliwogs were banned from Enid Blyton books following complaints that they were offensive. Margaret Thatcher was re-elected to make her the longest continuously serving Prime Minister since Lord Liverpool in the 19th century.

On the weather front, the year would end with hurricane winds battering southern England, making a mug of the BBC's weather forecaster Michael Fish's observation that there was nothing to worry about. 13 people died and dozens were injured, mostly by falling trees and buildings.

Corby suffered another blow, if not a catastrophe when Golden Wonder went up in flames in 1989. The crisp company had set up home in Earlstrees Road in 1964 and had been one of the town's major employers after the steelworks. The devastating fire destroyed the factory, leaving hundreds out of work. Alan Murphy was shift manager at the time and was the one who discovered the blaze and pressed the button for evacuation. The memory of that night gave Alan nightmares for years afterwards.

On a brighter note, Corby Railway Station was reopened after 21 years, albeit with just the one platform. The pedestrian bridge had long gone, as had the original Ticket Office and Waiting Room but that didn't matter. It was great to be able to catch a train again to Kettering, where you could connect to the rest of the country. Disappointingly, not everyone was enthused as just three years later, in 1990, the service was cancelled again. It would be another 17 years before Corby would lose its tag of "the biggest town in the country without a railway station."

It seemed to sum up the situation with Corby. Disconnected. Ten years to the millennium and we were all wondering where we would be, come the turn of the century.

Bibliographical Sources

(Books, Blogs, Newspapers, Magazines)

Charles Buchan's Football Monthly

Corby Iron and Steel Works -Steve Purcell

Daily Mail

Downham Market Weekly

The Guardian

Financial Times

The Isle of Wight News

Leicester News and Chronicle

Melody Maker (Published 1926-1999)

Musicians Only (Published 1979-1980)

My Life as an A "Z" Celebrity - Bip Wetherell

My Life - In the Eye of A Tornado - Clem Cattini

New Musical Express (Published 1952- 2018)

Northamptonshire Evening Telegraph

Richard Oliff Blog

Scottish Daily Record

Spectrum

The Times

Author Briefs

Authors Bip Wetherell & Clive Smith

Clive Smith was born in Corby and educated at Rockingham Road Infants, Studfall Juniors and Samuel Lloyd's Boys School. Following an aborted Bricklaying course at Corby Technical College, he worked in the C.W. Mills at Corby Tubeworks. He spent a couple of years on building sites before becoming full-time bar and cellar man at the Open Hearth in Studfall Avenue. Two spells in the EWSR tube making plant preceded a 35 year career at the Royal Mail, 30 of which was spent driving on the late and nightshift. In between times, he worked as a doorman, taxi driver, security man and part-time steward at Corby Rugby Club.

Clive was married to Sue for over 40 years before her passing after a long illness in 2014. Their son, Gareth, is a musician and Social Worker in Stockholm where he has lived since 2002. Their daughter, Carly, qualified as a Radiographer in 2004 and works at the world-renowned Christie Hospital in Manchester. Clive has three granddaughters, Polly, Ruby and Rose. Hobbies include travel, sport and writing.

As a feature writer, he has contributed to magazines and football programmes and has had three books published, "Its Steel Rock and Roll To Me", "Alive In the Dead of Night" in a collaboration with David Black and a biography, "Clem Cattini, My Life In the Eye of a Tornado" in collaboration with Bip Wetherell. Clive retired in 2013 and after losing his wife, Sue, in 2014, he travelled the world visiting the USA, South Africa, South America, Vietnam and all over Europe. He continues his hobbies of travel and writing and spending time with his family in Widnes and Stockholm to this day.

***

Bip Wetherell passed the 11 plus to go to Grammar School, then spent five years doing a Commercial Apprenticeship at British Steel. He left to work in the Head Office of Golden Wonder in the Accounts Department in Market Harborough, then started his discotheque business in 1969 after singing for various local bands. Bip worked at the Open Hearth where he met his future wife, Elaine Knight.

He decided to go to University to study English and First World War Poetry, whilst training to teach in Junior schools. However, the success of the discotheque business proved to be popular so he left Northampton University in his second year to concentrate on the business. He was married on in 1972, and his eldest daughter, Tamla, was born in 1973 and named after their favourite music.

Bip and his wife were promoted to landlord and landlady of the Open Hearth in May 1975 and then moved to The Nags Head March 1976. Their eldest son Glen was born in 1977. Bip lived in Middleton for 42 years and raised two more children Steven (born in 1981) and Louise (born in 1984). Steven is father to Holly and Harvey. Glen and Sally gave us Tabatha and Penelope. Tamla and Jon gave us Kai.

They bought their first night club in Kettering in 1980. They were also partners in a garage business with close friend Billy Masson. He still sang in bands part-time but moved a step-up reforming "Clem Cattini's Tornados" in late-1988. They gigged all over UK and Europe, the highlight of which was performing as a featured artist at the London Palladium.

Bip performing at the London Palladium

The Nags Head proved to be too small for the numbers generated so, along with several partners, they bought The Welfare Club in 1984 where they were entertaining 2000 customers every weekend.

Diagnosed with prostate cancer in 2005 and throat cancer in 2018, this meant the end of Bip's singing career so he took up writing. He has had two novels published entitled "Chopped" and "The Reluctant Assassin," a selection of 14 short stories under the name of "Cold Revenge" and finally a biography in collaboration with Clive Smith about the life of Clem Cattini entitled "My Life In The Eye Of A Tornado".

Bip's life story "My Life As A 'Z' List Celebrity" is a work-in-progress. Diagnosed with fibromyalgia restricted his previous hobbies of tennis and golf, although he is trying to get back into cycling through the generosity of his wife, Elaine, who graciously bought him an electric bike. They are now living in their new "eco" house on the hill as you come into the village of Cottingham.

Printed in Great Britain
by Amazon

38721927R00205